HOW TO LIVE
WITH EACH OTHER

HOW TO LIVE WITH EACH OTHER

An Anthropologist's Notes on Sharing a Divided World

FARHAN SAMANANI

P

PROFILE BOOKS

First published in Great Britain in 2022 by
Profile Books Ltd
29 Cloth Fair
London
ECIA 7JQ
www.profilebooks.com

1 3 5 7 9 10 8 6 4 2

Typeset in Dante by MacGuru Ltd
Printed and bound in Great Britain by
Clays Ltd, Elcograf S.p.A.

A CIP catalogue record for this book is available from the British Library.

ISBN 978 1 78816 389 7
eISBN 978 1 78283 636 0
Audio ISBN 978 1 78283 997 2

FSC
www.fsc.org
MIX
Paper from
responsible sources
FSC® C018072

CONTENTS

PART I

TRIBE

CHAPTER ONE

JOURNEYS

How can we live with those who are different from us? This is an old question and a tricky one. It may also be the most urgent problem of the twenty-first century.[1] In recent years, crises of difference have begun to crash in successive waves. In 2017, in Charlottesville, USA, the young activist Heather Heyer is murdered by a white supremacist, as others chant 'you will not replace us'. In Lebanon and Turkey, over 3.4 million Syrian refugees who have arrived since 2011 face the threat of double displacement as their presence generates growing backlash. In 2019, in Johannesburg, simmering resentment against migrants erupts into riots, targeting migrant-owned businesses and a local mosque. In 2015, Dylan Roof carries out a mass shooting at a majority black church in South Carolina. In 2018, Robert Bowers does the same at the Tree of Life Synagogue in Pittsburgh. In 2019, Brenton Tarrant kills fifty-one at a mosque in Christchurch, New Zealand. All three are found to be immersed in radical nationalist movements. In Poland new laws, passed in 2018, clamp down on references to Polish involvement in the Holocaust, casting the nation solely as a victim. Across the past decade, tens of thousands of migrants drown trying to cross the Mediterranean, as anti-immigrant groups in the US and France raise money to charter ships to patrol the waters, convinced those struggling to make the crossing pose a civilisational threat – voicing hope that even more will be lost to the sea.

There is a story that we tell: that difference always carries a threat. Whether marked by skin colour, nationality, religion, political camp or culture, this story tells us that living with others is inescapably threatening – that our own way of life risks being eroded by the ways others live. We imagine difference in terms of winners and losers, where, if others gain, we lose. This is not a story that we tell all the time, but it is old and familiar, and it has taken on many forms over the years. It sits at the foundations of Western democracy, informing our idea of citizenship, and most citizens will retell it in one way or another. Some may tell it about race or migration, imagining that the presence of newcomers or the economic success of minority groups poses a fundamental threat to their own interests. Others may tell it about political rivals, or those with different beliefs – imagining that the only way to respond to those who hold a different world view is to oppose them.

This story has tremendous power. It has this power, in part, because it is so well rehearsed. We tell this story over and over again, not only with words, but also in the designs of our cities, in the rules of our politics, in the ways in which we consume information. To call it a story, then, is not to say it is unreal. On the contrary, it becomes increasingly real in each retelling.

Democratic states are going through a major upheaval. In 2020, a major study from the Cambridge Centre for the Future of Democracy found that most citizens of democratic states, worldwide, were dissatisfied with democracy. For a range of countries, including the United Kingdom, South Africa, Australia, Brazil and the United States, faith in democracy has reached an all-time low.[2] Democracies are struggling to deal with political difference. Sometimes they grow more polarised, as divides become intractable and voters are pulled towards extremes. Sometimes they fragment, as values, agendas and groups multiply and become ever more niche.[3] Below the surface of formal politics, notions of truth and the possibilities for consensus and cooperation are splintering. Citizens are developing increasingly

distinctive habits of media consumption, interaction and connection, pulling away from each other in profound ways.[4] Even
in the face of seemingly global events, such as the Covid-19 pandemic, there is widespread disagreement over the realities we
face and the solutions we need – over science and belief, and
care and exploitation. Tangled with crumbling faith in democracy and public life, differences become volatile. Movements for
racial justice clash with emboldened nationalist movements.
Both clash with politicians eager to insist there was never any
issue to begin with.[5]

The challenges these upheavals pose is clear. What is less
clear is where they originate from. Are they the inevitable
product of an increasingly interconnected and mixed world? Or
are they, in the end, products of stories we tell about ourselves
and the world around us?

I believe it's the second of these two. The way we imagine
difference matters. And sometimes subtly, sometimes more
overtly, democratic states have long imagined difference as a
threat. But it doesn't have to be this way. This book investigates
how this story, where difference and conflict are inextricably
linked, came into being. It explores how this story gets acted
out by democratic institutions and through the everyday habits
of citizens. And, most importantly, it looks at how some citizens
are finding ways to tell different stories about difference, radically transforming the democratic tradition from within. This is
a book about the past, the present and the future – about an old,
familiar story that we continue to repeat, but also about how we
might rewrite the script.

❁

The first time I visited Kilburn, it was to attend a 'pop-up university'. A group of artists, architects and academics had come
together to run a series of events exploring the history, make-up

and politics of this busy corner of north-west London. The artists involved, I suspect, couldn't resist setting the scene a little. In the middle of the large, communal table around which the audience was gathered was a small display of books, knick-knacks and black-and-white photos of the neighbourhood – all set out on black cloth. At the centre, displayed like a religious tome, was an old architectural classic: *A Pattern Language*. Both the speakers and this book offered a similar message: places are defined by familiar patterns – a certain look to the shops and houses, certain trades and professions, certain places like parks, churches or community centres which bring people together in particular ways. To build a community meant recognising these patterns, learning how to draw on what was familiar and important, and then rearranging the elements.

Outside, after the workshop, I wandered down the Kilburn High Road, slightly baffled. If there was a pattern here, I was struggling to see it. The author Zadie Smith grew up near Kilburn, and the area provides the setting and inspiration for several of her stories. Here's how she describes a journey down the High Road:

> Polish paper, Turkish paper, Arabic, Irish, French, Russian, Spanish, *News of the World*. Unlock your (stolen) phone, buy a battery pack, a lighter pack, a perfume pack, sunglasses, three for a fiver, a life-size porcelain tiger, gold taps. Casino! [...] Boomboxes just because. Lone Italian, loafers, lost, looking for Mayfair. A hundred and one ways to take cover: the complete black tent, the facial grid, back of the head, Louis Vuitton-stamped, Gucci-stamped, yellow lace, attached to sunglasses, hardly on at all, striped, candy pink; paired with tracksuits, skin-tight jeans, summer dresses, blouses, vests, Gypsy skirts, flares. Bearing no relation to the debates in the papers, in Parliament. [...] The Arabs, the Israelis, the Russians, the Americans: here united by the

furnished penthouse, the private clinic. If we pay enough, if we squint, Kilburn need not exist. Free meals. English as a second language. Here is the school where they stabbed the headmaster. Here is the Islamic Centre of England opposite the Queen's Arms. Walk down the middle of this, you referee, you![6]

The Kilburn High Road runs like a spine, south-east to north-west, with streets branching off either side, leading to terraced Victorian homes, maze-like social housing estates or imposing mansions. As Smith's breathless description suggests, Kilburn teems with difference, reflecting a long, layered history of migration and political transformation. In the late 1800s, it provided a home to Irish families fleeing famine and Jews fleeing persecution who were often unwelcome elsewhere. Following the Second World War, they were joined by new arrivals from across Britain's current and former colonies who migrated in response to major British labour shortages and an urgent need to rebuild. Faced with prejudice and hostility, new arrivals often drew on informal networks of accommodating landlords and willing employers established by earlier migrants to find a foothold in the city.[7] In doing so, different generations of migrants got to know one another, establishing new connections, new identities, new ways of living. Today, Kilburn's diversity has multiplied even further, making it into a site of what the anthropologist Steven Vertovec calls 'superdiversity'.[8] Older Jewish, Irish and Caribbean migrants rub alongside more recent arrivals from Africa, the EU and South America, bringing with them different histories, faiths, languages, understandings and hopes.[9] Kilburn is not simply a place where the white British population is in the minority. It is one where no single group dominates and where our very language for describing difference seems to fray at the seams.

As these migrant histories build up, familiar categories break down. Many of the migrants arriving in the UK after the Second World War had been taught by colonial schools and administrators to view the UK as the 'motherland'. For them, migration was imagined partly as a sort of homecoming – an understanding supported by the fact that they arrived as full British citizens. When the ship *Empire Windrush* pulled into port on 21 June 1948, carrying the first group of post-war migrants from Jamaica, the London *Evening Standard* reported the event with the headline 'WELCOME HOME!'[10] In Kilburn, older migrants from India or Jamaica would sometimes nostalgically conjure up these feelings of connection and belonging.

In 1962, however, the UK rescinded the citizenship of most colonial and post-colonial subjects, and spent the subsequent decades creating ever-tighter restrictions on migration. Many of those who arrived after this point did so on the basis of 'family reunification'. For such migrants, life in Kilburn was not necessarily a matter of a general connection to the area, but characterised by one's place within relatively tight-knit networks of family and community.

In 1981, the UK government made it possible to strip British citizenship from people with migrant backgrounds – even if they themselves were born and raised in the UK – if their presence was deemed 'not conducive to the public good'.[11] Today, young people in Kilburn – the children or grandchildren of migrants – struggle to pin down what being British means to them. They feel at home in Kilburn, London and the UK, but they also know that unlike their white British counterparts, these roots could be pulled away at any moment. These layered histories of migration and citizenship shape different feelings of belonging, different identities and different ways of living. They make it difficult to talk about diversity simply in terms of national origins, as if all those from the Caribbean, Brazil, China or wherever else formed uniform, like-minded groups.

The difference that swirls through Kilburn, however, is not

just a product of migration. Surrounded by affluent neighbourhoods, Kilburn is a patchwork of different classes, professions
and circumstances – from refugees to retail workers, well-heeled
investment bankers to struggling artists. Forms of difference
multiply, intersect and fold in on themselves. Schoolchildren
exchange jokes in a swirling slang of hip-hop-inflected English,
Somali, Jamaican patois, Arabic and cockney. In the middle of
one of the UK's poorest housing estates, there's a small cul-de-
sac of former stables, converted into fashionable homes which
sell for over a million pounds. Streets of red-brick Victorian ter-
races are split between wealthy private owners and refugees
living in converted flats. Dance groups and anti-austerity activists encounter one another at the offices of a charity for Latin
American migrants; home-schooling families, artists and trendy
young Muslims mingle at a community centre. An Anglican
church hosts a post office, a café and a day-care centre, all within
its grand, vaulted hall.

Our interconnected planet was not born in the current age,
but in the colonial one. Surveying the Kilburn High Road, the
famed geographer Doreen Massey once wrote that, 'It is (or
ought to be) impossible even to begin thinking about Kilburn
High Road without bringing into play half the world and a
considerable amount of British imperialist history'.[12] Though
not always as readily apparent as in Kilburn, colonial histories
can be traced wherever migrant communities have put down
roots in Europe. Throughout the 1800s and into the early 1900s,
Europe experienced a migration boom, as Europeans left their
homelands to chase opportunities in colonised countries across
the Americas, Africa and Asia. Many others were deported as
bonded labourers. At a peak in the early twentieth century,
nearly 1.4 million people left Europe each year.[13] As a share of
the European population, this outpouring likely dwarfed migration in our present age, shaping the world in profound ways.[14]

Coupled with this was the slave trade. Between 1450 and

1900, 11.3 million African slaves were shipped across the Atlantic to the Americas and West Indies. Meanwhile, between 800 and 1900, a further 7.2 million slaves were shipped across the Sahara, 2.4 million across the Red Sea, and 2.9 million were sent from East Africa, bound for North Africa, the Middle East or Asia. The slave trade reached a grim peak in the 1790s, after European colonists took over older, Arab-dominated slave-trading routes. As colonial expansion and greed intensified, so too did the global demand for slaves.[15] Other forms of commerce, as well as indentured labour, played a further role in unsettling and resettling the globe – leading to Somali seamen coming to live in Victorian-era Cardiff, black entertainers serving in the court of Elizabeth I and Indian and Chinese labourers setting down roots in the Caribbean. Alongside these globe-spanning movements, colonialism also triggered migrations of a different sort, as colonial conquest devastated cities and villages, drew borders across far-off continents based on European rivalries, and created new hubs of economic activity and power – prompting large-scale migrations and mixing within colonial territories.

This upheaval created new channels of connection, linking people and cultures across the colonised world and back to Europe. Circuits of transport, communication, finance, trade, bureaucracy and governance along with missionary movements and the global exchange of goods created a highly interconnected world.

At the end of the Second World War these links and upheavals became the foundation for a new age of migration. While many displaced or struggling Europeans moved to America, those living in colonial or post-colonial nations opted to try their luck in Europe. As we saw in Kilburn, the need to rebuild nations including Britain and France led to active recruitment campaigns from current and former colonies. People from Vietnam and North Africa came to France, Indonesians moved to the Netherlands, and Indian, Pakistani and Afro-Caribbean migrants arrived in Britain. Meanwhile, economic booms and labour shortages in the 1960s led countries like West Germany and the Netherlands to develop international recruitment programmes that brought in migrants from countries such as Turkey or Morocco.

From these starting points, migration to Europe, alongside that to North America, has grown more diverse. Since 1960, the proportion of international migrants within the world has remained roughly the same, at around 3 per cent.[16] Today, however, these migrants hail from an increasingly diverse range of countries, regions and backgrounds.[17] In some cases, former colonial countries and metropolises have become hubs, creating new mixtures of identity, as would-be migrants stop off for a few months or years while they continue to search for a better life. In other cases, migration has contributed to a slow rise in the wealth of countries of origin, as migrants send money back to relatives or return to build homes or start businesses. In turn, economic development has made the costly journey overseas accessible to a wider range of people. Finally, just as the 1960s saw European states forming links with new nations to expand access to cheap labour, so too have more recent economic shifts opened up new migratory routes – from the end of the Soviet Union to the rapid industrialisation of China, to the expansion of the EU. Collectively, these changes have not accelerated migration, but they have diversified it, widening the range of backgrounds from which migrants hail. Today, those living in places where migrants have settled are often faced with an ever-growing kaleidoscope of difference.

As movement steadily reshapes the world, places like Kilburn offer a glimpse into what is likely to become an increasingly common future. Around 2045, the number of non-white Americans is expected to overtake the number of white Americans.[18] Meanwhile, in the UK, even if significant restrictions on immigration are put in place, and kept, the non-white population is projected to double, from 17.5 per cent to 35.6 per cent between 2016 and 2061.[19] Even when such trends may not play out nationally, they may take hold in large, globally connected cities.[20] More than this, regardless of where we live, today almost all of us routinely come into contact with difference – different cultures, viewpoints, beliefs and ways of living – through the internet, and through global commerce and media. As a consequence, the lives of citizens – whoever they are – seem to be growing further apart, or at least more distinctive. In 1984, the anthropologist Sandra Wallman published *Eight London Households*, a book where she explored how families in the 80s lived. She found that the households she studied were united by a strong sense of identity and belonging grounded in their local neighbourhood. In 2013, the German sociologist Jörg Dürrschmidt published an update to Wallman's study, which found little in the way of shared, local roots. Instead, Dürrschmidt's Londoners focused on cultivating a distinctive sense of personal identity. Drawing on the diverse offerings of the city, they crafted lives that were distinctively their own.[21]

In places like Kilburn, differences in nationality, language, income, lifestyle, profession, generation, gender, history, education, class, sexuality, social circles, ethnicity and belief all interact with one another. Yet if this swirling difference makes it challenging to spot a singular pattern, it doesn't mean that Kilburn is somehow being pulled apart by diversity. Rather, difference moves in and out of being ordinary and extraordinary, enriching and troublesome, as people build their lives.

Several months after my first visit, now living in Kilburn myself, I found myself at a garden centre one grey December afternoon, navigating plastic Christmas trees. I was with Paddy and Daisy, two old friends who had both moved to Kilburn in their twenties – Paddy from Ireland and Daisy from a small English village. Daisy was now in her mid-nineties, while Paddy was a sprightly seventy-nine. The pair met decades ago, through a tenants' association Daisy helped found for the residents of their tower block. The outing that afternoon had been arranged by a 'friendship club' Daisy was a part of – run by a local church. The visit to the garden centre was a sort of annual ritual, where each year they perused Christmas baubles and visited Santa's grotto, before settling in at a café with some tea or mulled wine. Paddy was not a regular part of the group, but he had come along to lend a hand and catch up with his old friend. As Paddy and I took turns pushing Daisy's wheelchair, weaving gingerly between overstuffed displays of ornaments, Daisy reminisced, sharing stories from the past, as Paddy nodded along.

When Daisy started the tenants' association, her initial intention was to push for simple improvements to their building. But she soon found herself with a stream of visitors asking for help with their bills, repairs or their family disputes. People came by to ask if they were allowed to decorate their council flat, but stayed to get her opinion on wallpaper swatches. Others would arrive, struggling with English, asking for help in understanding their rental or employment contracts – only to end up in tears, talking about the struggle of making a life in an unfamiliar place. Over time, as Paddy grew more involved in the tenants' association himself, he became involved in this living-room therapy, too. The association had begun to serve as a sort of stand-in family for those with few other sources of support.

With the occasional contribution from Paddy, Daisy told me about the relationships she had built with her neighbours, and of the stories they had told her: of the Polish handyman who helped residents make speedy repairs or alterations to their flats, without the council noticing; or the Pakistani lady who bent Daisy's ear about her struggle to connect with her daughter, who was much more comfortable in London than she was. Daisy told us how when she had first come to London, she found it a lonely, frightening place. In the stories of her neighbours, she recognised herself – disoriented, uncertain, determined to make a life. Paddy agreed. He had arrived from Ireland at a time when there was still considerable hostility towards the Irish – when they were stereotyped as lazy, criminal and unclean. For both, being able to connect with their neighbours helped make London home.

Ultimately, however, Daisy and Paddy both stepped back from the tenants' association. The requests for help were becoming overwhelming. But more than that, something was missing. Tighter rules around who was eligible for social housing meant that households moved around more often. Their neighbours started changing more rapidly. People were arriving from increasingly diverse backgrounds, and this made it harder to connect. The need for help, for sympathy and care was still there. If anything, it had grown. But the sense of community this once fostered seemed to disappear. The work shifted from an expression of care between neighbours, to providing a free and demanding service.

Up to this point, Daisy had led the conversation. But here, Paddy interjected to talk about his career as a gardener. He had worked for the Greater London Authority, and as a part of his duties he occasionally tended to the trees and flower beds that once flanked London's bustling Regent Street. Today, he lamented, most of the plants had gone. And he could see why. Towards the end of his years as a gardener, he was seeing more and more people damaging the plants he cared for, making it harder and harder to maintain them. It didn't help that many of the larger stores along Regent Street had come to be managed by wealthy foreign property investors or large multinational corporations who were collectively less willing to invest in the public spaces around them. He summed up his diagnosis decisively: the public spaces in London – just like his and Daisy's tenants' association – had declined because of 'all these immigrants!' Paddy looked at us and grumbled. 'No respect for anything any more.' In fact, he suggested, at this rate it wouldn't be long before London had no public space left. At this Daisy frowned, and gestured towards me – the brown-skinned, Canadian-born anthropologist, with a family history that had unfolded in the shadow of the British empire across three continents. 'But *he's* an immigrant!' she protested.

'You know what I mean,' Paddy responded, half irritated, half amused. 'Not like him!'

❊

Even for those who champion openness, living with difference can create real and weighty challenges. The efforts of refugees and migrants to establish new homes may conflict with the rights or aspirations of indigenous groups or settled minorities. Communities may disagree over the place of religious values in the school system, families may clash over different understandings of love and familial duty, and neighbours may quarrel over different understandings of gender and sexuality or stumble over language differences. These challenges often entail the tricky business of weighing up competing perspectives, values, hopes and fears, and cannot always be resolved by a simple insistence on acceptance, openness or equality.

These sorts of challenges have been connected to wider patterns which seem to suggest that diversity can pose a threat to our health, our communities and even the workings of democracy: locally, increases in ethnic diversity seem to trigger spikes in stress and declining feelings of well-being, as residents contend with changes to the fabric of their daily lives.[22] At a larger scale, growing ethnic diversity has repeatedly been shown to contribute to declining social trust and community involvement,[23] as well as to the unwillingness of citizens to act collaboratively and to invest in public goods.[24]

Declines in well-being, public trust, civic life and solidarity have likewise been linked to many other forms of difference as well – from income inequality to the splintering of media consumption into countless, relatively detached conversations.[25] Democracy relies on citizens trusting that their perspective and interests are represented. But minority groups tend to experience *lower* trust in their fellow citizens within democratic states.[26] Meanwhile, as differences grow, and shared beliefs and understandings splinter, even relatively powerful majority groups often come to view themselves as besieged minorities.[27]

If we believe the story about difference leading to conflict, then as the world grows more diverse, these patterns seem to foretell a future full of looming threat. Such fears increasingly drive democratic politics, stretching across the political spectrum. For the better part of the last two decades, immigration has been identified as the most pressing political issue by the British public,[28] and misgivings over immigration seemed to play a decisive role in driving the 2016 Brexit vote.[29] Similar preoccupations with migration can be found across a range of democracies, from the US to Italy, Germany and South Africa.[30] Conservatives talk nostalgically about the loss of national cultures and collective morality; self-proclaimed centrists fret about the prominence of 'identity politics'; and those on the left bemoan the decline of class-based solidarity or the ongoing ways in which minorities get excluded, misrepresented and vilified by more dominant groups. 'Fake news', 'alternative facts' and political division cause anxiety for people across a range of political camps – only no one can agree on who had the 'real' facts to begin with, or on how people ought to come back together. All these fears, in their own way, trade on an understanding of difference, where conflict is imagined as a near-inevitable result of living with others. If we truly believe this, then there is little that can be done except to throw up our walls and hunker down.

Yet there are plenty of signs that this may not be the whole story. For instance, there have been dozens of studies into the effect of diversity on trust. While findings vary from study to study, the overall pattern seems to be one where diversity does, in fact, have a negative impact on trust. Yet this overall effect is also very small – meaning that diversity cannot serve as the primary explanation for a waning sense of community spirit, or the diminished trust in democracies.[31] Meanwhile, when we look locally, we can find plenty of exceptions to this pattern, where growing diversity is in fact associated with growing trust and an upswing in civic engagement. These exceptions suggest that there is no *necessary* relationship between diversity and conflict. And, when we take a closer look at diverse communities, we can begin to find ways in which diversity can enrich life, shaping new forms of understanding and connection. Across all of this, there are hints of another story to be told – one which may seem unfamiliar, but which may emerge if we can only pause, and listen.

❋

This is where my own field of anthropology can help. 'Anthropology' comes from the Greek *anthrōpos*, meaning 'humankind', and *logia*, meaning 'study'. In its broadest sense anthropology is simply that – the study of what it means to be human. Unsurprisingly, this is a tricky question. As soon as you begin to survey the vast variety of human societies, it becomes quickly apparent that all sorts of different people define and experience their humanity in dramatically different ways. At the heart of anthropology, then, is a commitment to taking this difference seriously. Anthropology begins with a pause – with setting aside what we think we know, in order to hold space to listen, as best as we can, to what others are telling us.

Anthropology is a broad field. Over the years, anthropologists have developed distinct specialities. Evolutionary anthropology looks at humanity across our long collective history, drawing closely on psychology and physiology to try to understand what makes us distinct. Linguistic anthropologists look at how humans communicate, and how language shapes our lives. This approach is closely related to sociocultural anthropology, which looks at human societies in terms of the meanings, practices and feelings that fill everyday life and shape our rich cultural diversity.

This book draws together all three of these approaches, but I rely most on my background as a sociocultural anthropologist. That is to say, above all else, I treat the question of how we live with difference as a cultural matter – something whose answer is shaped by the specific ideas, practices and emotions that come together in a society. While anthropologists are often known for studying far-off societies, my own work comes from living and conducting research in the UK. Living in Kilburn for sixteen months across 2014 and 2015, I set out to understand how residents understood and dealt with their differences. How did they come together? How did they cooperate? When conflict arose, what differences caused it? And how did people from different walks of life come to feel at home in a place marked by continual change and swirling difference?

To answer these questions, I spent time with dozens of community organisations, as well as among the residents of Kilburn as they went about their daily lives. I conducted interviews, sat in on the meetings of community organisations, attended festivals, and got involved with organising events and projects. I followed activists as they attempted to combat evictions, get out the vote or fight climate change. I stayed up into the early morning with DJs from the local community radio station, I played football, Xbox and attempted strength training at youth clubs. I went to religious services, birthday parties and community kitchens. I hung out with young people on the street and chatted with parents outside the school gates.

The insights I have into our current divides are gleaned, in the first instance, from the lives of Kilburn's diverse residents.

Yet I am interested in Kilburn, not as a singular place, but as part of a broader story about human difference and democracy. And so this book weaves together stories from Kilburn with others from around the world and across history, to trace different ways of living with others and the lessons they may hold. Throughout these journeys, I hope to explore the world through an anthropologist's eyes by drawing on two key ideas: firstly, that we always build our understanding of the world *from somewhere*. Secondly that much of what we take for granted in our own lives can be shown to be the product of culture.

To understand how to think like an anthropologist, we can start with a simple question: what colour is a platypus? Anyone who has seen one should know the answer – they are clearly brown. To the naked human eye, that is. In 2020, scientists discovered that under a UV black light, platypuses glow in fluorescent shades of blue, green and purple. This discovery places platypuses alongside many other species, from opossums, to frogs, to puffins, whose colour appears completely different under UV – where flying squirrels glow with neon pink patterns and salamanders turn cucumber- or lime-green. Although we cannot detect UV light, many – perhaps even most – animals can. Where we may see a single, dull brown, other animals may see intricate patterns, striking colours or a bright shimmer.[32]

The anthropologist Gregory Bateson suggests that we understand the world by focusing in on particular distinctions within it.[33] Take platypuses. We might zoom in so closely to their fur that each strand appears different – one bleached by the sun, another darker, another thicker, another frayed. We might also zoom out to the extent where it appears as a single, uniform object – fur. We might take the platypus as an individual, or we might treat it as part of a larger unit, such as a burrow, a species, or an ecosystem. It's possible to move between many of these perspectives, although to zoom in on individual strands of hair and zoom out to entire ecosystems, we many need some additional tools and skills – a microscope, for instance, or the ability to calculate patterns in the behaviour or numbers of species. Crucially, however, we can only take up one perspective at a time – we can see a uniform brown, or switch on the UV and see the glow of green and purple. We can pay attention to the varied behaviour of individual critters, look at what unites them into a single species, or look at them as part of bigger ecological patterns. Every possible perspective involves emphasising certain aspects and suppressing others. To understand the world, then, we always take up a distinctive, partial viewpoint.

Some distinctions are shaped by our biology. We see brown and not neon blue because of the way our eyes work. But anthropologists have shown that even our biological capabilities do not take shape independently of culture. Not all languages distinguish between green and blue, for instance, while other languages may name shades such as green using a wider and more subtle range of terms than we do in English. Speakers of languages that do not make blue/green distinctions struggle to distinguish between these shades, while those who use more precise categories are able to pick out more subtle differences in colour.[34] Just like other animals, our bodies – the workings of our eyes or the design of our vocal cords – attune us to our environment and to those around us in specific ways. But to a far greater degree than other animals, our cultures also do the same, channelling our capacity to perceive and understand the world in particular ways.

For anthropologists, culture entails everything that shapes the way we experience and understand the world. Culture goes well beyond language to encompass bodily habits and our physical environment as well. Routine tasks, such as carving wood or filling in spreadsheets, and social habits such as studiously ignoring strangers on the bus or asking visitors about the health of their families, are all a part of culture. So too are the things around us – from woodcarving tools, to buses and homes.

Scientists and politicians, Israeli factory workers, Japanese stock traders and academic philosophers all possess distinctive cultures.

Culture is a system for drawing distinctions – for instance, whether we differentiate between green and blue – which attunes us to the world. As human beings, culture doesn't get *between* us and nature, it *is* our nature. The brain of a newborn human weighs only 25 per cent of its eventual adult weight – far less than any other closely related primate. The other 75 per cent of our brain's development occurs after birth.[35] Our ability to see, smell, move, talk, taste, think and feel; our sense of balance, our capacity for emotion and empathy, and much more – are only capable of developing through interaction with the world beyond us. These capacities develop in distinctive ways in relation to specific cultural environments. There is no experience of the world, no way of thinking, that is not mediated by culture.[36]

On an individual level, our ways of seeing and knowing might be shaped by blending, layering or moving between different cultures. There's the culture of our families and schools, our media, our workplaces and communities. This variability also means that collective cultures are never totally uniform, and that they tend to continuously change over time.

Taking culture seriously gives us a different purchase on the world. The anthropologist Janet Carsten, who works in Langkawi, Malaysia, writes about a prevalent local understanding that siblings are made by being fed on the same substance. Children born to the same woman are considered siblings. But so too are those breastfed by the same woman, as well as those who are raised in the same house and fed rice from the same hearth. Blood, milk and rice are all substances capable of making people into siblings, and becoming related is a process – requiring feeding, care and connectedness.[37] This is no more or less reasonable than the Western understanding that siblings are defined by birth and genetics. Those who insist on this definition could be rightly challenged as to why shared genes are no guarantee that siblings will care for one another, or act in similar ways. In both cases, people are simply operating on different understandings of what siblings and families are, or ought to be. We are drawing different distinctions.

Recognising that culture is everywhere – that it shapes all human knowledge and experience – leads us to a different way of understanding ourselves and others. If all understanding is mediated by culture, then the first step to learning about others is to really delve into their own cultural perspective. Anthropologists sometimes refer to this commitment to trying to understand the world from the standpoint of others as 'taking seriously'. This involves exploring how others' perspectives and experiences are, for them, just as natural and meaningful, real and rational as ours are for us. When Bedouin invoke the mischievous acts of djinn to account for misfortune, when indigenous groups in the Amazon say that they have seen people turn into jaguars, or when conspiracy theorists suggest that the world is run by shadowy cabals, anthropologists do not respond by dismissing these views or by trying to debunk them. Instead, they try to suspend their own perspective and ask what makes these things true for those who hold them? When anthropologists try to understand others, their guiding question is not, '*In what ways are these people wrong?*' but rather, '*In what ways are they right?*'

Anthropology works a bit like a pilgrimage or quest – a journey to somewhere distant and unfamiliar that eventually brings us back home, transformed. While understanding others may require us to step back from our own ideas and values, it also allows us to return to them with a richer perspective. In part, these journeys offer us lessons from other places that may be valuable to us. More than this, though, they allow us to recognise how we too occupy a specific position in the world – how our likes and dislikes, our sense of what is true and false, wrong and right, no matter how fundamental they feel to us, are not universal, but in fact shaped by our own cultural environment.

On the one hand, this means that any moment of learning about others also helps us understand ourselves. Take gender, for example. Within Western culture, most people understand gender as a way of distinguishing the variations that exist in human biology. Bodies vary in terms of height and strength, chromosomes, reproductive organs, secondary sex characteristics, such as breasts or facial hair, and certain capabilities such as the capacity to get pregnant. Western culture groups these variations within two primary categories: female and male.

But these traits don't always stick together biologically in the way this clear-cut definition suggests they do: there are people with both breasts and beards; there are those with female sex organs who can't get pregnant. And these variations are not uncommon. In fact, 1.7 per cent of babies – nearly 2 in every 100 people – are born with physical variations that do not fit typical male or female patterns.[38] This percentage grows even larger if we factor in people who come to feel that the body they are born into does not fit them, or who may lack certain reproductive capabilities – which are not things that can be measured at birth. To insist on having only two gender categories works against acknowledging these differences, while also marking them out as deviant, as something gone wrong. Yet there are other, equally common physical variations that we do acknowledge, and do not treat negatively – such as twins, who make up between 0.6 per cent to 4.5 per cent of births, depending on the country (with identical twins being even rarer, at 0.4 per cent).[39]

The fact that this way of talking about gender is distinctly cultural becomes clear when we look beyond ourselves. Across South East Asia, a range of atypical gender identities were often associated with significant political or spiritual power. For instance, the Bugis people of Indonesia traditionally recognise five gender categories – including a category of people known as *bissu*, who were seen simultaneously embodying all aspects of gender together, evading easy categorisation. Rather than being outcasts, *bissu* were respected ritual specialists, seen as bridges to the gods, guardians of royal regalia and status. Similarly, in India, *hirjas* are a group of hermaphrodites and eunuchs, closely associated with the mother goddess Bahucharā Mātā, and an aspect of the god Shiva.[40] In North America, different First Nations groups had a range of widely accepted gender categories which were seen as neither typically male or female – with these different categories nowadays grouped under the modern term 'two spirit'.[41] Meanwhile, in many cultures, twins *are* considered to be quite troublesome – as embodiments of dangerous spiritual forces, or as threats to family stability and the social fabric.[42]

Seeing beyond ourselves is challenging. Without an outside viewpoint, we cannot recognise that we are *not* seeing certain distinctions. If you can't distinguish blue and green, because your language doesn't support this, you are unlikely to realise you are missing something, unless you come across somebody who sees things otherwise. Yet the more effort given to understanding an outside perspective in its own terms, the more it provides us with insights into our own worlds. Looking at other cultures allows us to stop seeing our own culture as natural or universal.

Recognising ourselves as cultural creatures also allows for a different sort of self-examination. Moments where people trip over differences emerge not just between broad cultural groups, but within them as well. These moments of friction suggest gaps in perspective. In many cases these gaps are ordinary and harmless – I say tomato, you say tom*a*to. In other cases, however, these gaps point to the ways in which our cultural frames might incorporate stories or perspectives that pull us in different directions. Both comparison with other cultures, and the capacity to recognise the frictions and tensions in our own cultural worlds, open our eyes to new ways of living.

❄

The value of taking an anthropological perspective becomes apparent when we return to Daisy and Paddy. For some, Paddy's rant about migration is easy to characterise as lazy prejudice. His protest – 'Not like him!' – might be seen as a defensive move, an attempt to avoid accusations of prejudice, while still allowing him to insist that *most* migrants cause trouble. Meanwhile, others may think the troubles Paddy associates with migration seem spot on – after all, public resources are only sustainable if everyone chooses to value them and appreciates their significance. And, *by definition*, diversity involves variations in values and understanding.

Listen closely, however, and Daisy's and Paddy's lives tell of a more complex story. The tenants' association they ran thrived by becoming a place to forge common bonds between neighbours from diverse backgrounds and parts of the world. Yet it also shut down because people's needs were becoming too varied and too complex. Both Paddy and Daisy seem to share an idea that some migrants cause trouble or division, while others may become friends, collaborators or even surrogate family – without necessarily providing clear criteria for identifying who falls into which category.

In popular media, online debate and by listening to the most vocal activists across the political spectrum, our differences seem stark. In debates around racism or diversity, we are often confronted with images of brash, unapologetic racists, or of woke activists who speak as though they have it all figured out. However, most of us tend to hold much more complex, even contradictory views. Just like Paddy and Daisy, the meaning and stakes of 'difference' take on shifting forms. For them, 'immigrants' are never just immigrants, and strangers are never just strangers. Rather, the value found in others seems to vary across situations and circumstances. Almost all of our attitudes are marked by this sort of complexity. So, for example, in the UK, one 2013 poll found that 70 per cent of all British citizens were in favour of a multicultural Britain. And yet, among the same group of people, 54 per cent also said that they thought immigration had been a bad thing for Britain, while 47 per cent thought that 'having a wide variety of backgrounds and cultures has under-mined British culture'. If we imagine that all these responses have to do with just one understanding of diversity, then these contradictions are baffling. But if we recognise that diversity comes to be experienced in different ways, and within different frames, these shifts and swings in attitude begin to make sense. It might be tempting to label this inconsistency hypocritical – or at best confused. Yet, taking it seriously, it serves as important evidence of tensions within our own societies that pull us in different directions.

Listening to Daisy and Paddy's story helps reveal what these tensions are, pointing to two intertwined political crises, both of which Daisy and Paddy know all too well. On the one hand, they are first-hand witnesses to the slow stripping away of civic resources from communities, neighbourhoods, cities and towns – a trend observable in many nations today. In the UK, between 2010 and 2017, local councils have experienced a 26 per cent drop in funding, forcing them to close youth centres and libraries, to end English-language classes for migrants and to lock the gates of public parks.[43] In the US, neighbourhoods where the average home was built after 1979 have just over half as many social advocacy organisations as older neighbourhoods. In turn, the prevalence of such organisations remains a strong predictor of how active residents are in civic life – meaning that in newer neighbourhoods, locals engage less.[44] Meanwhile, other spaces where Americans often mingle, including parks and shopping malls, are likewise on the decline. More and more, urban planning and policy across the globe are literally squeezing out the space for encountering and getting to know others. As Paddy and

Daisy can attest, these public resources are often what enable different groups to build commonality. Shared space and shared time allowed their tenants' association to flourish, to forge new bonds and to overcome a range of challenges – right up to the point where things became overburdened, and collapsed.

Civic resources are more than just spaces to meet and socialise, just as civic life is sustained by more than just formal organisations. The capacity to take part in community life is closely tied up with the time and resources we have available to us, making poverty and inequality crucial factors in determining the strength of our democracies. This is especially true when it comes to bridging difference and building common ground. These processes can be deeply rewarding, but they are also slow and messy, requiring time and capacity that not all citizens can spare. These tensions reflect a broader struggle over value: As long as demands to produce *financial* value dominate our lives and dreams, we will always have less capacity to cultivate other forms of value – such as care, belonging, friendship or understanding.

On the other hand, Paddy and Daisy are living through a crisis of storytelling. In many ways, immigrants, strangers or political rivals are fictional characters. They take on life not through our direct experience, but through the stories we tell about them. In a democracy the stories we tell matter, because some of the biggest decisions we are asked to take don't simply affect ourselves or the people around us, they impact the society of strangers in which we live. Our ability to make these political choices is closely bound up with the sorts of stories we tell.

To take just one example from contemporary Britain, a sweeping study at the University of Oxford found that the words most commonly used in reporting on immigration were 'mass' and 'illegal'.[45] Despite illegal immigration making up a small proportion of overall immigration, and immigrants making up only around 14 per cent of the UK population, the story the

British most often tell of migration is one of a lawless influx that threatens to engulf the country. The tone of such stories has been shown to play a major role in shaping public attitudes.[46]

These stories have tremendous power, taking on a life of their own. In doing so, however, they can also become detached from our own experiences, sometimes even without us realising. Just like Paddy, we are willing to dismiss broad stereotypes or popular images when they are applied to those we know personally. Even though we may claim to have little patience for atheists, or voice little desire to befriend right-wingers, we often make exceptions when those atheists or right-wingers happen to be our family or friends. Meanwhile, these personal connections do little to alter our beliefs in the broader stories we tell about those who are not like us. And so, for Paddy, despite being friends with people from all over the world, the abstract idea of immigration as a threat helps him understand the slow degradation of the public spaces he cares for, and once tended.

According to the big, familiar story about difference, the social tensions we face, including the loss of civic resources and our struggle to tell meaningful stories about our lives, are *caused*, at least in part, by growing diversity and difference. This book, however, makes the opposite argument – that there are, in fact, other political forces which undermine our capacity to live with difference, to the point where it has come to look as if difference itself is the problem. Responding to the increasingly common declaration that the tensions and conflicts of our present moment reveal that 'the multicultural experiment' has failed, Zadie Smith wrote: 'As a child I did not realize that the life I was living was considered in any way provisional or experimental by others: I thought it was just life.' At the heart of this book are stories like Paddy's and Daisy's – stories of 'life', often lived alongside unfamiliar others, and marked by harmony and tension, ups and downs, just like any other life. Together, these stories challenge the idea that diversity itself is the problem, while helping us recognise where the roots of our current struggles really lie, and how we might cultivate something different.

This argument unfolds over the rest of the book. It follows an anthropological journey, first setting out to learn from unfamiliar perspectives, before turning inwards to look at tensions and lessons for living otherwise from within Western democracy. This journey begins by posing a pointed challenge to the idea that group divisions and conflict are somehow just a part of human nature. Chapter Two confronts this idea by flipping the perspective and looking instead at how we have evolved to connect to one another. By focusing on two key abilities, empathy and abstraction, I look at how these capacities can work to cultivate both connection and division, depending on how they are used. Chapter Three looks at how different groups across the world imagine human difference. Against the idea that our group differences are always fixed and opposed, I aim to show the surprising fluidity of group identities, but also to highlight how even such fluid identities can come to be seen as fixed and as powerful motivators of action.

Equipped with the idea that there is nothing inevitable about group conflict, the next three chapters dive back into the history of democracy, leading up to the twenty-first century, to look at how democratic societies have come to imagine and manage difference. In Chapter Four, I explore how two of the key traditions of democracy – liberalism and civic republicanism – have also equipped us with two very distinct ways of imagining and relating to difference. Where liberalism tends to see differences in terms of fixed identities and universal essences, republicanism attempts to approach the question of what differences make a difference as a matter of ongoing negotiation. The fixed ideas of difference involved in liberalism allow for strong claims about rights and equalities that have played a crucial role in twentieth-century movements for justice, while the civic republican vision of difference as negotiable allows people to form commitments to one another that go beyond the calculus of opposing identities. In Chapters Five and Six, I explore the potentials and limits of each of these approaches, in relation to one another.

The final three chapters look at how different citizens are transforming democracy from within by weaving these two traditions together in new ways. Chapter Seven takes on our current 'post-truth' moment, and highlights the important role 'enchantment' can play in rebuilding faith in public knowledge. Chapter Eight attempts to rethink liberalism not as a quest for universal claims and laws, but as a practice of storytelling, capable of holding more space for diverse lives. Finally, Chapter Nine looks at how to rebuild public life as a 'commons' that can sustain both equality and difference, together.

Anthropology teaches us that we only ever understand the world from a particular perspective, and that we can only transform this perspective by relating it to others. This book takes up this lesson in two important ways. Firstly, it is an attempt to rethink democracy from *within*. Often commentary on the state of democracy – whether from journalists, public figures or academics – is written in a critical, detached tone. This detachment creates a sense of authority, as if the writer is standing above the fray, looking down. Yet it also means that the solutions offered can seem similarly detached from everyday life. It can be hard to work out how to act on the lofty criticisms offered, or how to enact the solutions that are proposed. Here, I also try to explore problems and solutions, but I try to do so in a more grounded way. I rely on everyday concepts such as storytelling, love or community, or on ideas that are strongly embedded in the democratic tradition, such as liberalism and civic republicanism. In doing so, I hope to offer a perspective that does not break with the current world but gets stuck into its problems and possibilities, in order to map how, exactly, we might journey elsewhere.

Secondly, throughout this book, I play with the idea of inside and outside. Democracy promises equal representation and equal rights to citizens, regardless of who they are. I try to both interrogate and extend this promise by frequently writing in the collective 'we'. This is not to suggest that everything in the book applies to humanity as a whole. Rather, it is an invitation to think relationally – to ask how the perspective at hand might resonate with or trouble our own, how it might fit within or fall beyond the current promise of democracy. This is the journey this book follows: setting out to learn from everyday lives, to tell a different story of what it means to live with difference.

CHAPTER TWO

NEAR AND FAR

In the aftermath of the Second World War, the world scrambled to understand the cruelties and complicities of the conflict. Historians, politicians and scientists struggled to understand how ordinary Germans were swept up in the genocidal fervour of the Nazi regime. Meanwhile, the Allied nations also had their own choices to face up to, whether in initially acting to appease the Nazi government, dismissing early reports of the unfolding Holocaust, or closing their borders to refugees fleeing death. For many post-war thinkers, the scale of these horrors suggested something savage at the heart of human nature. A portrait began to emerge of humanity as red in tooth and claw, capable of doing almost anything when acting in the name of our tribes and nations.

In an unpublished memoir, the novelist William Golding wrote with self-loathing that, 'I have always understood the Nazis, because I am of that sort by nature'.[1] Before he gained fame as an author, Golding was a schoolteacher. Fascinated and repulsed by what he saw as an innate human capacity for cruelty, he used teaching as a chance to observe and experiment with the savage impulses of his pupils. Leading a school trip to Figsbury Ring, a Stone Age monument in south-west England, he divided his pupils into two groups, and encouraged one group to defend the site while the other attempted to capture it. Later he would describe his wide-eyed horror as he watched the warring groups move close to outright murder.[2] His observations of his students and his brooding reflections on his own inclinations informed the grim picture Golding painted in his best-known novel, *Lord of the Flies*. The novel depicts a group of schoolboys, stranded on an island, who quickly fracture into warring factions before descending into sadistic, superstitious and violent behaviour. Golding imagined his novel as a portrait of humanity's true, dark heart. He declared that 'you could have taken any bunch of boys from any country and stuck them on an island, and you would have ended up with mayhem.'[3]

In 1954, the same year *Lord of the Flies* was published, the pioneering social psychologist Muzafer Sherif conducted an experiment, masquerading as a summer camp, in Robbers Cave State Park, Oklahoma. In his native Turkey, Sherif had witnessed the Armenian genocide, and had been exiled for speaking out against the government's support for Nazi Germany. Like Golding, Sherif was fascinated by the human potential for cruelty and division when collective identities were at stake. At Robbers Cave, he divided his twenty-two adolescent campers into two opposing teams. While Sherif watched from the sidelines, the boys quickly developed a violent rivalry, thrashing one another's cabins, stealing and destroying possessions, and ending up in furious, bloody brawls.

In 1961, the science writer Robert Ardrey popularised the work of the anthropologist Raymond Dart and Austrian zoologist Konrad Lorenz in his book *African Genesis*. Dart had studied the fossilised remains of one of our early ancestors, a species known as *Australopithecus Africanus*, which were often found alongside primitive tools. He found that the shapes of these early tools often corresponded to the wounds found on *Australopithecus* skeletons – suggesting that many of them had died violent deaths at the hands of others. Linking violence to emerging tool use, and identifying tool use as the major force behind the evolution of modern human intelligence, Dart argued that conflict and violence played a fundamental role in shaping humankind. Lorenz took this a step further. Based on his studies of conflict in other species, especially birds, Lorenz saw aggression between groups as a fundamental human trait that could not be denied. At best, he argued, it could be channelled into more productive forms of conflict and competition – such as the cold war space race taking place at the time.[4]

As scientists, novelists and politicians painted an increasingly menacing picture of our tendency for division and conflict, the world grew ever more mixed. The upheavals of war and the end of colonialism left millions seeking new homes. The image of humanity as a vicious, tribal species seeped into the popular imagination, mingling with older stories about insurmountable divides between nations, cultures and peoples. This vision of division and conflict came to colour the ways in which migrants were received. In 1968, the British Conservative politician Enoch Powell made a now-infamous speech in which he voiced the fear, shared to him by one of his constituents, that 'In this country in fifteen or twenty years' time the black man will have the whip hand over the white man.'[5] Powell believed conflict was an inescapable result of different groups coming together, and that migrants were fundamentally motivated to seek 'actual domination, first over fellow-immigrants and then over the rest of the population'. Channelling a prophecy of war from the Latin epic *The Aeneid*, Powell declared: 'As I look ahead, I am filled with foreboding. Like the Roman, I seem to see "the River Tiber foaming with much blood".' Met with sharp criticism for stirring up unrest, Powell was hurriedly dismissed from his high-up post within the Conservative Party. His firing triggered widespread protest, and a year after his speech, a national poll found Powell to be the most admired man in Britain.[6]

Shaped by the horrors of war and genocide, these ideas not only painted a savage view of human nature but, more subtly, they also insisted on a grand, zoomed-out perspective. The Second World War was a truly global conflict, embroiling countless millions and impacting life on every continent. The cold war, which followed, likewise had implications for life across the world. To make sense of such events, people searched for or promoted stories that had a similarly vast scope. In conversations about human nature, simple, sweeping stories often prevailed – ones which equated biology with destiny, and which offered little room for variation. To different extents, thinkers such as Golding, Sherif or Dart were quick to equate what they saw in the classroom, in experiments or in prehuman remains with a portrait of humankind as a whole. They saw themselves as uncovering core human *tendencies* which drove behaviour across the species.

What would change, though, if we asked the question differently? What if we looked not for *tendencies*, but *capacities*? What if we looked at our biology not as destiny, but as equipping us with certain tools? What if we tried to figure out exactly what these tools can, and can't, do?

※

Daniel and Kev seem unable to agree on anything, but they have been close friends and business partners for decades. They were the sort of scrappy, hustling, jack-of-all-trades entrepreneurs who can be found in any city, dealing in anything and everything. Daniel ran a small corner shop, where the front room was piled high with old electrical goods, many of which he had refurbished himself. Hi-fi systems, TVs, computers, synthesisers and a jumble of various parts for repair were arranged into teetering piles. These were the big money makers, but Daniel's daily stock in trade lay in his other speciality – produce. For years, Daniel prided himself on being the only one to sell fresh fruit and vegetables on the Caldwell[7] estate, at a time when few were willing to open up shop in such a place. More recently, Daniel had encountered some competition, but as times changed, so did he. Working alongside Kev, he began supplying produce to local schools and businesses, while picking up other sources of income, offering their services in everything from home repairs to running a football team.

Whenever they heard about a potential new supply of electrical goods, or received a request for their services, the pair worked out whether to pursue the job, and who would do what, with a minimum of words. They never established a formal agreement around their partnership, and the written accounts of the various purchases and deals that sustained their business were kept to a minimum. Instead, they trusted one another implicitly. Kev entrusted Daniel with his van. When Daniel improvised a way to park, and got slapped with a fine, Kev was happy to treat this as a shared expense, recognising that he likely would have done something similar himself. When Kev sourced items for Daniel to sell, Daniel took him at his word on the price, unless he felt that Kev himself was being ripped off. Kev likewise trusted Daniel to handle the selling on – to find a fair price and pay him fairly. When things went wrong, the two would debate the best way forward, but they rarely put the blame onto one another. In their endlessly shifting attempts to get ahead in London's tough economy, the two were almost like an old, happy couple – familiar, forgiving and closely attuned to one another.

None of this was apparent, however, from how they spoke. Kev could frequently be spotted in Daniel's shop, sometimes stopping by for a quick hello, his English mastiff in tow, other times hanging out for hours. Regardless, the pair often ended up in an argument. These debates were so frequent, and the gulf between Daniel's and Kev's views so vast, that you'd be forgiven for suspecting that Kev was visiting with the primary intent of antagonising Daniel.

Daniel was a relentless optimist. Now in his sixties, his family moved to the UK from Jamaica shortly before Enoch Powell's inflammatory speech, when he was still young. They were the first black family on their street. At school, Daniel learnt how to avoid the older children, who would try to corner him and beat him up, or stop by to pelt his home with stones. This same prejudice followed him into his career. Training as an electrical repairman, he found himself constantly working to diffuse the distrust and hostility of his teachers and, later, of colleagues and managers – who often treated him like he was moments away from stealing something valuable and making a run for it. Daniel dreamt of one day running his own shop, but no one was willing to trust him with any major responsibility.

While these experiences may have turned others bitter, Daniel took them as a lesson in the value of self-sufficiency. He sought out opportunities to build up his skills – carpentry, electrical repair, jewellery repair – and to work independently, until the point where he was entirely devoted to his entrepreneurial wheeling and dealing. Visiting Daniel in his store, I would regularly find him wearing a mischievous grin, gently teasing a customer or strategising with Kev. Daniel had a particular talent for coaxing seemingly irreparably broken appliances back to life – though his modifications could sometimes leave his customers perplexed as to what they were looking at. Sometimes, in response to these looks of bafflement – at his improvised creations, or at the towering piles of gizmos and parts that loomed over the produce in his shop – he would declare, with a wry smile: 'What can I say? I'm a genius.'

Despite the teetering towers of electrical goods, and the sometimes dubious-looking fruit and veg, Daniel's shop was a fixture of life on the Caldwell estate. Throughout the day, people wove in and out, sometimes saying a brief hello, sometimes getting drawn into a longer chat. Commuters swung by on their way to work, parents stopped by with kids in tow after school, and residents popped in with dogs or clutching cups of tea from the nearby café. This openness was something Daniel had worked carefully to cultivate. When visitors to the shop started to share personal struggles, or griped about the news, Daniel withheld judgement, instead offering a combination of sympathy and humour that kept people talking. The square just outside Daniel's store was a favoured meeting spot for a group of young men with reputations as toughs, drug dealers and troublemakers. In private, with others, Daniel would readily curse out these young men for the smashed liquor bottles and other debris, their intimidation of passers-by *and the noise*. But in person, he favoured a friendlier approach, zeroing in on what they held in common, asking after their families or drawing them into conversations about music and hi-fi systems.

Kev, meanwhile, was a cynic. He was convinced that almost everyone around him was driven by self-interest and greed. Above all else, Kev distrusted the unfamiliar, and had an almost knee-jerk mistrust of migrants. Cultural differences were signs of irreconcilable interests. For Kev, proof of the damage immigration had done to the UK could be found right by Daniel's shop, in the groups of boys who gathered outside. Rattling off cases where people had been stabbed, shot or mugged on the estate, Kev was hostile and standoffish, not only with the young men, but with their families and friends as well. His anger frequently took on racially charged tones, and he was prone to describing the estate's struggle with crime as a 'black' problem – even though those involved came from a range of backgrounds. In fact, although Kev wouldn't talk about it himself, members of his own family had been caught up in local criminal activity.

Despite his grouchiness, one thing Kev did enjoy was arguing – with Daniel and with others. He took evident delight in holding forth on the moral bankruptcy of government policy, or of a particular local organisation. Daniel's own approach to these arguments varied. Sometimes he happily minded his own business, sometimes he jumped right in, either mischievously or with full sincerity. Immigration was one issue where Daniel often challenged Kev. But Kev tended to remain unmoved.

There were exceptions to Kev's cynicism: there were people from a range of backgrounds, like certain community-development workers, residents, friends, and of course Daniel, who Kev sincerely respected. If these individuals came up during one of his diatribes, Kev would often pause to make an exception for them – 'not George, of course, he's all right' – but these concessions had little impact on his overall perspective.

Daniel and Kev remained close friends and collaborators. Ultimately, Daniel seemed able to shrug off Kev's cynicism, even as it echoed the discrimination he faced growing up. Meanwhile, Kev was often willing to suspend his mistrust of enterprises, projects and people championed by Daniel, if it allowed the two of them to pursue new opportunities together. The two men embodied a strange sort of friendship: tightly knit yet deeply divided.

In Powell's 'rivers of blood' speech, he presented conflict between groups as inevitable – as a basic reality of human life. Over fifty years later, this fatalistic view has run up against the simple reality of people from diverse backgrounds living side by side across the world. These everyday lives have helped paint a less stark, more nuanced picture, where conflict is far from inescapable. Experiences such as Daniel and Kev's offer important clues for understanding our human capacities for living with others. On the one hand, Kev and Daniel can look past each other's strongly held views and forge a relationship by working together. On the other hand, the closeness of their friendship has done little to change the broader views they hold. Although this may seem like a contradiction, there is a wealth of current research that suggests that attitudes towards diversity vary when we encounter difference face to face, and when we think of it abstractly.[8] This pattern, of relating to difference in different ways across varied scales, points to the workings of our two core capacities for relating to others: empathy and abstraction.

Empathic connections are deeply personal, intuitive and

often highly compelling. Abstract, symbolic thinking provides us with a way of relating to those beyond our immediate social circles. Both capacities give us powerful tools for understanding and building bonds with unfamiliar others. Both, however, are characterised by certain trade-offs which limit the ways in which we can use them. These two capacities can work in tandem, but as shown by Daniel and Kev's complicated friendship, they can also pull us in contradictory directions.

＊

In the early 2000s, at the University of Liverpool, the evolutionary anthropologist Robin Dunbar made a curious discovery. By that time, it was well accepted that forming relationships with others was a demanding task – both in terms of time and mental resources. In fact, Dunbar's own work played an important role in uncovering the relationship between the size of primate brains – including those of humans – and the sizes of the social groups they tended to maintain.[9] Famously, Dunbar had guessed that, based on the size of our brains, the average human social group would tend to number around 150 members. From an extensive survey of human groups, past and present – in workplaces, in Roman army units, in small villages or nomadic clans – Dunbar found that group size almost always ranged between 130 to 150, confirming his hypothesis.

But Dunbar suspected that even within these everyday social circles, we didn't give everyone the same share of our time and mental resources. To explore this, Dunbar and his colleagues dived into a wide range of studies charting how much time people spent around others, and what sorts of relationships they formed. They found a spectrum of connectedness, trust and care. On one side of this spectrum are our most intimate relations, which rely heavily on our capacity for empathy. For most of us, we have three to five very close relations, who provide our most trusted and familiar connections, and then another set of around fifteen others, still close but slightly more distant, who are good friends, close family or important sources of care. Meanwhile, on the other side are hundreds, or even thousands, of more distant connections, whom we often relate to in abstract, symbolic terms, understanding them through the lens of stereotypes, roles or simplified traits – people like doctors, shopkeepers, teachers, politicians and those we know only by name. In between these two extremes lies almost everyone we know, who we tend to connect with through a combination of empathy and abstraction. The average human group of 130 to 150, for example, holds itself together by precisely that combination. Meanwhile, groups that rely on more intense forms of cooperation, such as bands of hunters, or artisan workshops, tend to be much smaller, topping out at around 50.

Our closest relations, characterised by implicit trust and deep care, take shape through our capacity for empathy. Empathy can be understood as the capacity to take on the perspective of others. Often, we talk of empathy as if it was a single ability. The human brain, however, has a suite of related abilities for taking on the perspectives of others.[10] We frequently mirror actions, emotions, movements and bodily sensations, often automatically, as if we were experiencing these things ourselves. Seeing someone else about to get punched may cause us to flinch, while witnessing sadness may make our own eyes well up. We follow the eyes or gestures of others to form intuitive guesses about how they experience the world. And, in conversation or at a distance, we can model others' minds within our own – sometimes automatically, sometimes reflectively – to try to anticipate what they might be thinking or feeling. We often speak of empathy as a generally positive way of relating to others, and as one associated with positive feelings such as care and compassion. But these different forms of perspective-taking can be used in a variety of ways. Empathy allows us to deceive or connect, anticipate, manipulate or learn. Together, these empathic tools play a fundamental role in shaping our sense of who we are and of how the world works.

As newborn babies, we start off without any sense of self, or of the world. In fact, we lack awareness of where our bodies stop and where everything else around us begins. We cannot recognise ourselves in the mirror and we cannot distinguish between people, other creatures and things. We learn these distinctions through empathy, starting off with mimicry. In early infancy, we imitate adults, pulling faces or mimicking gestures, and adults often playfully imitate us as well. Through this intimate, caring play, we gradually learn that our own physical sensations – the changing of perspective as we move our eyes, the thrill of surprise, or the feeling of tensing muscles and weight when we grab an object – may correspond to the actions and experiences of others.[11] As we learn the correspondences between ourselves and others, we also begin to realise that the glances, gestures, emotions and responses of those around us teach us about the world.[12] An object being lifted slowly may indicate that it is heavy, a grimace may point to a source of pain. In doing so, we move from mimicry to *joint attention*.

Following the attention of others teaches us that they have a different perspective to our own, and gradually this enables us to model their minds. At around two months old, we automatically mimic the smiles of familiar adults, whereas later in our first year, automatic mirroring drops off and instead we begin to react *in response* to the feelings others display – for example, responding to a look of disgust with anger or hurt.[13] We begin to recognise expressions and actions as judgements, and we realise that these judgements reflect on us, as well as the wider world.

These processes of mimicry, joint attention and mental modelling shape us in profound ways. They establish habits of thought and action, sensing and emotion, that become the foundation for further learning and exploration throughout our lives. Imagine, for instance, that as small children we notice that every morning our mother goes out to fetch water, gracefully perching a clay pot on top of her head. We may feel a pang of anxiety when she leaves and a rush of relief when she returns. Perhaps we attempt to mimic her, trying to lift pots onto our own heads, as if to say we are ready to accompany her. We know from our mother's ease that these pots *ought* to feel light and stable, but to us they are heavy and cumbersome, so perhaps, when we play, we start by trying to balance a soft toy on our head instead. If we cry when we drop the toy, or wobble precariously, our mother may step in, gently replacing the toy or placing a firm hand on our back to correct our posture. When we are older, we accompany our mother, and we learn that her journeys were not only about fetching water – they gave her a chance to catch up on local news, and to chat to other women about their respective families.

As we grow, parts of the world are internalised, etched into our muscle memory, the habits of our senses or the pathways of our memory. As young adults, we may carry our own pot, with a familiar ease. This culturally specific practice has shaped us in a number of ways. It has cultivated habits of poise, strength and attentiveness that attune us to the world around us. It has made us familiar with feelings of departure and return, labour and care. It has made us aware of what women discuss when men aren't around. Through this process of learning, we develop a vocabulary of security and attachment. We have learnt to trust that loved ones who leave will return, to become secure in our time alone, and we have learnt to read emotions in particular ways – the flash of anger when, while playing, we nearly break a valuable pot, the friendly smiles from others as we begin to accompany our mother, the hidden meanings behind local gossip.

Whatever our upbringing, these sorts of childhood experiences give us a template for engaging with the wider world and navigating new experiences. These templates, these bodies of empathic knowledge, play a powerful role in shaping how we think and act. First, since empathic knowledge is acquired gradually through everyday routine and experience, and since it is built upon bodily habits and unconsciously operating capacities, it can be challenging to recognise it as *knowledge* – as something that is learnt, and that can be relearnt. Rather, the understandings and habits acquired through our empathic abilities – our notions of family, our ways of expressing joy, anger or sadness, our practices of gender, livelihood or ritual, and much more – can simply feel like a reflection of how the world *is*. Secondly, since empathic knowledge weaves together different dimensions of experience – habit and emotion, skill and understanding – such knowledge can often become invested with huge emotional significance. Finally, empathic knowledge can often exceed the grasp of language. It's not that language – the categories we use or the stories we tell – plays no role in shaping empathy; in fact, it can play quite an important one. Rather, because of the tacit and emotionally charged nature of much empathic knowledge, it can be very hard to capture the *full extent* of such knowledge within language. It can be impossible to fully communicate to others the importance of our closest relationships or our most fundamental values. All this means that empathically rooted understandings can be especially hard to argue with. Yet precisely because they are tacit, emotionally rich and hard to describe, empathic understandings exercise a powerful pull on us throughout our lives.

As empathic knowledge accumulates, it shapes real, meaningful differences in our sense of self and how we experience the world. For decades, psychologists used a simple test, known as the mirror-mark test, to figure out when children became self-aware. A sticker or marking is covertly placed on a young child's forehead, and then later they are shown their reflection. The idea is that those who reach for or attempt to remove the mark have recognised the image in the mirror as themselves. Having a mental image of oneself as an entity in the world is seen as a crucial first step in being able to engage in future planning, symbolic reasoning and other fundamental human abilities, so mirror self-recognition was considered a particularly important milestone.

In recent years, however, psychologists conducted the mirror-mark test across different cultures and found striking differences. While Western children are often able to pass the test between eighteen and twenty-four months old, non-Western children have been shown to struggle – even up to the age of six.[14] Yet it turns out that non-Western children excel in other forms of self-awareness that Western children struggle with. In one experiment, conducted with Scottish, Zambian and Turkish toddlers, Scottish children were shown to be better at recognising their own image in the mirror-mark test. But Zambian and Turkish toddlers outdid the Scottish ones in a second test, which required them to move an object partly trapped under their own body. Before the tests, the researchers also observed how parents and children interacted, and found that the Scottish children received much more verbal interaction, while Zambian and Turkish children received more physical interaction. Verbal interaction got children used to thinking of themselves symbolically – as beings which could be represented, by a name, a description or, indeed, a reflection in a mirror – while physical interaction trained children to think more about themselves as a physical entity. It turned out that all three sets of children were developing mental images of themselves at a similar rate, but, guided by different cultural forms of parenting, they were doing so in very different ways. As we grow up these distinctive notions of selfhood grow deeper, grounding different conceptions of what it means to be human.

Yet if empathic learning can shape feelings of difference, it can also help do the opposite. Although childhood plays an especially strong role in shaping our sense of self, empathic learning never stops. Humans, whether children or adults, are instinctively empathic. We compulsively take on the perspective of others, to the point where it is difficult for us *not* to follow the gaze of others, or to internalise the judgements modelled by those around us – even when we think others are in the wrong.[15] Likewise, we are intuitively drawn towards mimicry. When instructed to solve a puzzle by imitating a demonstrator, we compulsively mimic not only the essential actions, but irrelevant ones as well. Human children do this, as do adults, but chimpanzees do not.[16] Such over-imitation is motivated by a desire to fit in, to respond to the potential cultural cues around an object or situation, and to understand the minds of those around us.[17] Most of these processes are unconscious, with conscious and deliberate forms of empathy often layering on top of, or operating in parallel to, this automatic empathic tuning.[18]

Empathy can enable us to cross all sorts of boundaries in surprising, even radical ways – especially when honed from an early age. In Eastern Siberia, the Yukaghir people live by hunting elk, bear and other creatures. To do so, hunters are said to transform themselves, abandoning their human forms to become hybrid, animal-like creatures, able to seduce their prey into giving themselves up as food. Practically, this involves hunters donning skin and furs from the animals they are tracking and, crucially, mirroring the movements of their prey. To us, it may be difficult to believe that the Yukaghir actually undergo transformation. Yet to watch them hunt – as the Danish anthropologist Rane Willerslev[19] has done – is to realise that they are able to connect with their prey on a fundamental level; their swaying and animal calling really do work to put prey at ease, and even draw prey towards waiting hunters. Willerslev describes this as a profound act of empathy where hunters and prey take on part of an animal's being.

If empathy is powerful enough to cross species boundaries,

it can certainly do the same with ethnicity. In Kilburn, on the Caldwell estate, if it was a Friday afternoon, you could reliably find many of the estates' younger mothers gathered in a small church hall. Each Friday, staff and volunteers transformed the space into a cheap and cheerful community café. A welcoming atmosphere, affordable food, and the opportunity to momentarily leave children in the hands of volunteers and catch up with friends made the space one of the busiest and most diverse places on the estate. In the bustling play area, young children from different backgrounds zipped around, balancing one another on see-saws or figuring out, with the help of volunteers, how to share toys without coming to tears.

These close encounters often meant that children went on to form lasting, meaningful friendships. One summer, on the last Friday before the start of the school year, two best friends were brought in by their beaming parents, wearing their new school uniform. One child was from an Afro-Caribbean family, the other white British. The first was beaming in her new uniform, proudly showing it off, but her friend looked crestfallen. While they were being paraded around, a café volunteer noticed this and bent down to tell the girl that her uniform really did look lovely. 'But we look the same now!' she protested. 'How will people tell us apart?' While, to us, the idea that skin colour marks a meaningful – or at least visible – difference may seem self-evident, close, empathic relationships can make such notions simply unthinkable.

Less radically, but perhaps even more importantly, the café also worked to transform the lives of adults. Parents typically broke off into familiar groups, not unlike in a high-school cafeteria. Here, the Filipinos, some with their own children, others nannies with their charges; there the Eritrean mums, most of whom arrived as refugees; here a tight-knit squad of women from black Caribbean and white European backgrounds. Despite this clustering, people often ended up thrown together. Those helping watch the children would bond over the shared travails of parenting, or of immigrant life in the UK. Overheard conversations would spill over to include neighbouring groups. A full house could mean having to find a seat at a new table, while rushing to help a weeping child could lead to a connection with their mother. The forms of joint attention and shared experience involved in parenting and in sharing the lively space helped parents see something of themselves reflected in others, and enabled them to connect across different backgrounds. Over the course of months or years, you could often watch the friendship groups of regulars grow increasingly diverse.[20]

At a larger scale, empathic connections can even remake group boundaries and transform collective identities. In colonial Rhodesia – modern-day Zimbabwe – as members of different tribal groups moved from villages into newly developing cities in search of opportunity, a huge shift occurred. As these new migrants experienced urban life together, many of them began to discard their old ethnic identities and adopt new or different ones. Where people may have once insisted that ethnic identities were ancient and immutable, in less than a generation these changed entirely. This shift was not simply a matter of tactical urban camouflage, where migrants adopted new identities to blend in or chase opportunities. Rather, it was a deep, personally felt shift, made possible by the new forms of togetherness city life enabled. Joking with erstwhile strangers in public canteens or working together in new jobs played important roles. However, one of the most important ways in which ethnic identities were reinvented was through participation in dance teams, which mixed together elements from different ethnic traditions.[21] The shared attention, coordination and exhilaration of dance has a powerful ability to create a lived, visceral sense of commonality and togetherness.[22] These charged experiences of being in tune with one another, especially when sustained over time, run roughshod over seemingly inflexible distinctions.

Casting our minds back to those post-war researchers, we can see that the picture isn't as clear as it first seemed. In the Robbers Cave experiment, Muzafer Sherif was determined to show how group conflict came easily to the campers, and by extension, to humanity. Recently, however, the Australian psychologist Gina Perry has revisited a number of the key studies used to support a tribal, conflictual view of human nature. She has found evidence that these were heavily manipulated. In Sherif's case, before the study that made him famous, he made two previous attempts to run summer camp experiments, which turned out very differently. At a camp in Middle Grove, New York, simply allowing the campers a day to interact freely before they were divided into teams was enough to make them resilient to all the experimenters' efforts to stoke division.[23]

Empathy, however, is rarely neutral, or universal. We cultivate our capacities for mimicry, joint attention and mental modelling within particular environments, which channel these abilities in specific directions. Meanwhile, our motivation to fit in – to tune into what is normal, acceptable or valued in our immediate environment – makes our empathic abilities even more selective. When reading emotion during a conversation, our empathic abilities have a harder time with less familiar faces and modes of expression, often resulting in gaps across cultures or ethnic groups.[24] Tellingly, even among people of the same cultural and ethnic background, introducing the very idea that we belong to opposing groups – say, two opposing teams in a competition – serves to diminish our ability to empathise with one another.[25]

These failures of empathy have less to do with limits on our actual empathic abilities, and more to do with culturally guided habits around how and when we use these abilities. In a clever experiment, a team of Italian and French researchers made white and black African Italians watch a video of a needle slowly being pushed into a human hand. Imagine this – does it make you cringe? When the hand matched their own race, volunteers cringed as well – a quick, automatic response, with the nerves in their hand firing as if they had been jabbed themselves. When the hand belonged to the other race, however, these empathic responses were slower or absent. The experimenters then showed both groups the same video, but this time featuring a violet hand. With the alien, violet hand, participants' automatic empathic reactions once again kicked in. The experiment showed that it is not difference or unfamiliarity per se that inhibits empathy, but the cultural understandings we attach to this difference.[26]

Empathy is physical, intimate, close to the chest. But it does not require physical presence. Modern media and public figures have become increasingly adept at triggering empathic reactions – whether compassion, anger or attachment – at a distance. The anthropologist William Mazzarella explores how advertising, populist rallies and new forms of media gain their power through creating a sense of immediacy and vitality – a sense that audiences are connecting directly with someone or something, in a way that resists being captured in words. Especially at a distance, however, empathy operates through culturally specific repertoires of connection – what Mazzarella calls 'archives of experience'.[27] Whether Donald Trump inspires you, makes you angry or leaves you cold, whether the slow-mo shots of laughing friends in a Coca-Cola commercial feel authentic or contrived, depends in large part on how you have previously learnt to tune in and respond to such performances.

Taken together, the possibilities and limitations of empathy create a tricky situation. On the one hand, empathy is a powerful ability, which allows us to connect to others across a wide range of seemingly significant divides – even to connect across species. Empathy can not only shape, but transform our fundamental sense of self; it can forge close, committed forms of care, cooperation and connection – such as those evident in Daniel's and Kev's relationships – in ways that can cut against our firmly held convictions and prejudices. On the other hand, our capacity for empathy is never neutral or all-encompassing. Rather, from a young age, it develops in relation to our environment, which makes it easier to empathise with some over others. This same process that underpins empathy can also work to create a sense of deep difference, where our feelings of selfhood, attachment and security, of how to understand and navigate the world, do not line up with those of others.

Even when we *can* extend empathy towards unfamiliar others, we face another, crucial limit: empathy is highly taxing. Empathy draws heavily on our mental, emotional and physical resources. It is such a costly ability that people seem to have an unconscious urge to avoid exercising it too widely or too often.[28] The taxing nature of empathy was a challenge that Robin Dunbar noticed even in other primates. Species that tended to form larger groups needed to put more time into bonding activities to maintain harmony within their groups – to the point where this was putting pressure on the hours available in the day. For humans, there are often distinctive advantages to living in larger groups – from greater security to the ability to divide up tasks or cultivate specialised skills.[29] Many of these benefits, however, often come from groups where it simply isn't possible to maintain strong face-to-face relationships with every member. There are also benefits to cooperation or harmony *across* groups, but here, empathy becomes even more demanding: psychologists have shown that trying to connect with people from unfamiliar backgrounds takes up even more mental capacity than trying to connect with those who are more familiar.[30] Observing these patterns in both primates and humans, Dunbar argued that empathy alone was not sufficient to hold most human groups together. This is especially true in relation to the scale of modern, urban life. In Portugal, for example, research on mobile phone use shows that residents of Lisbon, with a population of around

560,000, have twice as many people they maintain contact with than in the town of Lixa, with a population of 4,233.[31] These extra connections not only stretch our time more thinly but are also more likely to be with people from less familiar backgrounds.

❋

Fortunately, we have another powerful tool at our disposal – symbolic thinking. This capacity is the foundation of imagination, speech, language and literacy. Symbolic reasoning plays an important role in virtually all of human life.[32] In the words of anthropologist Roy Rappaport, 'Humanity is a species that lives and can only live in terms of meanings it itself must invent. These meanings and understandings not only reflect [...] an independently existing world but participate in its very construction.'[33] Empathy and symbolic reasoning are not opposed capacities. Throughout much of our lives they are closely entangled. Yet they relate to one another in different ways – reinforcing one another in certain moments and tugging in opposite directions in others.

Symbolic thinking can be more or less abstract. Abstraction refers to the capacity of language to create representations that capture an *idea* of the thing they refer to. As the anthropologist Webb Keane puts it, 'Concepts and categories typically involve some degree of abstraction and generalisation of what might otherwise be very specific, concrete circumstances, the results of which can be applied more widely.' Our collective evolutionary history is marked by the emergence of more abstract forms of thinking and communicating over time.[34]

Where other primates used physical touch as a way of building connections, we came to use language as well – conversation and story, gossip and imagination.[35] Unlike most animal communication, human language is highly symbolic. We don't simply use sounds to indicate things in the immediate present, like an approaching predator. Instead, we often use language to *represent* things – to indicate the *idea* of a predator. Unlike the physical environment, representations are easy to manipulate – even in improbable ways. Manipulating representations enables us to imagine new possibilities, new ways of understanding and acting on the world. For instance, witnessing a fox hunting a rabbit, or a hungry polar bear attacking humans, we might categorise these as relationships between 'predator' and 'prey'. These categories enable us to ask a number of imaginative questions: What makes a creature a predator? What do the bear and fox have in common? Is it their sharp teeth? Their cunning? Are these qualities accessible to others? Is it possible for the rabbit to hunt the fox? Or for humans to hunt the bear?

At an even more abstract level, we are not only capable of using symbolic reasoning to think, question, imagine and plan, but also to reflect on language itself – to ask how language represents and relates to the world. We can do this by putting our thoughts and ideas into a physical medium, such as the written word, as well as by sophisticated communicative forms such as poetry.[36] Although the prehistory of poetry or epics is hard to trace, we know that written language appears later on in our evolutionary history, and seems to reflect a shift in thinking. For instance, decorated graves are some of the earliest forms of human art. While our early ancestors and close relatives – such as Neanderthals – buried their dead, grave decorations seem to involve more than simply respect or a concern for hygiene. These decorations *represent* the dead – they refer to their presence in life, and perhaps even after death, as something distinct from their physical being. In this way, media such as writing, art or poetry raise questions not only about how the material world is arranged, but about how concepts are formed, how they relate to one another, how they work as descriptions, how they gain or lose power. Questions of how and when things become meaningful or true open the way to various forms of testing and probing into the unknown world, including that of modern science.[37]

Abstraction is the key quality of language that enables us to connect with unfamiliar others. The act of capturing the world around us in various representations untethers thought and communication from the here and now. It allows us to imagine and talk about distant, far-off places, inhabit the past or the future, and imagine new possibilities. To the extent that language is shared, these possibilities become accessible not only to ourselves but to others. In the words of the pioneering linguist Charles Hockett, humans have 'the capacity to say things that have never been said or heard before and yet to be understood by other speakers of the language'.[38]

When it comes to connecting with others, abstract thinking allows us to extend our understanding beyond that provided by face-to-face relations and the limits of our existing knowledge and our empathic capabilities. In some relations, symbolic reasoning works in tandem with empathy – channelling it, supplementing it or substituting for it in different ways, moment by moment. The terms we use for kin and family are good examples. Concepts such as 'sister', 'husband' or 'godparent' offer culturally specific templates for relationships, setting expectations for how we ought to understand and act towards others, and for how we ought to evaluate our relationships as good or bad. Even as we forge relationships that are uniquely our own, we continue to use these templates as points of reference. In the process we render these categories less abstract by grounding them within specific experiences. Meanwhile, in more distant relationships, abstract reasoning can play a more dominant role. Categories such as 'teacher', 'doctor' or 'boss' can provide the primary script for how we interact with less familiar others. At even greater distance, abstract concepts such as 'migrant', 'citizen', 'billionaire', 'human being' or 'politician' provide us with ways of thinking about and relating to people we may have never met. All these forms of symbolic reasoning extend our social worlds far beyond the horizons of what could be accessed through empathy alone.

As with empathy, however, the potentials and limitations of abstraction go hand in hand. Going back to Gregory Bateson, concepts are ways of marking out 'differences which make a difference' – breaking down the endless variability of the world by putting things into boxes.[39] This makes certain forms of understanding possible at the expense of others. For instance, Inuit people categorise polar bears not quite as 'predators' but as *fellow hunters*. Whereas the term 'predator' imagines an oppositional relationship – one where humans may well be on the losing side – understanding polar bears as fellow hunters allows for a respectful appreciation of the danger they may pose, but stresses commonality. One consequence of this is that Inuit people are attuned to learning from other 'fellow hunters'. For instance, hunting seals when they are swimming under Arctic ice is a notoriously tricky business. Inuit hunters, however, mimic techniques learnt from polar bears to lure seals towards breathing holes in the ice. Another consequence of this categorisation is that Inuit people understand hunting not as a destructive or extractive process, but as one that is essential to maintaining processes of natural flourishing – as bodies sustain other life and (human or animal) souls travel to be reborn. When a 2010 Canadian government study reported that the numbers of narwhals in the high Arctic seas had increased from 30,000 to 60,000, Inuit elders attributed the increase to more intense hunting, not less.[40] These concepts open up certain imaginative possibilities while closing down others.

Abstraction takes the vast complexity of the world – the wide range of ways we can see and think and feel – and narrows it by putting things into generic categories. But everyday communication often opens things back up by reconnecting abstract concepts with local contexts and extending and enriching their meaning in the process. It does this in a number of related ways.

Firstly, everyday communication typically involves ongoing conversation, allowing for meaning to be reworked over time. Rather than trying to pin down exactly what we mean in precise terms, ongoing conversation allows us to speak, weigh up the responses and reactions of others, and then respond accordingly – fine-tuning our language in relation to others, across the flow of everyday life. We can, for example, say 'I love you' to a partner in the first instance, and then, gradually, over time, figure out what exactly this means in terms of caring for one another, living arrangements, commitment, children, work and much more, as life unfolds.

Secondly, everyday communication makes meaning collaboratively, through a process of give and take. Our ability to express ourselves is dependent on the capacity of others to interpret, identify with or respond to what we say and do. As such, concepts, ideas, stories, conversations, art, ritual and much more are made collectively, infused with meaning from a range of perspectives.

Third, everyday communication allows us to play with language and extend its meaning in new directions by drawing on familiar frames of reference.[41] By evoking concepts, such as ballerinas *en pointe* on their toes, fencers on guard, and 'pointed' remarks, hip-hop artists in the 1990s were able to talk about style and performance being 'on point', and have this new term make sense. In turn this made it possible for teenagers in the mid-2010s to talk about grooming and fashion as 'on fleek'.

Fourth, and finally, everyday communication brings language to life by connecting it to experiences, habits, emotions and events. Meaning goes far beyond what categories themselves convey. A familiar notion, popularised by Franz Boas, one of the founding figures of American anthropology, is that the Inuit have fifty words for snow. Actual lists vary by dialect, but a recent study found that the dialect of Inuit spoken in Nunavik, Quebec, has at least fifty-three terms for snow, including words such as *utuqaq*, ice that lasts year after year, *matsaaruti*, snow wet enough to ice a sleigh's runners, or *auniq*, 'rotten' ice, filled with holes.[42] The fact that so many terms exist is tied closely to the rhythm and challenges of everyday life in places like Nunavik – but, more than this, these terms come to life only in relation to particular experiences. They rely on the ability to detect subtle shifts in the snow underfoot, on experience in icing sled runners, or on a broader cultural understanding of natural rhythms, where, at certain times of year, both plants and ice 'rot'.

All four of these ways of grounding language comple-ment and reinforce one another. In a famous essay titled 'The Storyteller', the philosopher Walter Benjamin explored what made traditional forms of storytelling – oral epics, craftsmen sharing tales, or yarns from returned sailors – so powerful. He highlighted how traditional stories often changed across each retelling, as storytellers drew on their own perspective and worked to connect stories to whoever their audience was. Such stories, Benjamin emphasised, were often ambiguous. Charac-ters were sketched roughly, allowing many people to identify with them. Plots unfolded with an air of mystery, or a fairy-tale logic, enabling listeners to draw their own conclusions as to the significance of what had transpired. And these stories rarely ended definitively – they could always be continued in new ways. All this made it easier for people to imaginatively step into or connect with traditional stories – to invest in their nar-rative and draw on their ideas by weaving these into the frame of their own lives. Storytelling worked as an unfolding conver-sation; it treated meaning as a collective possession, drew on familiar frames of reference and tapped into lived experience.

To communicate with wider audiences, however, or to enable us to relate to more distant strangers, language must operate at a more abstract level. Writing in 1936, Benjamin con-trasted storytelling with two genres prominent in his day – the novel and 'information' (giving newspapers as an example of the latter). Novels and news, Benjamin claimed, worked much harder to impose a particular interpretation. They told you in more clear-cut terms what characters were thinking or what motivated them. They told you why events happened and why they mattered. They often relied on more generic categories, such as 'healers', 'migrants' or 'citizens', capable of applying to a range of different people and situations in broad strokes. They were written to ensure that a wide, general audience could comprehend them. In short, they were more abstract – relying more on fixed categories, rather than on the play and complexity of everyday communication, to supply their meaning. These features made both the novel and information capable of travelling more widely. Yet these same features narrowed the ways in which people could relate to these genres and make the stories they conveyed their own. This involved a sort of meeting in the middle. Today, psychologists have shown how reading novels can sometimes extend our capacity for empathy, allowing us to understand and identify with unfamiliar characters and to map these understandings onto other situations.[43] Yet Benjamin argued that to make lives legible in this way, novels also had to narrow the possibilities available for interpretation – limiting how widely their stories could be identified with or used as guides when compared to traditional storytelling. 'Information', given by the daily news, or in dry reports from experts, was even narrower – not simply turning people into characters, but casting them as anonymous statistics. Benjamin's misgivings have been backed up by other recent psychological work showing that people extend relatively more compassion to tragedies and challenges that play out on the scale of their own social worlds – individuals or small groups – than they do to similar issues affecting thousands or tens of thousands.[44] There is a trade-off, then, between the reach of our stories and their capacity to relate to local worlds. Understanding more distant others often means doing so in thinner terms.

As empathy and symbolic reasoning tangle together and pull apart, they cultivate distinctive patterns of understanding, giving shape to different perspectives that don't always align. In certain situations it's possible for empathy and more abstract forms of symbolic reasoning to pull us in contradictory directions, just like in Daniel and Kev's complicated friendship. Their close collaboration relies on a highly empathic, practical understanding of one another, which does not implicate broader categories of difference. Meanwhile, their stubborn political differences remain locked into abstract stories, which are shaped, repeated and reinforced in circuits of media and debate stretching way beyond Kilburn, making it difficult to contest these stories at a local level.

This tug of war between empathic and abstract understandings can play out in a range of different ways across the political spectrum. Don Black runs Stormfront, one of the web's largest and most prominent white nationalist sites. His wife Chloe works as a spokesperson for a charter school set up to support underprivileged black and Latino children. When questioned about this awkward link, Chloe seemed to struggle to see how her work and her support for her husband were incompatible. This pattern – where close connections become exceptions to principled commitments – echoes the familiar defence following an accusation of racism: 'I can't be racist! I have black friends!' The contradictions that emerge point to something more complex than bad faith or simple defensiveness. They reveal the ways in which empathic and abstract understandings have the potential to slip past one another, and they reveal the need for political approaches that can address both forms of knowledge at the same time.

Whether interwoven or pulling apart, when it comes to how we live with difference, we need to work with not one but two different tools for connecting with others. Although empathy and symbolic understandings share some common foundations, and often build on one another, they are also capable of pulling in different directions. Harmony in one arena does not guarantee harmony in the other. Since the Second World War, we've come to understand that we are capable not only of division and conflict, but of creative, transformative forms of connection and cooperation as well. However, we are only just beginning to understand the way these capacities play out across different dimensions of life. To find better ways of living with others requires us to resist treating difference as something that takes the same form everywhere we encounter it. Instead, we must treat this as a varied challenge and craft different ways of relating to others, near and far.

CHAPTER THREE

US AND THEM

'Don't get me started on *them*,' Fawzia scoffed, 'that group has problems!' Taken aback, I asked her what she meant. Originally from Somalia, we'd been talking about the challenges she faced supporting her children at school, having not been through the British education system herself. Assuming I was being helpful, I suggested that she might be interested in a local, community-run 'homework club'. The club, founded by a group of migrant parents, was guided by similar anxieties around how best to support their children in an unfamiliar system. Together, they had managed to hire two teaching assistants from nearby schools to provide after-school group tutoring at affordable rates. While children were with the tutors, parents would gather themselves – partly to manage the logistics of the club, to keep track of the finances and plan publicity, but largely to form a sort of talking shop over tea and snacks. Knowing that others had been through similar struggles – living as refugees, feeling caught between cultures, or navigating the ins and outs of life in Kilburn – parents used the club as a venue for collective problem-solving, offering each other sympathy, advice and support. This, I thought, sounded just like what Fawzia needed.

Clearly, I was wrong. Annoyed, Fawzia continued, explaining that by focusing on academic success, the group had got it all wrong. The problem wasn't whether children were getting enough support, she insisted, but that the British school system was not teaching them the right values. Her children were struggling, and the older ones frequently acted out. To her, this was because they had little connection to their heritage. They did not speak Somali, nor did they know their own history. The traditional values that she believed had the potential to offer her children guidance and strength were vanishing in front of her own eyes. They were too British.

Fawzia was uneasy not simply because her Somali heritage was important to her. She was also aware that even as her children tried to embrace a British identity, they constantly faced barriers. At school they were shoved around, had their homework stolen, were called names or were simply shunned. For her children to have to face all this, and then for them to want, more than anything, to be like their classmates, broke Fawzia's heart. She saw in her Somali heritage a way out of this trap – a way of living that didn't rely on the affirmation of bullies or on success in a school system where they would always be seen as catching up.

Across North America and Western Europe, people like Fawzia are the subject of intense debate, and are often met with demanding and contradictory expectations. On the one hand, minority groups are pushed to take part in public life: to learn national languages, adopt majority cultures and become active in their communities. At the same time, as minorities become more visible, they attract increasing resentment. They're blamed for taking away jobs, diluting national culture or putting pressure on local resources. Sometimes, no matter how well they blend in, the mere sight of someone who looks a bit different in public is enough to trigger hostility. In 2015, one of the UK's most beloved television programmes, *The Great British Bake Off*, was won by Nadiya Hussain, a hijab-wearing Muslim, born and raised in Luton. At the time, Nadiya's victory triggered a wave of snippy commentary, questioning whether she was British enough to deserve the title. A few years later, when she wrote in a national newspaper about how she celebrated Christmas, she triggered further backlash, this time for adopting British traditions that supposedly weren't hers.

This 'double bind'[1] relates to a problem that anthropologists themselves have had to face when dealing with questions of identity. On the one hand the varied ways in which different cultural groups relate to others show that there is almost nothing fixed about how we form our identities. There are no universal ways of marking difference. Traits that we may imagine to be significant, such as skin colour or place of birth, are routinely disregarded by various cultural groups. On top of this, anthropologists, historians and others have, for decades, been chronicling how individuals are often able to move between seemingly exclusive groups. Definitions of race or nationality get rewritten all the time.

Yet we treat identity with deadly seriousness. We kill and die for nations and ethnic groups. We use racial categories to judge character. We treat locality as destiny. Although we may be able to recognise some forms of identity as fluid and negotiable, we treat others as innate. Whether it's our nationality, political creed, family, gender or ethnicity, there are facets of identity that feel fundamental to who we are – to the extent that giving up these identities feels impossible to imagine. These two perspectives paint a radically contrasting picture, where our group differences appear at once fixed and fluid. How can both be true at once?

These contradictory perspectives are apparent not only in the demands migrants and minorities are faced with from the outside, but also, often, in the ways in which majority and minority groups alike approach their own identities. For many years, Fawzia had talked about starting a local Somali community group, primarily supporting parents in providing language and cultural education. Her disenchantment with the homework club gave her the spark she needed to get things going, and just a few weeks after we spoke, she organised a planning meeting. At the meeting, a small group of friends, acquaintances and strangers – all around Fawzia's age, most born in Somalia – gathered to discuss what sort of support they wanted to see. Among those in attendance were Zahra and her husband. When it was their turn to talk Zahra explained that they had come because they were particularly interested in organising something for isolated older people in their community. They suggested linking up with another Somali cultural organisation nearby to help jump-start their own efforts – and to provide a wider network that could better combat elders' loneliness and isolation. There was an awkward, uncertain pause, until someone else volunteered a different suggestion, and the discussion moved on as if Zahra had never chimed in. Whenever they were asked about collaboration with other Somali organisations, Fawzia and her closest co-organisers would become evasive – reluctant to take up the suggestion, but also reluctant to articulate why.

Researchers have highlighted how in the UK, Somali cultural organisations have struggled to bring Somalis together across clans.[2] Traditionally, every Somali belongs to one of six major clan families. With the outbreak of civil war in 1989, Somalia splintered violently along clan lines. The majority of Somalis in the UK are refugees who fled the civil war, and, scarred by their experience, many of them brought a distrust of other clans with them. In turn, many British Somali organisations have, openly or covertly, been set up for specific clans – and even when this has not been the case, some British Somalis have been wary of turning to organisations whose affiliations are unclear. Fawzia never explained her own wariness around cooperating with other organisations, but by the time her group was up and running, other Somali families in the neighbourhood were voicing the same sort of scepticism she had voiced towards the homework club – it served certain interests and supported certain values, but not others.

Fawzia's story reveals an interplay between two contrasting

understandings of identity. In certain moments she treats Somali identity as an open question – where a group of friends and strangers can gather around a table and define it themselves. In other moments, it serves as an already established foundation for ethical guidance and dignity, marked by seemingly irreconcilable divides that make cooperation impossible. In one moment, she expresses frustration at the closed, exclusive attitudes of those around her, and in another she adopts a similarly closed stance herself. From the outside, these shifts look contradictory, even incoherent. To resolve this contradiction it may be tempting to argue that one of these perspectives is somehow false or inauthentic. But the very fact that both perspectives remain compelling to Fawzia – and to so many others – suggests the need to take an anthropological perspective, and ask how it may be possible to see both perspectives as true *at the same time*. But it also suggests that this sense of truth may emerge not from one perspective taken in its own right, but from how each perspective meets and modifies the other. From an anthropological perspective, the relevant question is not *whether* groups are fluid *or* fixed, but *how* groups might be fluid *and* fixed, dynamic and deadly serious, all at once.

❋

We tell three major stories about what makes group identities fixed and inescapable. The first imagines groups – especially ethnic and racial groups – as defined by biology, often by shared blood. The second sees groups as the possessors of distinctive shared traditions – unique and irreducible ways of existence. The third claims that thinking in terms of 'us and them' or 'self and other' is a basic psychological tendency. Over the course of the twentieth century, all three of these stories have been pulled apart by anthropologists who have turned to the wide record of human diversity to show that none of these ways of thinking about group identity are, in fact, universal.

The oldest story has to do with biology. Even before Charles Darwin, European thinkers were talking about national, ethnic and racial identity as a matter of shared descent. Darwin's theory of evolution and, more recently, the discovery of DNA, gave renewed life to these ideas. Until the middle of the twentieth century, anthropologists held to their own version of this story. Already specialised in studying kinship, anthropologists had long argued that different ethnic groups were primarily defined by descent – especially when state structures were not present. At the time, it was common practice for anthropologists to spend their time unravelling who was related to whom, in order to produce staggeringly elaborate family trees. The goal of this exercise was to show how villages, clans and nations were built by layering formal roles on top of networks of blood ties – binding politics and kinship tightly together. Clan-based African societies such as Somalia were taken as quintessential examples of the power of kinship to unite people.[3]

There are six large Somali clan families: Dir, Daarood, Isaaq, Hawiye, Digil and Rahanweyn.[4] These clan families are then subdivided into different clans, sub-clans, lineages and familial groups – with membership in all these groupings inherited through one's father. Many Somalis claim to be able to trace the lineage of their clan family right back to the Prophet Muhammad's family and speak of their ancestry as a mix of Middle Eastern and black African.[5] The Somali term *reer*, meaning family but also implying a sense of origin, is used flexibly to refer to different groups, ranging from smaller family units to large clans, encompassing society in kin terms. Historically, *reer* guided everything from trade to politics to marriage. The anthropologist I. M. Lewis once characterised Somali society as organised around 'genealogical' ties 'bred in the bone' and running 'in the blood'.[6]

In 1969, the Norwegian anthropologist Frederik Barth

challenged the prevailing view that ethnic identity was rooted in blood relations – and with it, the idea that such groups were innate and inescapable. Tracing a wide range of anthropological studies, he found that in almost every case, you could find exceptions to the idea that ethnicity was defined by innate qualities like genetics. Looking at the cases of the Yao in China, the Pathans in Central and East Asia and the Fur in South Sudan, Barth revealed how groups which insisted on their unchangeable character actually allowed people to change membership all the time. The Yao practised adoption, resulting in about one in ten members of each generation coming from other groups. Despite this, adoptees typically came to be considered fully Yao – a change worked through rituals, such as incorporating children into ancestral obligations and marriage. Meanwhile, members of the Fur, who were farmers, would often leave to join the nearby Baggara, who were nomadic cattle herders. Changing their way of life and their customs was generally seen as a change in ethnic identity. Despite these frequent exchanges, the Yao, the Fur and the Baggara all frequently spoke of their groups as unchanging, and often characterised themselves all as kin.[7]

A similar flexibility is apparent when it comes to ethnic groups writ large – which often blur and blend into one another. Historically, many ethnic groups have expanded by incorporating other groups – often growing their political power in the process. Among countless examples, there are the Sinhalese kingdoms of Sri Lanka, the Tonga in Zambia and the Baganda in Uganda.[8] America's so-called 'white' majority is another example. This seemingly uniform category is composed of migrants from a range of different backgrounds, including many who, historically, were cast as distinctive and 'inferior' racial groups – such as Jews, Italians or the Irish.[9]

What Barth realised was that asserting an innate identity was fundamentally symbolic. People might speak of their ethnicity using the language of blood, but in practice they are often highly flexible as to who does or doesn't qualify as a member. Anthropologists came to realise that when the people they studied said that their clans, villages or nations were all related, they were often telling stories. This is not to say that they were lying. Rather, in many cases, people were evoking a sense of relatedness as an ongoing process. Familial ties were spoken into existence or cultivated over time. Since Barth's time, this flexibility has been found in groups across the world and throughout history – whether in terms of nationality, ethnicity or race.

Barth was writing at a time when ideas of race and ethnicity were beginning to shift, from emphasising biology and descent towards emphasising shared culture. Yet, rather than offering a clean break, ideas of cultural distinctiveness often drew on the language established around race. For instance, in Enoch Powell's 'rivers of blood' speech, where he predicted a future of widespread violent racial conflict, Powell professed a cultural understanding of difference – where group identity was not a matter of bloodlines, but one of social networks, upbringing, values, traditions and habits. Even though these differences weren't biological, Powell still imagined them as inherited, inflexible and irreconcilable, making it difficult for people to transcend culture or for cultural groups to coexist. A few months after his speech, Powell flatly proclaimed his view that 'the West Indian or Asian does not, by being born in England, become an Englishman'.[10] Again, anthropologists played a role in perpetuating this perspective.[11] Many of Barth's contemporaries mapped forms of culture neatly onto seemingly distinct groups. In response, Barth not only challenged descent-based notions of group identity, but culturally bound ones too. When it came to culture, he argued, it was easy to find examples of groups which claimed unity but which varied widely in their perspectives and practices.

To account for how groups maintained a sense of identity,

Barth argued that at their core ethnic groups were defined by key 'boundary markers'. Rather than uniformly sharing forms of culture, Barth argued, groups pinned their sense of distinctiveness on a small set of key cultural forms – ways of dressing, elements of language, stories, histories, rituals, skills, icons, core beliefs. These cultural forms worked to stand in for the distinctiveness of groups as a whole, creating a *sense* of fundamental commonality and shared destiny.

Barth's insight rings true even when we look into some of the most divisive conflicts in recent history. A striking example of how symbolic boundaries create identities emerges from the history of the former Yugoslavia and its bloody break-up in 1995. In Yugoslavia, Bosnians, Croats and Serbs had lived together in a complex mix of peace and compromise since the start of Communist rule in 1945. The three groups shared a mixed history; in some places peace had been the order of the day for as long as anyone could remember. Elsewhere, people carried the memories of past nationalist agitation or of violent clashes. Nonetheless, during the Communist era, thinkers and leaders from all groups championed the idea of a unified Yugoslavia. For many citizens, this unity was a lived reality. Many areas experienced high-rates of intermarriage. Serbian, Bosnian and Croatian functioned as distinct but mutually intelligible variations of a shared language. Customs and cuisines were shared, borrowed, tweaked and exchanged.

Leading up to the bloody 1995 civil war, enterprising politicians and military leaders worked hard to repaint this history as one of enduring, irreconcilable differences. For instance, in an infamous 1989 speech the Serbian nationalist leader Slobodan Milošević invoked the 1389 Battle of Kosovo to paper over centuries of complex coexistence with a narrative of primordial conflict. He openly owned this rewriting of history, declaring: 'Today, it is difficult to say what is the historical truth about the Battle of Kosovo and what is legend. Today, this is no longer important.'[12] Nationalist leaders also spoke of the three languages not as related, but as though they were mutually unintelligible.[13] Today, following the conflict, the three groups not only occupy separate states, but insist on the distinctiveness of their own languages, making modifications or reviving archaic terms to engineer this distinctiveness for themselves.[14] As barriers to communication and exchange grow, the three groups drift further apart and become increasingly distinct. Despite this, linguistic distinctiveness may remain a primarily symbolic boundary – people claim that the three languages are unintelligible to one another, but translation-based experiments suggest otherwise.[15] Depending on the boundaries we set up, ethnic identities can be made, or unmade, with astonishing speed.

It turns out that clan, in Somalia, is similar. Local ways of speaking about clan always used the language of biological descent and relatedness. For many years anthropologists took this at face value. Today, however, it's clear that this talk about kinship involved a fair amount of poetic licence. In principle, closely related families, lineages or sub-clans supported one another in commerce, warfare and negotiation. Historically, however, this ideal was 'often more honoured in the breach',[16] based on the actual relations between groups at any given time. Even the tracing of bloodlines could be a fluid practice. In different circumstances, one could claim descent from different ancestors associated with particular wars, alliances or events, to tell different stories of who one was *really* related to. Esteem and political influence stemmed not from lineage, but from the ability of leaders to participate in political life, negotiate contracts and forge new alliances – which often involved re-narrating one's ancestry in creative ways.[17] In other words, rather than treating descent as a fact of nature, many Somalis used ancestry as a flexible metaphor for how people could be connected. Its very flexibility allowed them to reimagine their identity and the political possibilities of the world.

Barth wrote during an era of cultural reckoning, when efforts to grapple with the impact of the Second World War met and mingled with growing challenges to gender inequality, racism and colonialism. Partly inspired by Barth's work, a new idea began to take hold. 'Otherness' became a particularly important boundary marker. Psychologists, social scientists and philosophers – many from colonial or post-colonial countries – argued that group identity was often defined in opposition to outsiders. Lacking a uniform, unchanging identity of their own, ethnic groups conjured up fixed, highly stereotyped images of others – age-old rivals, lesser races – as a way of maintaining their sense of distinctiveness and superiority.[18] This emphasis on otherness was entangled with the workings of power, but for many thinkers there was something fundamentally psychological about it too. The self, at its core, could be seen as defined in opposition to the other.

Again, however, the idea that we have an innate tendency to define ourselves in opposition to others falls apart when we take an anthropological perspective. Take the Nayaka hunter-gatherers in South India, studied by Nurit Bird-David. The Nayaka live in very small groups in the forest. They have a very open understanding of kinship, and of Nayaka identity, considering anyone who is present with them to be *sonta* – a term that at once means 'like us' and 'relatives'. Anyone can be considered *sonta*, and Bird-David observes that distinctions that may appear important to Westerners, such as a person's place of origin, their parentage, skin colour or physical features, simply go unnoticed in determining who counts as a relative. Even members of other species can be considered *sonta*. The Nayaka, argues Bird-David, have 'no mental map of ethnic groups and divisions',[19] simply a notion of people (and animals) as related in different ways. Over the years, groups such as the Nayaka have enabled anthropologists to understand that opposition is far from the only way to think of how collective identities are defined and made to relate to others.

Anthropology shows us that there is almost nothing fixed or fundamental about group identities at all. They are formed by categories we draw and act out, and it is always possible to think of ourselves in other ways. However, acknowledging this also creates new challenges. How do we then understand the intense feelings and commitments that flow from group identities? How do we make sense of what happened in the former Yugoslavia or Somalia, where group divisions boiled over into bloody civil war? Unquestionably, the manoeuvring and motivations of powerful actors – Milošević in Yugoslavia, or Somalia's Mohamed Siad Barre – play a crucial role in hardening boundaries and stoking division. Yet, if we are to insist on an anthropological perspective, we should be wary of the idea that 'power' tells us the full story. We also need to understand what makes group identities feel so compelling and natural to ordinary people themselves. If group boundaries are flexible and culture is fluid, why do they often feel so inflexible and solid?

※

It starts with belonging. 'Home is the return to where distance did not yet count,' wrote John Berger, the renowned British art historian, reflecting on experiences of immigration, loss and change.[20] For each of us, there are places, scents, sounds and people that anchor our sense of who we are and where we belong. For each of us, belonging is the feeling that our sense of self *fits* with the world around us.[21]

Belonging is hard to capture. This sense of 'fit' is often tangled and multifaceted. The designer and academic Roger Coleman writes about one form of it in East Anglia, in the rural east of England.[22] When he and his wife decided to raise and butcher a pig, they quickly realised they were in over their heads. They turned to their neighbours, Mr and Mrs Horrey, for help. Over the course of a single day, the Horreys helped them butcher a daunting 239 pounds of meat into sausages, bacon, lard and much more. The Horreys divvied up the work in a gendered manner, foisting this same division onto Roger and his wife Fran. It was only after making it through the mammoth task that Fran figured out that this division of roles was tied to the demands and rhythms of rural life. As Roger puts it:

> There was simply too much to do to the pig. One person alone could not manage it, and any arbitrary division of labour would mean that a couple might or might not know how to deal with their pig [...] The sexual division of labour here meant that each couple shared all the knowledge necessary for survival, for preserving their food against times of shortage. Each part was indispensable, and preserved within an oral tradition of skills for survival which were passed on by example, by helping with the task and by talking [...] about how things are done.[23]

The Horreys inhabit a world marked by subtle and overt divisions – of gender, skill, time and place. These divisions, however, are not simply categories imposed upon them in ways that feel alien or constricting. Instead, they are divisions that underwrite their capacity to understand, experience and act within the world. A gendered division of labour not only allowed the Horreys to organise their day and manage their tasks, but it enabled them to cultivate distinct skills – different forms of dexterity, differently honed senses, different bodies of memory – that complemented one another. These skills shaped their sense of who they were and what they could and couldn't do, but they also connected them to the world. Their sense of what it meant to be a man or woman related to particular elements of their surroundings, to the smell of coming rain or the seasonal behaviour of livestock. With others, gendered divisions gave them a way of naming and transmitting these often tacit skills, shaping the language they used to relate to others such as the Colemans. This same gendered division gave the Horreys a template for relating to one another and a foundation for their sense of self-worth. We have seen, earlier in this book, how there is nothing innate or inescapable about the particular gendered categories the Horreys lean on. Yet, for the Horreys, these categories take on a feeling of naturalness as they become woven into a web of correspondences – where bodies, skills, categories, feelings, relationships, objects and a given environment all come to fit with one another.

This sense of 'fit' becomes the foundation for belonging. Such foundations may be anchored in single places or they may be more widely dispersed. They may be many or few. Our feelings of belonging can be contradictory: we may feel at home in both the bustle of the city and the quiet openness of the countryside; our sense of home may incorporate feelings of both safety and pain. Belonging can feel incomplete, or like a past memory or future dream. What evokes this sense of belonging will vary for each of us, but however we come to feel it, belonging is one of our most fundamental and compelling needs.

Belonging often emerges at the intersection of empathic and symbolic understandings. Social psychologists have explored belonging in terms of our need for relationships with others, characterised by long-term bonds and mutual care. This need is closely related to many of the forms of empathic early learning detailed in the previous chapter, such as imitation, joint attention and the formation of early attachments.[24] But these same mechanisms extend our sense of belonging to reach beyond individual relationships to encompass our physical and cultural environment.[25] Language and culture offer us a repertoire of templates – concepts, images, practices – that underpin our ability to think, act and understand ourselves. The material world around us provides similar scaffolding. Writing with a pen, riding a bike or using a smartphone may lead us to develop particular mental habits and routines that rely on these external objects.[26] Without these supports to hand, we may find ourselves at a loss – unable to recall a certain event without flicking through photos on our phone, suddenly grasping for the right words to express ourselves in a second language in which we are otherwise fluent.

We often take belonging for granted. The sociologist Floya Anthias argues that we typically begin to reflect on what belonging means to us only when we feel out of place. She writes,

> It is precisely when we feel destabilised, when we seek for answers to the quandaries of uncertainty, disconnection, alienation and invisibility that we become more obsessed with finding, even fixing, a social place that we feel at home in, or at least more at home with; where we seek for our imagined roots, for the secure haven of our group, our family, our nation.[27]

For instance, with regard to language, the anthropologist and historian Lisa Mitchell has traced how the idea of a 'mother tongue' emerged only from the early-modern era.[28] As European states consolidated their authority over diverse local communities and worked to shape unifying national cultures, people began to compare the merits of different local languages and dialects. Promoters of different languages were prone to insisting that *theirs* was the most authentic and rich – attuned to the complexities of human experience – while emphasising the relative poverty of others. This question, of what languages could and could not represent, only emerged once Europeans began to regularly encounter other languages, grounded in other worlds and webs of correspondence.

In South India, where Mitchell works, efforts to champion different languages as authentic markers of local identity began in the nineteenth and twentieth centuries, taking off after

British colonial rule ended. As in Europe, bringing languages into contact with each other raised questions about how a language corresponded to experience and conveyed meaning – making it harder to take these correspondences for granted. The way people understood language shifted. Language went from simply being a means of communication to a distinctive expression of deep-seated identities. Some languages were even personified as gods. Language began to be described as something that could command feelings of *abhimānam*. This term can be understood to signify deep affection, but it also incorporates a sense of devotion, pride and love, as well as a sense of desire, or even a desire to injure others. To feel *abhimānam* is to feel that your essence is defined in close relation to whatever you feel *abhimānam* towards – in this case, a language. Popular movements to recognise various languages involved activism and demonstrations, but also violent clashes with police, fasts to the death and self-immolation. Partly at stake were the ways in which having an officially recognised language made it easier to access opportunities, ranging from university to government jobs. But the widespread, deeply passionate efforts of language champions show that the stakes ran deeper – involving a fundamental sense of belonging.[29]

Anthias points to why these feelings of belonging – and their loss – can be so powerful, describing them as 'feelings of being part of a larger whole'.[30] Belonging provides an important explanation not only for how group identities can come to feel so real and solid, but also for the sorts of things ordinary people become willing to do in the name of collectives. Our capacity to think and feel is always shaped by our cultural worlds, and our feelings of belonging capture this sense of entanglement with culture. The loss or upheaval of a cultural world can come to feel like the loss or upheaval of one's whole sense of self.

There is a politics to belonging that has to do not only with how belonging is cultivated or defended, but also with how different feelings of belonging get mapped onto particular cultural markers. Cultural worlds are never without differences in perspective, tension and disagreement. Everyday language may be rich, but it may be richer in capturing and valuing men's experiences than women's. Skills, habits, values, relationships, feelings and objects may correspond, but they rarely do so seamlessly. As Anthias puts it, 'The collective places constructed by imaginings of belonging gloss over the fissures, the losses, the absences and the borders within them.'[31] If worlds never quite add up, then the question of how feelings of belonging get attached to group identities is never a straightforward one.

In Mitchell's account of language politics in the South Indian state of Andhra Pradesh, the movement for linguistic and political recognition entailed compromises. Middle-class professionals often championed local language as a way of angling for opportunities and power – positioning themselves as the elite representatives of an authentic people. Less well-off citizens took up these same causes to access opportunities in a system where patronage, political representation and dignity were determined by who could lay claim to 'authentic' cultural and linguistic identities. These contending interests shaped which forms of language were recognised and promoted as genuine markers of local identity, and which were excluded and suppressed. Language politics, in other words, was never simply about championing the pure, collective voice of a given people – but about a struggle to name and channel diverse interests and attachments into particular visions of purity and collectivity. Inevitably, it benefited some more than others.

Closely tied to this question of politics is one of ethics. How do we inhabit, challenge or step beyond given frames? Although collective identities may not specify every facet of life, they rely on key boundary markers – values, practices, ideas, customs – to which each member must figure out their own relationship. In a now classic anthropological study, Lila Abu-Lughod writes about how Awlad 'Ali Bedouin women take dominant cultural ideas about public male honour and private female modesty and use them to carve out domestic, women-only spaces. In such private spaces, within tents and homes, women gossip and joke, conspiring to resist arranged marriages by organising a chorus of resistant voices within the family or by appealing to tradition. Women forge close bonds through sharing secrets; poking fun at men and their preoccupations with status; sharing grief; discussing family issues; and reciting poetry. Within, and sometimes beyond, the forms of Bedouin culture, they weave a space of defiance, intimacy and care. But the terms by which these women value themselves and other women – the ways in which they secure their own sense of belonging – do not necessarily line up with the ways in which men view or value them.[32]

Similar efforts to carve out ways of inhabiting cultural identities, or to contest these identities outright, can be seen within Kilburn's Somali community. When Aisha first arrived in the UK as a teenage refugee following the outbreak of the Somali civil war, she relied heavily on the Somali community in and around Kilburn for support. Family friends offered her places to stay, and support in establishing a life. These same people, however, also placed her under intense scrutiny, both as a single woman and as someone who was curious about life in the UK. Whether she was meeting up with friends or attending language classes, older relatives or family friends would frown and question if it was really appropriate for her to be so independent.

I first met Aisha, many years later, when she helped lead a meeting of a local campaign group. The 2015 national elections were coming up, and the team was eager to use the occasion to get the parliamentary candidates to commit to work on a range of local issues – among them addressing the crowded, squalid housing conditions faced by many refugees and social tenants in the area. Over the following weeks, I ran into Aisha at several more events, each associated with different groups – charity fundraisers, or residents' association meetings – making it clear just how involved she was in the area. As we got to know one another, Aisha would tell me stories from her past, tracing how her understanding of what it meant to be Somali had changed throughout her life.

Aisha met her future husband by chance, waiting for the bus with a friend. Overhearing them chatting he asked them where they were from – and, on hearing they were Somali, offered them a lift. He was charming, but Aisha recalls feeling shy and flustered at the offer. Her friend accepted for them, but Aisha panicked internally. What would her host family think if they found out? Was he flirting with them? What did he want? Aisha had begun to fantasise about marriage, seeing it as a route to a more independent life, freer from the watchfulness of others. In the Somali community, marriage conferred status and autonomy. It would mean an end to depending on the hospitality of others. In the car, as her friend chatted brightly with the stranger, Aisha remembers feeling a mixture of disappointment and relief that he wasn't interested in her. Yet as they parted, he told Aisha that he would like to see her again. Their courtship was smoothed along by the fact that he was well known in the Somali community, seen as someone respectable. Soon, he proposed.

Marriage, however, wasn't what she imagined it would be. Soon after their wedding, Aisha began to realise that her husband could be just as controlling as the family friends she had been living with. Like them, he would assert his authority as a matter of tradition. He would jealously quiz her over her time at work or with various community groups, refuse to do housework and shirk childcare responsibilities, all by insisting that she needed to behave like a proper Somali wife. When they eventually got divorced, Aisha's husband started telling others that Aisha had abandoned her heritage and faith. To her surprise, Aisha found many of her friends and relatives were willing to believe these allegations, trusting her husband because he was a man and because of his connections to the local community. Exhausted by endless gossip, she eventually drifted away from the Somali community.

When we met, Aisha was leading a very different life. She worked at a local school and volunteered at the refugee charity that first helped her out. She was completing a diploma in therapy, was involved with a group of refugee women running a catering business, served as a school governor, ran with a jogging group, was learning to swim and was an active, proud mother. Through these different activities, she had built a large network of friends, who she often spoke about with self-effacing gratitude – expressing appreciation to those who were able to see past the colour of her skin, her hijab or her imperfect English. She talked about all the moments when she wanted to try something new – learning to swim or running a business – only to be met with her old anxiety that people would judge her, followed by her surprise in finding people who were welcoming and supportive.

In many ways, Aisha challenged conventional ideas of what it means to be Somali. She remained deeply wary of the community's capacity for judgement and exclusion. Yet, despite this, she insisted that she still felt Somali in her heart. She struggled to say what this essential, enduring Somali identity consisted of, but she was convinced it still mattered. She was teaching her kids the Somali language, even though she saw no point in taking them to visit Somalia. She was especially passionate about the plight of Somali refugees, and animated – but also wary and sensitive – when discussing issues related to Somalis: sending money to family overseas, the role of religion, female circumcision, English-language skills.

Over time, something peculiar began to happen. After many years of being shunned by most other Somali women ('They think I'm mad,' she once declared), Aisha began to find herself being approached for help. She had previously been branded as un-Somali, but now, she explained, women were saying, 'You are Somali, but you are doing things differently, so we need your help.' She had come to be seen as someone who could navigate between tradition and the new possibilities and challenges of life in the UK. By 2015, she was involved in supporting a range of other Somali women facing similar circumstances: they had become primary breadwinners, they were struggling with husbands stuck stubbornly in the past, or they had recognised that their children were leading very British lives and building new identities of their own and they wanted to connect with them.

Collectively, Somalis in the UK are redefining Somali identity. Faith in Islam, which also allows people to build cross-cultural links, has gained in importance, as have activism, art and a new role for women in public life. These transformations have been imagined not as a break with the past, but as new approaches to old values and traditions. For example, the traditional value once placed on men's ability to make rousing speeches or recite poetry now informs a reinvigorated appreciation of poetry, music and art. While historically, deliberating over politics or local affairs was seen as a mark of male leadership, today women's participation in art, and in cultural and community groups, makes it possible to challenge men who spend too much time at home or at cafés, talking endlessly about politics but remaining removed from other facets of collective life. Together, Aisha and her friends are resisting the assumption that people like her ex-husband have the final say in defining what counts as Somali.

These varied, complex, even inconsistent positions – these different ways of being Somali or Bedouin, or inhabiting any other sort of identity – often remain tied to a sense of shared essence and intertwined fate. Aisha feels an enduring sense of Somali-ness despite her travails and uncertainty, just as the Awlad 'Ali Bedouin women Abu-Lughod spoke with may have ridiculed men's obsession with honour, but slept with guns under their pillows, ready to fight off Egyptian authorities attempting to further constrict Bedouin life. In fact, the power and pull of collective identities can emerge not despite but *through* the variability and complexity they encompass.

Writing fifteen years after Barth, another anthropologist, Anthony Cohen, built on Barth's original insight.[33] Working on the Shetland Islands in Scotland, Cohen quickly found that islanders shared a strong sense of a common Shetland identity, marked by particular symbols – fishing or herding sheep, or the importance of locality – key boundary markers, in Barth's sense. However, these shared symbols meant very different things to different people. For some, locality was about family and mutual support. For others it was an oppressive but inescapable force, characterised by gossip and surveillance. To some 'community' may have referred to those at the pub, while for others, it related to fishing. The symbols locals used to define their common identity, Cohen realised, were all marked by a high degree of flexibility. Locality, community or fishing worked as symbols of islander identity not because everyone agreed on what they meant, but because they could be meaningful to different people in different ways. As he put it,

> Symbols […] do more than merely stand for or represent something else … They also allow those who employ them to supply part of their meaning … their meanings are not shared in the same way. Each is mediated by the idiosyncratic experience of the individual … Symbols do not so much express meaning as give us the capacity to make meaning.[34]

Group bonds, he argued, were forged by the process of making meaning in plural, personal, varied ways, but nonetheless, together.

Aisha's story shows that this sort of unifying flexibility that lurks under the surface of our collective identities can exist not just between different people, but across the course of a single life. It shows that our collective identities not only draw us together across different experiences, but also ground our sense of who we are, even as we change. In this way shared identities feel profoundly important, not *despite* the diversity within them but precisely *because of it*. The categories that define us – and others – work like containers, providing thin parameters of difference that we fill with the fullness of our own, personal sense of belonging. Even when Aisha and those around her disagree over what Somali-ness means, they feel implicated in each other's interpretations. Aisha feels hurt when others paint her as betraying her Somali heritage. Others feel the impact of the criticisms from Aisha and others when they challenge male behaviour. Across these tensions, there is a sense that these are issues and questions that inescapably tie individuals into collectives, even when they disagree.

This makes identity into something paradoxical. On the one hand, this ability of collective identities to accommodate diversity suggests there is no *fundamental* link between the identities we inhabit and the forms of belonging we come to feel, forge or contest. Rather, forms of belonging come to be *mapped onto* identities in different ways. We use identities as a common shorthand for our own sense of belonging, even if these feelings of belonging vary in significant ways, person to person. This makes identity into something messy and dynamic, always plural, always changing. On the other hand, this very richness – the feeling that our identities anchor our sense of self, even across variation, and connect us with a wide range of others – can also make identity *feel fundamental*. Identity can take on an innate, universal quality. And that which lies beyond the present scope of our understanding of identity can feel profoundly alien.

❋

Human history is full of examples of cultures where group membership is relatively open, boundaries are blurred, and where ideas of otherness do not oppose notions of self. All this reveals how fluid the identities that bring us together, or hold us apart, can be. At the same time, the historical record is full of charged conflict carried out in the name of party, clan and nation – reminding us just how serious, ferocious and fixed group identities can become. Fixity and fluidity can work to both oppose or reinforce one another. Experiences of fluidity can help underwrite a sense of fixed identity and deep difference. But when it comes to deep difference, there are three other factors at play.

The first is that we may have a natural psychological tendency to think in rigid, categorical terms about human difference. Anthropologists have long recognised ethnic categorisation and stereotyping as providing a sort of cognitive map – distilling a complex world into a smaller set of simpler, more stable categories that are easier to think with.[35] On top of this, however, we may also have an instinct for thinking about categories as inherently fixed. The lives of the Vezo people of Madagascar are particularly revealing in this regard, because culturally their understandings of identities such as gender and ethnicity are especially flexible – taken as something 'achieved gradually and progressively throughout life, and even after death, rather than ascribed and fixed definitively at birth'.[36] The anthropologist Rita Astuti, who has lived and worked with the Vezo for several decades, has come to find that in many spheres of Vezo life, gendered distinctions are absent. Kinship, for example, is not distinguished by gender. People trace their family lineages simultaneously through maternal and paternal descent – resulting in people identifying a great number of kin. Likewise, while the full process of pregnancy and birth is only associated with those who are biologically female, the Vezo draw an equivalence between the capacity of men's semen and women's vaginal mucus to trigger a process of gestation, and also talk about men as capable of attaining a pregnancy-like state that can come from eating food provided by a woman's male lover.[37] These understandings of what bodies are, and how they matter, shrink the distinction between biologically male and female bodies, in comparison to our own understanding. Similarly, ethnic identity – whether one belongs to the Vezo, or to the nearby Masikoro, for example – is described not as a matter of descent, but as a product of where one lives, what one eats and how one makes a living. Children born to Vezo parents are not immediately thought of as Vezo themselves, 'as they are not yet competent at "struggling with the sea"'.[38] Meanwhile, to go from living on the coast and fishing to living inland, raising cattle and farming ('eating grass' as the Vezo put it), is to go from being Vezo to being Masikoro – and vice versa. Those who undergo such changes are recognised as having changed identity.

Despite all this, when quizzed about whether certain cultural or physical traits are inheritable, Vezo children, in particular, often give much more categorical answers that do not reflect the fluid notions of identity the Vezo profess. Children's answers generally contrast with the more culturally proficient responses of adults – though adults too can be caught out, or at least slowed down by cleverly worded questions about innate versus acquired traits. Based on this picture, and working in collaboration with psychologists, Astuti has argued that we have an innate psychological tendency towards thinking in terms of relatively fixed, categorical *types*. Yet, she stresses, this tendency does not amount to destiny. Vezo culture works both to minimise and to channel this tendency in distinctive ways. For instance, when the Vezo do, occasionally, think in more fixed terms about gender and bodies, they do not base these categorisations on the same physical traits – such as genitals – as we might. Instead, for the Vezo, whether a baby is born facing upwards or downwards is considered a matter of innate biology – as newborn boys are considered to understand the taboo of looking at their mother's vagina.

Next, distributions of power and institutional dynamics can play an important role in rendering identities more or less fixed. The sociologist Andreas Wimmer has been one of the most vocal advocates for understanding ethnic identities in terms of political opportunities and structures.[39] He has emphasised both that elites often play a disproportionate role in defining the boundaries of group identities, but also that the boundary markers that prove most compelling are often those which enable both elites and regular people to identify and fight for interconnected interests. Likewise, Wimmer places significant emphasis on states and other institutions in shaping ethnic boundaries. As modern states began to develop, they had to centralise power, wresting control from feudal lords and relatively autonomous cities and towns. In doing so, modern states required new terms of legitimacy. Governing elites reached into history and local customs to create a picture of 'the people' who they could claim to represent. These portraits of identity fit some subjects better than others. Meanwhile, colonised and enslaved people often found their identity defined for them, typically in stark, dehumanising terms. Groups faced a choice – influenced by their relative access to power – over whether and how to take up or resist these representations of themselves.

Today, states and other institutions continue to play important roles in facilitating access to resources – from jobs to security, to charity funding. As we saw in Mitchell's account of language politics in Andhra Pradesh, the ways people imagine and present their identities often relate to the opportunities available. A similar example comes from anthropologist Gerd Baumann's work in the late 80s and early 90s in Southall, west London, where he finds a diverse cast of residents – Afro-Caribbeans, Pakistanis, Gujaratis, Punjabis, white Brits – wrangling over how to define themselves. A predominant sense of separate cultures endures, Baumann argues – largely thanks to government policies that offer funding for community centres or language classes on the basis of ethnic-group membership, believing that this provides the best way of allocating resources. But whether in experimenting with new genres of music – such as the hip-hop and pop-inspired revitalisation of Bhangra, which helped inspire a new pan-Asian sense of identity – or through political activism – such as the women who came together to form Southall Black Sisters – Baumann also found spaces where people felt able to embrace more inclusive or experimental framings of identity that challenged dominant distinctions between groups.[40] Baumann's work points to how, when the possibility of survival, advancement or dignity becomes caught up with adhering to particular formulations of identity, these categories can come to feel weightier.

The relative power of different groups will change how they respond to these institutional incentives and pressures. Whether on the streets of Southall, or in the midst of the Somali civil war, sometimes ordinary people adopt relatively fixed notions of identity because they are not in a position to easily contest these – and because this approach may offer the best chance of survival. During the Somali conflict, acts of war were often attributed to clans as a whole. In turn, all members of that clan became potential targets. Clan affiliations became a quick way to parse the interests and intentions of others, in a context where getting this right was a matter of life and death. In London, too, Aisha's struggles reflect the difficulty of contesting identities from a less powerful position.

A third and final reason why some identities can come to feel especially fixed stems from the ways in which different cultures imagine the notion of 'identity' itself. Although Barth reminds us that identities are defined by symbolic boundaries, groups differ over how rigid, encompassing or changeable such boundaries may be. For groups such as the Nayaka in India, identity is not opposed to difference, and is not something which is strongly bounded. For others, such as the Korowai, who live in the lowland forests of southern Papua New Guinea, virtually everyone whom one does not live with is considered an outsider. At the same time, any outsider can become an insider – a friend, a neighbour, kin.[41] Different groups cultivate distinctive grammars for recognising the diversity that exists within and beyond them, and for drawing distinctions between themselves and others.

※

Surveying the vast scope of human diversity, we can witness the countless ways people have found to come together, even across the most stubborn differences. These efforts are often messy, uneven and constrained by circumstances, but they are also a testament to the human capacity for forging cultures of creativity and connection. In turn, this poses a radical challenge to the sorts of political questions we might ask. Rather than asking whether a certain group belongs in a certain place – whether we ought to welcome more migrants or insist on a unified national culture – we might instead ask why certain groups come to be treated differently in the first place. What is *our* cultural and political inheritance? What sets the terms of difference in our societies? And how might these terms of difference be rewritten?

PART II

ROOTS

CHAPTER FOUR

WE THE PEOPLE

Fluorescent lights buzzed overhead, reflecting off the chipped linoleum floor. The meeting was packed and, despite the hour, the debate was going strong – even if things were getting a bit circular: 'But there have to be mosques somewhere in the city! Why do they have to pray in the park?' Someone else perked up, 'They are Shia. There are no Shia mosques nearby. You wouldn't tell a Catholic to go pray at an Anglican church, would you?' A local councillor jumped on this to add, 'I don't think there is enough space. Eid is a big occasion. Lots of people must go out to mosque, and I think they fill up … They have nowhere else to go.' 'But there are mosques! Why do they need to come to a park? They must be able to find a mosque somewhere in London …' Chairing from a table at the front, Arjun discreetly checked the time on his phone and briefly winced, before regaining his composure. The meeting had run well over time.

Arjun spent much of his life surrounded by suspicion. It was rarely of his own making. A tech freelancer in his early fifties, he devoted a significant amount of his time to various community projects – including chairing a small group of volunteers who helped to run events in and maintain the local park. Arjun had a trim, salt-and-pepper beard, a flat cap that rarely left his head and eyes that creased deeply when he smiled. Years of community work had made him well known. He could hardly walk down the street without being greeted by a parade of neighbours or quizzed about ongoing projects. He was proud of this work, and this pride sometimes spilt into possessiveness, but for the most part he was amiable and open. Most of the distrust he met with was not personal – it clung to the work he did in Kilburn. Whether repurposing disused land for a vegetable garden, organising a litter clean-up or planning the annual community festival in the park – there were always people quick to assume that these efforts would do more harm than good. The festival would be a noisy, unwanted disruption. New trees would spoil the view. New benches would only attract loud, antisocial drinkers. Arjun's usual optimistic response to these complaints was to invite people to join in these projects – or at least to come and talk it over with others who might see things differently.

This time, the issue had to do with the Muslim festival of Eid al-Fitr – one of the major events in the Islamic calendar. The celebration attracted a surge of worshippers, too numerous for the space in the local mosque. Muslims in London struggle to find prayer space – while there is roughly one church for every 850 Christians, there is one mosque for every 2,600 Muslims, many of which are small, improvised, informal spaces.[1] To alleviate these cramped conditions, the local council had given permission to the mosque in question to hold Eid celebrations in the park – an hour or so of prayer in the morning, followed by a festival that spilt into lunchtime and wrapped up in the afternoon. In the past, however, some residents had complained that the event had been foisted on them without any consultation. More than this, there were allegations: that women or dog walkers were being kept out of the park by private security guards, or that non-Muslims were told that they weren't welcome at the supposedly public festivities. People knew someone, who knew someone, who had a bad experience of the event. To discuss these concerns, Arjun's park group had organised a discussion forum with the support of representatives from the mosque and local councillors. Arjun hoped the discussion would challenge preconceptions, but also prompt the organisers to act on any areas of legitimate concern.

Even before the discussion, it seemed people had already made up their minds. To help publicise the meeting, Arjun and his group followed their usual approach of sticking up flyers around the neighbourhood. A few days later, they found their flyers had been torn down.

Met with mixed responses, the Eid event went ahead as planned. On the day, following prayers, children raced between food stalls and a bouncy castle while adults milled about, greeting friends and family. At the edge of the crowd, I spotted Arjun. He was pleased with how the event organisers had responded to concerns about openness – arranging a variety of entertainment, advertising the event as open to all and briefing volunteers and security on welcoming non-Muslims. But, he added with exasperation, he wished that some of those present at the public discussion – several of whom belonged to other community groups – had made an effort to engage with the subsequent planning themselves. Or at least to show up. People seemed happy to judge suspiciously from a distance, or circulate rumours, but rarely put in the effort of seeing for themselves, up close.

Then, perhaps in an attempt to address me as the resident anthropologist, he concluded with a striking statement: 'That's the problem with the digital age – everything is communicated but no one is going to talk to you! Actually, the real problem is with the development of script – the written language – because before that you only had what people would say, so you had to listen – really listen to them, and make sense of everything in terms of what it meant for them. When you can write things down, you can take people's words from them!'

Whatever the motivation behind it, there is a sense of the sweep of history in Arjun's comment – a sense that the struggles he faces today began, in some form, long ago. For Arjun – and for a great many others – these struggles revolve around questions of how we can understand one another and work together. For many of Arjun's neighbours – and even for Arjun himself – these challenges were made harder by growing diversity. Diversity multiplied the perspectives that need to be bridged. The presence of unfamiliar others can cause people to retreat into suspicion and distrust, prompting them to cling to existing assumptions, making it even harder to negotiate between different perspectives.

Yet the way these struggles have been shaped is cultural. As Arjun points out, these possibilities start with our basic capacities, such as symbolic thought, but are filtered through a vast array of cultural tools that have been built around these capacities. It doesn't stop at writing. It's also things like community meetings and public festivals. We may not always recognise these as 'tools' but they very much are: community meetings may bring strangers together, while staging this encounter as a debate. Public festivals may frame encounters as more joyful, but also more anonymous. These tools allow us to think about and relate to others in specific ways. And like apprentices learning a craft, the more we take up these tools, the more we too are shaped by them, leading us to develop distinctive skills of understanding and connection.

In Western democracy, our thinking about how to design tools for connection has been guided by two dominant political philosophies: liberalism and civic republicanism. These philosophical traditions are marked by centuries of contested history, often traced back to Ancient Greece. Both have profoundly influenced Western culture. In broad terms, as the name suggests, liberalism is a tradition concerned with *liberty* – that is, the freedom of individuals or collectives to shape their own destiny in a way that is meaningful to them. Similarly, republicanism is a political tradition where government is considered to be a public matter. Republics are states ruled by, and for, the public. At this broad level, there is overlap between these traditions, and many democratic nations were founded or operate as *liberal republics*. Both traditions have also played a major role in shaping cultural understandings of what it means to live with difference. However, despite other areas of overlap, liberalism and civic republicanism imagine human difference in very different ways. Each sets out distinct principles for how to live with those who are different.

A quick note: these terms are often associated with specific political parties – such as the Liberal Party in Australia or the Republican Party in the USA. As traditions for living with difference, however, liberal and civic republican approaches can be found across the political spectrum. When discussing these traditions here, I am not referring to any political wing or party, but to something far broader.

Much of the commentary on liberalism and republicanism has approached these as attempts to define how people can live meaningful lives and live in a just society. However, I want to show that both traditions have also been preoccupied by questions of what it means to live with difference, and that we can gain important insights by centring such questions. The questions of human destiny and justice most often foregrounded are posed in highly abstract terms, with a sort of top-down view – as matters of principle, to be explored by governments, high-court judges and academics. Of course, ordinary people confront such questions, but when they do, it is through their everyday lives and relations. In other words, questions of human meaning and justice are often approached not in the abstract, but as practical questions of how to live well with others. Ideas matter. But taking an anthropological approach reminds us to pay attention to the social life of ideas – how they become real and compelling.

※

Another thinker grappling with the implications of the Second World War was Hannah Arendt, who fled Germany as a Jewish refugee. Arendt is responsible for penning our best-known account of the trial of the Nazi leader Adolf Eichmann, who orchestrated much of the Holocaust. Arendt's account famously coined the phrase 'the banality of evil', which she used to capture her impression of Eichmann as a committed bureaucrat. Arendt understood Eichmann as motivated not by Nazi ideology but by the requirements of his job and his need to belong and be affirmed as part of an organisation.[2] Arendt's depiction of Eichmann as a dutiful functionary has since been challenged – there is evidence suggesting that Eichmann believed in the Nazi final solution with clear conviction.[3] But there may have been other reasons Arendt had come to understand the roots of evil as buried in everyday routine and habits of thought. Arendt had fled Nazi Germany with her mother in 1933, and in 1941 left Vichy France for America. With the Nazi regime having rescinded the right to citizenship of all German Jews, Arendt and her mother were stateless.

In New York, the American government issued Arendt with an 'Affidavit of Identity in Lieu of Passport' – a document acknowledging her identity and her presence, but not her right to be in the US. She was in limbo.[4] In her landmark book *The Origins of Totalitarianism*, she writes about how, for millions of refugees like her, the idea of 'universal' human rights, and invocations of an innate, shared humanity, were an empty promise. 'The Rights of Man, after all, had been defined as "inalienable" because they were supposed to be independent of all governments; but it turned out that the moment human beings lacked their own government and had to fall back on their minimum rights, no authority was left to protect them and no institution was willing to guarantee them.'[5] For Arendt, the post-war refugee crisis was also a crisis in the moral and political authority of modern states.[6] If the legitimacy of states came from their

claim to represent and safeguard the rights of those they governed, what did it mean to suddenly have a group of people
who could not claim to be represented or protected anywhere
in the world? How representative and legitimate could states be,
if none of them could manage to represent the stateless? What
did it mean when these states were the cause of statelessness in
the first place?

Finding an answer to these questions would occupy Arendt's
career. She realised that if the very category of humanity was up
for debate – if states such as Nazi Germany could effectively strip
it away, while others such as America, England or France could
hesitate, debate or refuse to acknowledge it, then appeals to an
innate humanity could not be enough to guarantee the survival,
much less the rights and dignity, of anyone. The failure of the
international human rights regime set Arendt off in pursuit of a
different way of thinking about political recognition. Her work
led her to the ancient Greek philosopher Aristotle, and to an
attempt to rekindle an ancient democratic tradition which she
believed was dying out.

The history of Western democracy is often imagined as
beginning in ancient Greece. Over the centuries philosophers
like Arendt have returned to the era as a source of inspiration.
From the American founding fathers to the thinkers who shaped
the French Revolution, many even imagine ancient Greece as
a prototypical example of the systems we live in today. In this
vision of history, the work of Aristotle and his teacher Plato play
a foundational role. But the pair had very different ideas about
politics and difference. Overtly and covertly, their different ideas
have been woven into democratic traditions and institutions,
infusing modern-day democracy with a set of contrasting ideals.
Liberalism imagines humanity as defined by core essences that
cut across our differences and form the foundation for public
life. This thinking about human essences can be traced back to
Plato. Civic republicanism, meanwhile, imagines humanity as

defined by processes of collective negotiation, where people work out what ought to define them, together. This notion of human difference as malleable and politically negotiated can be traced back to Aristotle.

The philosopher Alfred North Whitehead once quipped that the whole European tradition of philosophy might be characterised as 'a series of footnotes to Plato'.[7] Whatever the truth of this statement, Plato's ideas provide a good way of understanding one of the major ways in which democracies have come to imagine difference. Plato argued that all things possess fundamental, immaterial essences – what he called 'forms' – and that these essences were what determined the nature of reality. This idea comes out in different ways across much of Plato's thought, but one of the most famous examples comes from his allegory of the cave. Writing in the voice of his own teacher, Socrates, Plato describes a group of people who have always lived in a cave, chained to the wall. All they can see are shadows on the cave wall, made by objects and puppets passing in front of a fire, which burns behind them, out of sight. The prisoners do not see the shadows as shadows, and do not know of the objects which cast them, nor the fire behind them – all they experience are shadows, and so to them these shadows are all there is to reality.

Plato describes the philosopher as one who is able – slowly and painfully – to make the journey out of the cave, out of ignorance, by looking behind the apparent forms of reality, layer by layer, and discovering the underlying truth. Plato relates each of these forms in the cave to something within his own world: the shadows represent physical reality; the objects and puppets, works of art and culture; the fire, political ideology. Behind everything else, Plato argued, were unchangeable ideal forms that existed beyond space and time. For instance, there exists the form of an apple. This form is the essence of apple-ness. It is everything that makes an apple an apple. All the apples that we see here in the physical world are imperfect expressions of this form. Plato took this further, and believed something similar existed for ideas, too. Just as there is an ideal form of an apple, there is also an ideal form of justice, truth or goodness. It was the role of the philosopher to look beyond the surface of reality and try to understand these essences as closely as possible.

Plato's allegory of the cave comes from *The Republic*, his long work on the nature of justice. There he also develops a political theory that puts his vision of philosophical inquiry front and centre. Presenting an imagined utopia, Kallipolis, Plato argues for a system where a philosopher elite rules the rest. He points to various reasons why philosophers deserve to rule and why they will be regarded as ideal rulers by other citizens. For example, he claims that philosophers are motivated solely by the love of wisdom, and so will not *want* to rule. However, the chief qualification of philosophers is that, through rigorous inquiry, they strive to understand what is good. Plato believed that a universal form of goodness existed. By striving to rule the city according to the principles of goodness, the philosophers would enable citizens to lead good lives and, recognising this, the citizens will support their rule.

This rule required both recognising and transcending the essential differences between citizens. Plato believed that citizens fell into different classes, each with a distinct essence. Different classes were motivated by different things, such as desire or heroism. It was the role of the ruling philosophers to orchestrate the lives of citizens so that all citizens were able to live according their own essence and in harmony with the universal essence of goodness. Plato criticised the democratic system of nearby Athens for lacking common standards for assessing what was good and just. Democracy was filled with too many different voices and therefore prone to chaos. Grandly, he declared, 'no city could ever be blessed unless its features were traced by artists who used the heavenly model'.[8]

Aristotle took his teacher's dedication to rigorous inquiry

much further. He strenuously challenged Plato's idea that reality was determined by unseen, immaterial 'forms'. Instead, he argued that the nature of reality could only be understood by exploring the basic physical properties of the world around us – an approach that pointed the way towards modern science. Unlike Plato, however, Aristotle separated his understanding of philosophical inquiry from political life. Politics, as well as the pursuit of justice and virtue, he argued, were matters of *practical knowledge* – knowledge gained through personal experience, not unlike learning to sculpt or dance, rather than something that could be gleaned in the abstract. Unlike knowledge of the natural world, practical knowledge was not necessarily singular or stable – it was something worked out continuously, within specific contexts.

When it came to politics, Aristotle focused on this process of working out, writing that, 'The citizen in an unqualified sense is defined by no other thing so much as by sharing in decision and office.' Political participation was vitally important, then, not simply for making good decisions, but for leading a virtuous life – which required making the best use of human capacities. In particular, politics involved using the capacity for *logos* – a term meaning both 'reason' and 'speech', which Aristotle saw as central to human nature – to deliberate and build a consensus on the common good. In public assemblies, politicians would set out and attempt to pursue visions of virtue and prosperity. What made these visions virtuous and worthwhile was not some objective, external measure of good, but their ability to persuade others and inspire them to action. This exercise of *logos* was highly dramatic, relying not only on logic but on passionate emotion and the weight of one's own experiences and deeds, conveyed through powerful rhetoric.[9]

Hannah Arendt was a keen student of Aristotle. For her, the promise of this public, dramatic exchange was the promise of human recognition. 'With us from Germany,' she wrote 'the word assimilation received a "deep" philosophical meaning. You can hardly realize how serious we were about it.'[10] But it wasn't good enough. However 'assimilated' German Jews were, however much they looked and acted and thought like Germans, it didn't stop their persecution. For Arendt, the evils of the war and the failures of the international human rights regime stemmed from the thinness of categories like 'citizen', 'German' or 'human' when stretched by conflict. It was a failure to truly recognise the humanity of Jews and other persecuted, displaced peoples, not in terms of abstract categories but directly and personally. Of Eichmann, she wrote: 'The longer one listened to him, the more obvious it became that his inability to speak was closely connected with an inability to think, namely, to think from the standpoint of someone else.'

In Aristotle's civic politics, Arendt recognised a possibility for a deeper recognition of human worth – a recognition of others not in terms of fixed categories or stable selves, but as a matter of mutual interdependency and intertwined fate. By striving to build consensus through passionate speech and proof of great deeds; by exposing who you were and what you stood for; and by demanding that others respond to your presence and your words in their own efforts to adjudicate what was right and good, each citizen was given a deep, mutually binding stake in the political community. Here the ability to speak and to be recognised was deeply bound up with the ability to listen to and recognise others. 'The public realm,' Arendt wrote, 'was the only place where men could show who they really and inexchangeably were.'[11]

Aristotle's conception of politics as public, collective *logos*, however, is marked by a tension between uniformity and difference. On the one hand difference – especially individual difference – is fundamental to the process of political deliberation. Politics is driven by the ongoing negotiation of different perspectives, and the deliberative process draws the best elements of each individual perspective together. On the other hand, Aristotle worries that too much difference may make it too difficult to reach a consensus. He writes that those who rule, 'tend by their nature to be on an equal footing and to differ in nothing', and that this mattered because 'in the case of persons similar by nature, justice and merit must necessarily be the same according to nature'. As such, despite all the importance he puts on political participation, Aristotle simultaneously argues that politics ideally should be restricted to an aristocratic elite.

Aristotle feared variation not just between people, but across time. He believed it was necessary to maintain a coherent tradition of justice. Most people don't follow the law because they have reasoned through its righteousness, but out of habit and deference to authority. The more laws are changed – particularly laws that set out the overarching principles of collective life – the more the power of habit and authority are eroded. Meanwhile, to be able to speak about the common good at all requires some shared, stable templates for value, meaning and action. In this sense, tradition makes politics possible, rather than standing in the way of it.

In revisiting Aristotle's thought, Arendt struggled with these exclusions. Ultimately she stuck to the idea that politics was a distinct sort of activity that not everyone may be able to engage in. She seemed to recognise this vision of the common good as both deep and fragile – deep because it bound people in mutual recognition, interweaving histories and identities, and fragile because this collective striving could easily be undone by divisive, self-interested concerns, or an excess of difference.

❊

These two political philosophies – one a search for fixed, universal truths, the other a process of collective deliberation – emphasise different human capacities. Plato's thought points to the importance of abstract reasoning – of looking behind the appearances of the physical world to arrive at a universally applicable understanding. Aristotle's, in contrast, emphasises our ability to tell stories and evoke emotions, to express our perspective and experiences and to recognise the perspectives and experiences of others. These two ways of thinking about how we arrive at political answers, and how we understand our collective humanity, are not the only possibilities out there. But they are a useful guide for understanding the historical foundations of democratic states. Plato's thinking about singular essences starts off a search that has led towards modern-day liberalism. Meanwhile, Aristotle's emphasis on deliberation, mutual recognition and practical action has found its own expression in political arrangements often characterised as civic republicanism.[12]

For republican thinkers from Aristotle onwards, civic republican ideals tend to derive their value in relation to one another. Face-to-face deliberation, and the forms of mutual understanding it produces, have been understood as closely intertwined with a range of other ideals: just rule; solidarity; maintaining investment in the political process; sustaining and strengthening collective traditions. It is this intertwining, this mutual dependency, that gives these ideals much of their value and meaning. It forges a political collective – a group of people who understand themselves as sharing and shaping a common fate. Civic republicanism makes it possible to continually negotiate and redraw the lines between insider and outsider, self and other. In practice, however, philosophers and statesmen alike have tended to see collective identity as something that needs to exist *prior* to political deliberation. Throughout history, civic republicans have emphasised shared status, identity, values or tradition as largely *foundational for*, rather than as *resulting from*, face-to-face negotiation.

Therefore, the story of those political endeavours that have been self-consciously shaped by republican ideals offer a limited record of whether or how republican politics allow us to bridge differences. Such projects have tended to put disproportionate emphasis on shared tradition and identities, offering a relatively closed vision of republicanism. We can gain a different perspective, however, by looking at forms of politics grounded in mutual recognition[13] and richly resonant with republican ideals, but which come from places that may not see themselves as part of a Western civic republican tradition at all.

In the Amazon rainforest, for instance, the anthropologist Joanna Overing has lived with the Piaroa people, on and off, for decades. The Piaroa live along the banks of the Orinoco River in Venezuela, and make their living through a mix of gardening, fishing, hunting and gathering. Overing adds that 'They are referred to by their neighbours as "the intellectuals of the Orinoco", and indeed they do have a love for intellectual debate, particularly over metaphysical aspects of everyday life.'[14] Everyday life has a metaphysical quality because the arts of living, such as gardening, childrearing, making blowguns or building houses, are seen as capabilities possessed and safeguarded by celestial gods. In Piaroa myths, these everyday capabilities have overwhelming transformative power – the power to sustain or destroy life, or civilisation.

These powers drove the creator gods to conflict and destruction before they were finally locked away for safekeeping. Today, at birth, and then at stages throughout life, human beings inherit a small share of these cosmic skills, making them who they are. This inheritance is very much an individual matter – the power to create, be productive and transform the world is seen as handed from the gods directly to individuals, linking individuals with the divine and giving them tremendous potency. As such, the Piaroa place great value on individuality and autonomy. Yet, to truly use these skills well requires coming together, thinking and acting alongside others, and for the sake of them.

This is done not through any rigid social structures or strict hierarchies – the Piaroa do not cooperate because they are made to by leaders or law. Rather, cooperation is sustained, and made worthwhile, through ongoing effort. A Piaroa marriage, for example, takes place when a man hunts down some food and presents it to a woman, and she cooks it for him to eat. This simple ritual, uniting the skills of hunting and cooking, is renewed throughout the marriage – making marriage not a fixed status, but a continuous project. The same might be said for other forms of status and relation as well – they are never written in stone. Through shared efforts to care for one another, and through ongoing debate over how they should live together, the Piaroa make community an ongoing process. Not only that, but this same philosophy of negotiated togetherness is used to establish peace and alliances between the Piaroa and other Amazonian peoples – many of whom subscribe to similar philosophies.[15] As Overing puts it, 'For the Piaroa, the idea is that those who in the first instance are dangerously "different in kind" ... become "of a kind" through the process of living together.'[16]

Meanwhile, the Chilean anthropologist Marcelo Gonzalez Galvez writes about the rural Mapuche people, who live across the southern and central reaches of Chile and Argentina. Where the Piaroa put great emphasis on individual autonomy, the Mapuche stress individualism of a different sort. They insist that personal experience is incontestably true, and that 'what each person experiences is unique, and no other person can replicate it'.[17] For the Mapuche, the stuff of reality – substances and spirits, objects and laws – is *generated* by individual experiences and actions. Perception, thought and action are understood as forces that create and shape the world, producing a multitude of parallel realities that remain inaccessible for those outside them.

This belief leads the Mapuche to argue that it is impossible to assess the truth of what others claim, since truth and reality are inescapably individual matters. It may seem like this belief would make it hard to sustain a society of any sort. After all, how can we trust one another, cooperate or even communicate when we have no way of grasping what others might be talking about? The Mapuche solution to this problem is to emphasise the importance of shared experience. If, in Gonzalez Galvez's words, Mapuche 'truth is a property of a person's ongoing inter-action with the environment',[18] then joint interaction works to produce joint truths.[19]

The lives of the Piaroa and Mapuche provide vivid illustra-tions of how face-to-face dialogue and negotiation can work to bridge differences. They foreground a dimension of possibility not often emphasised within the European tradition of civic republicanism, but which nonetheless fits well within its pre-cepts. The differences they bridge are not small ones. The Piaroa are practised in crossing gulfs of both individual and group difference, just as the Mapuche build understanding across irre-ducible notions of truth, even while both groups recognise that these respective differences are deep, even sacrosanct.

These visions of deep difference hold important parallels to Western society. Here, too, individualism is celebrated and fiercely guarded. Many of our most valued rights – the ability to make our own choices, think for ourselves or speak freely – are cast in an individualist mould. Yet individualism is also seen as posing an ongoing challenge to political life, and as a potentially corrosive force – eroding trust and connection, while fuelling greed and conflict. Tied to this individualist outlook is a growing disagreement over the nature of truth – marked by quarrels over fake news, conspiracy theories and disputed science.

Yet, in contrast to the Piaroa and Mapuche, our response to these gulfs of difference is very often not to negotiate them per-son-to-person, but to insist on common standards that apply for us all. In diverse societies, such exercises in standard-setting are increasingly challenging. If we want to insist – not unlike Paddy in Chapter One – that public life ought to be governed by a sense of collective decency and solidarity, who sets the terms? If we insist that the truth is out there, and shouldn't be up for debate, how do we deal with the fact that our opponents, with whom we disagree, make the same claim with equal confidence? If we insist on our own standards by saying we have science, rationality, God or justice on our side, how do we address the fact that these categories don't share the same meaning or pull for others. Whose god, which science?

※

These questions can feel vast and dramatic, even unanswerable. But they are also prosaic. We pose them in countless small ways every day. Back in Kilburn, they are precisely the sorts of questions Arjun finds himself grappling with when confronted with sceptical locals who believe that the projects he champions will cause disruption, or will change the fabric of the place into something rough and unfamiliar, just as passionately as he believes that they will do good. How, then, to reconcile different ways of valuing, knowing or feeling? How to deal with the insistence that there is enough space to celebrate Eid indoors, despite evidence to the contrary? How about the unverifiable gossip that depicts the Eid celebrations as a covert privatisation of public space, the stories of someone – walking a dog, wearing a sundress – who was chased out of the park by a gruff security guard, in the name of piety?

Nancy had been familiar with these stories for years. She had long lived on an estate just off the park, and had been loosely involved with Arjun's voluntary groups. To her, the rumours had a ring of truth to them. Some Muslims considered contact with dogs as violating the state of ritual cleanliness required for prayer, known as *wudu*. She had seen one of her Muslim neighbours react with some discomfort around Simba, her ageing bichon frise. Still, she knew of other Muslims who were friendly, even adoring towards Simba, and she had come to discover that any frictions that emerged could usually be talked out.

Frustrated with the rumours, Nancy decided to conduct an experiment – taking Simba for a walk in the park, in the middle of the festivities. A few days later, I visited Nancy at her flat. She was beaming from her success. The revellers had welcomed her warmly; they complimented Simba; she chatted to them about their colourful dresses and stylish hijabs. Nancy wasn't really surprised: her experience of Kilburn had taught her that there was almost always something worth discovering about most people and places. To her, living in Kilburn meant: 'We don't avoid, we embrace!'

Piaroa and Mapuche customs reveal a way of valuing individuality, individual experience and personal knowledge, without sacrificing the possibility of common understanding, mutual regard and shared belonging. This is achieved through living shared lives, working closely together and having open conversations about what is collectively important. For both groups, individuality is realised, not diminished, by coming together. Life with others broadens our capabilities, expands our horizons of understanding and experience and enriches our sense of self. Individuals realise their individuality through participation, while collectives become infused with the individuality of their members.

Yet, to discover this, people must first commit to being and working together – they must put their individuality, or even their group identity, on the line and become open and vulnerable to others. Overing uses the term *conviviality* to describe the Piaroa commitment to living in light of one another. She talks about this interweaving of lives as an exercise in 'trust' – a faith that openness to others will lead somewhere worthwhile; a faith expressed in action. Convivial trust is a good way of describing Nancy walking her dog during the Eid celebrations. A year later, Nancy shared her story at the fractious meeting chaired by Arjun. It did little good. What was, for Nancy, a lived experiment in trust was, for the rest, just another story among others. The debate wore on.

As modern states developed, authority became centralised – first in the figure of the monarch and later in parliaments. Both monarchical and popular rule relied on increasingly large bureaucracies to manage commerce, taxation, security and public welfare. These shifts bred an increasing awareness of the distance between the lives of ordinary citizens and the state, and helped give rise to the modern concept of civil society. Today, civil society is understood as a sphere where people come together voluntarily to imagine, deliberate over and pursue forms of common good.[20] While – as we will see – liberalism has come to dominate the high-level workings of the modern state, this vision of civil society remains heavily influenced by civic republican ideals. Charities, community organisations, mutual-aid groups, activist and campaign groups take up the civic republican vision as a matter of everyday politics. Nancy's story reveals the potential of this everyday civic republicanism to also work as a practice of bridging differences. Her personal mantra – 'We don't avoid, we embrace' – was a product of her long-standing involvement in community groups across Kilburn. She'd learnt that the potential for common ground and shared understandings were often not visible at a distance, but required close personal engagement to become apparent.

While Nancy's story reveals the potential of everyday republican politics to bridge differences, what happens when those around her don't share her willingness to trust, or don't trust her own claims? This is one of the challenges of civic republican politics – at its heart, it is a politics centred on active participation. It requires face-to-face relationships and a belief that we are part of a collective. For those not already engaged in these relationships and forms of participation, it can be challenging to draw them in. Even when people are in the same room, face to face, they may hear but not listen.

Throughout the history of civic republicanism, political leaders have experimented with the question of inclusiveness. From the Venetian republic, dominated by aristocratic and merchant elites, to the Dutch republic, where the ruling class of regents tried to maintain a balance between elite interests and popular legitimacy, or the Corsican republic grounded in traditions of village democracy, different republics drew varying boundaries around who was included in political deliberation, and on what terms. In many instances, tradition and commonality played an outsized role. These were often seen as necessary for enabling people to trust and to understand one another in the first instance – in order to make the whole process of civic deliberation possible. Even in the cases of the Piaroa and Mapuche, people understand that coming together is worthwhile – because of a shared metaphysical tradition and because of well-worn habits of association. This need for tradition and commonality can accommodate some forms of diversity but not others. Differences between individuals, united by common traditions or identities, are seen as crucial to civic deliberation. Contact between traditions and groups, however, is seen as running the risk of eroding the taken-for-granted authority of tradition, and of destabilising identities.[21]

A different perspective on tradition comes from the history of Islamic rule in Spain. From the eighth-century conquest of the Iberian peninsula by the Umayyad Caliphate until the 'reconquest' in the late fifteenth century, by the Catholic monarchs Fernando and Isabel, much of modern-day Spain was under the authority of Muslim rulers. The new state, known as Al-Andalus, was governed by royals and their courts, with little accountably. Despite this, the era of Muslim rule is widely remembered as a golden age of harmony and exchange between Christians, Muslims and Jews. The three religions were granted similar rights and freedoms, including the freedom of belief, and representatives from each religion were incorporated into the ranks of administrators and courtiers who oversaw the state. Philosophy took on a new liveliness at the meeting of these traditions. The Muslim thinker Muhammad ibn Rushd wove ancient Greek thought with Islamic reflections, prompting the European rediscovery of seemingly 'lost' thinkers such as Aristotle and Plato. Inspired by ibn Rushd's work, the great Jewish thinker Moses ben Maimon (often known as Maimonides) set about producing a code of Jewish law that remains influential today. Many others set about translating works from different traditions of knowledge, building a formidable body of scientific, social and philosophical thought. Complex mixtures of tradition took physical form in lush, grand monuments such as the Alhambra palaces or the great mosque of Córdoba. And beyond the courts, in practices of trading and working, marriage and worship, ordinary people developed creative customs of coexistence. The cultural historian Amerigo Castro popularised the notion that Al-Andalus was a kingdom of *convivencia* – of conviviality.

This romantic portrait has gone through cycles of cheerleading and criticism. Historians have challenged the image of an age of tolerance by pointing to moments of tension and bloodshed. Maimonides was exiled following a change in rule. Following a failed coup by a Jewish vizier, a mob turned its anger towards the Jewish population of Granada, resulting in a massacre. Christians turned against Muslim neighbours during the Christian 'reconquest' and the subsequent Spanish Inquisition.

Seeking to cut through this debate, the historian Brian A. Catlos traces a sweeping history not of idealistic tolerance, nor of dogmatic division, but of simple interdependence.[22] For ruling elites, this interdependence was characterised by the need to maintain power – starting with the need of the incoming conquerors to establish legitimacy and stability. For those within the ranks of courtiers and administrators, mixing and understanding often came out of a desire for power or prestige. Ambitious Christians would vie for lucrative administrative positions by studying the Quran to learn Arabic, with some of them having epiphanies and converting in the process. Muslim governors promoted Christian administrators to keep the peace and promote prosperity. Most importantly, for ordinary people, interdependence came from living together – from mixing in artisan workshops, haggling in markets and the web of relationships formed through inter-faith marriages. It came from religious leaders preaching about the mixed, complex world around them, or borrowing from other faiths to create new hybrid traditions.

All required tradition – to an extent – in the form of shared languages or collective cultural touchpoints. More than this, however, coming together required people to *get under the skin of tradition* – to renegotiate spiritual practices, or mix different languages into the flow of everyday life. This came not through unchanging beliefs, but through settings that facilitated such mixing: diverse royal courts, bustling universities, artisan workshops, schools of translators, and priests or imams who would officiate mixed marriages. Practice trumped belief; solidarity came not from dogma but from structures that supported everyday experiments in living. These structures were often fragile, open to challenge or political capture. When they crumbled, were seized by power-hungry leaders or were simply absent, lives broke apart, often in bloody fashion.

Places such as Amazonia, Kilburn or Al-Andalus may not self-consciously position themselves within the republican tradition. Nonetheless, they not only provide rich illustrations of key republican ideas but also help push against certain limitations within this tradition. Hannah Arendt distinguished civic action from everyday subsistence and creativity (what she called 'labour' and 'work'), to paint political action as a rarefied domain of heroic achievement. Others have put significant stress on the need for shared traditions or a strong sense of collective identity. Yet when we focus on our capacity for negotiating difference – when we look at how people cooperate on an everyday basis – these limits become much less stark. Civic republican politics become a matter not of great historical feats and unwavering traditions, but often, simply, of everyday interaction.

Still, if this perspective expands the limits of civic republicanism, it does not eliminate them. The capacity for everyday cooperation remains reliant on forms of trust embedded in belief and habit, and in institutions that support everyday cooperation. In large, diverse societies, where beliefs, habits and the level of participation in civil society vary widely, these requirements can leave republican politics especially fragile and uncertain, as people like Nancy and Arjun know all too well.

※

'We hold these truths to be self-evident, that all men are created equal, that they are endowed by their Creator with certain unalienable Rights, that among these are Life, Liberty and the pursuit of Happiness.' This historic proclamation, found near the start of the American Declaration of Independence, anticipates the Universal Declaration of Human Rights adopted by the United Nations shortly after the end of the Second World War. The Universal Declaration of Human Rights begins by pronouncing that 'recognition of the inherent dignity and of the equal and inalienable rights of all members of the human family is the foundation of freedom, justice and peace in the world'. Between these two grand statements, issued 170 years apart, there's a long history of thinking about human nature and political rights which sits at the heart of most democracies today. In the broadest sense, all truly democratic states are republics – ruled, in principle, by and for the people. But from the Enlightenment onwards the principles of civic republicanism gradually came to lose their force, ceding influence to a new tradition: liberalism.

As with civic republicanism, liberalism is a debated, diverse tradition. Amid this debate, however, many elements of liberalism have become engrained in the workings of democracy – often to the point where they are widely seen as common sense. Notably, the idea that politics is rooted in the universal – that political legitimacy comes from what is 'self-evident' – is fundamental to modern democracy. Although most often discussed in relation to rights and justice, universalism also carries important implications for how people connect across difference. Liberalism assumes that whatever their differences, people also share certain 'self-evident' commonalties that render them equal in certain ways. These commonalities form the foundations of citizenship and political life.

Universalism emerged as a political ideal during the Enlightenment, running from the late 1600s to the early 1800s. This was the era in which some of the first and most foundational experiments in modern democratic government took shape. The French and American Revolutions, which overthrew royal rule, and the dramatic shift of power in Britain away from the monarchy and towards parliament, all unfolded over this period. Europe was moving out of a period when religious divisions caused bitter civil conflicts and bloody wars. In England, Henry VIII's split from the Catholic Church marked the beginning of a back-and-forth power struggle and led ultimately to the English Civil War in 1642. In Spain, the Christian reconquest of Granada led to an ultimatum in 1501 – that the Muslim population either convert or leave. In the early 1600s, all the descendants of those who converted were expelled anyway. In Germany, simmering tensions between Protestants and Catholics expanded into a struggle between powerful European rulers, leading to the Thirty Years War, which encompassed much of Europe and was one of the bloodiest events in European history.

By the time of the Enlightenment, these tensions had quieted, but not vanished. Understandably, there was a desire to find forms of government that could peacefully and fairly accommodate diverse faiths. These challenges played out against a backdrop of dramatic technological, social and commercial transformation, which exercised a profound influence on the new democratic visions of revolutionaries and reformers. The European world was moving away from familiar communities and local geographies to encompass an increasingly wide range of relationships, many of which were symbolic and impersonal.

In seventeenth-century England, the philosopher Joan Tronto notes,[23] life was largely understood in terms of the household and the family. This provided the setting for daily labour and interactions, and embodied the moral standing of its inhabitants. By the eighteenth century, however, the growth of markets and long-distance trade, alongside the spread of publishing, journalism, post and other forms of long-distance communication, created a world where 'individuals were expected to cope with large numbers of people in daily life, to travel more, to think more in terms of a "public"'.[24]

As the Industrial Revolution picked up steam, changes to everyday life began to accumulate: the firm and the factory replaced the household as the centre of economic activity; mechanical timekeeping synchronised daily rhythms across vast distances; science – in manufacturing, agriculture and even psychology – arranged the world into types and categories, creating standardised frameworks for navigating the world; and the growth of capitalist competition linked lives and livelihoods on ever-greater scales. The result, writes Tronto, was that by the end of the eighteenth century, there was an increasingly widespread belief among Western Europeans 'that they had, through their actions, a formidable ability to shape the world in which they lived'.[25] Everyday life came to be seen as influenced by a vast body of diverse, anonymous strangers, and everyday actions were seen as capable of affecting this same unknown public. This new vision of a mass, impersonal, yet interconnected society coincided with a growing belief that ordinary people deserved a stake in the political process. Politics couldn't only be led by, or accountable to, elites. Political communities needed a way of including people of different beliefs fairly, but without any one group dominating.

This simultaneous expansion of social worlds and of the political sphere posed a thorny problem for the political thinkers of the day. How could a political system guarantee justice and fairness between people who could not make themselves directly known to one another? Tronto traces this problem across the lives of several eighteenth-century philosophers, including that of the Scottish thinker Adam Smith. Smith is most famously remembered as the father of modern capitalism. His writings praise the social benefits of market exchange. One of his most famous statements is that, 'It is not from the benevolence of the butcher, the brewer, or the baker that we expect our dinner, but from their regard to their own interest.'[26] For Smith, however, 'self-interest' was not characterised by the desire for material gain, but by the desire for recognition – for being valued, accepted and understood by others.[27]

In his early writings, Smith was decidedly civic republican – developing a theory of 'sympathy' as a binding political force that enabled people to secure and offer recognition by acting with regard to the perspectives of others. Sympathy, Smith believed, was a basic human capacity enabling strangers to understand one another and to act in concert. Over time, however, Smith grew unsatisfied with this model, coming to realise that sympathy became much more challenging or inconsistent across large social distances. Revising his earlier work, he put greater stress on rationality and self-interest. As with sympathy, Smith saw rationality and self-interest as basic human qualities, capable of generating political and personal recognition between strangers. The difference, however, was that Smith believed rationality and self-interest unfolded in more uniform and predictable ways than sympathy, providing a better guarantee of working at a distance. Although often remembered as a champion of free-market exchange, Smith was interested in markets primarily for how they might be able to allocate recognition and value. Markets orchestrated forms of common good across an anonymous public – he didn't believe in treating free markets or economic exchange as ends in themselves. Tronto highlights how Smith, alongside other prominent Enlightenment thinkers, embraced increasingly universalist visions of humanity and templates for political life, in response to an expanding, increasingly diverse social world.

Universalist ideas reflected a sense of an increasingly large, interconnected society, but they also helped to create it. In the early twentieth century, suffragettes argued their case by evoking images of innate essences, even across clashing arguments. Some claimed that women deserved the vote because they were naturally more peaceful and compassionate than men, while others made their case based on claims of fundamental equality. In 1897, in Berlin, the world's first gay rights organisation, the Scientific-Humanitarian Committee, fought for equality by deploying a language of natural rights and the idea that differences in sexuality were part of human nature. And in the late eighteenth century European movements to abolish slavery experienced a sudden growth and surge of energy. Historical accounts of this rise to popular consciousness vary, but almost all accounts incorporate an understanding that during this time the horizons of the world shifted.[28] If it was possible for wealth drawn from plantations in the Caribbean to enrich landowners in southern England, then it was also possible for English abolitionists to challenge this globe-spanning institution. Abolitionists frequently drew on accounts of universal human capacities and essences. For instance, Adam Smith's ideas about the human capacity for sympathy and self-interest were used to argue that the British slave trade was both inhumane and economically misguided – privileging slave owners by suppressing free markets and the general prosperity they brought.[29] The emergence of ideas of universal human nature was gradual, patchy and often self-contradictory. Yet these ideas provided abolitionists, and other campaigners for equality, with a new grammar for thinking about connection beyond the known social world.

Even prior to the Enlightenment era, there had been a growing tradition within European political thought of justifying political orders in terms of natural law. Forms of citizenship, state power and decision-making were related to particular visions of innate human nature.[30] This quest for human essences drew on a tradition that linked Plato's search for ideal forms with the budding development of modern science, which privileged the search for patterns and generalisations, formed into theories and laws. Drawing on this history of thought, political thinkers increasingly came to treat what could be generalised and fixed as a privileged form of knowledge, while anything cast as specific, personal and particular came to be viewed with an air of suspicion. In the fledgling days of the United States, James Madison – often hailed as the father of the American constitution – grappled with the question of what it meant for a democratic system to be responsive to popular interests and opinions. Madison was especially wary of two threats: the power of majorities to impose their will unfairly onto minority groups, and the power of well-organised, factional interests to cause division and strife. Madison's answer to these threats was twofold. On the one hand, he defended the absolute right to political, religious and moral belief, partly in the hopes that cultivating a diversity of views would fragment the power of large factions. Meanwhile, alongside other key figures such as Thomas Paine, he stressed the importance of a system of *representative* democracy, where it was representatives – not the people themselves – who deliberated over political decisions. Standing above the messy diversity of the masses, representatives were capable of identifying and drawing together common threads of interest and belief.

Liberalism, then, is a political system that trades on abstract, idealised representations. Concepts and categories, not personal relationships, are what shape the major question of who counts as a rights-bearing citizen, and more ordinary questions of how to weigh up competing political claims. In the civic republican tradition, the capacity of people to participate in political life is seen as flowing from difference – from the different perspectives they bring to processes of collective deliberation. In contrast, the liberal tradition argues that people deserve a political stake because they hold some essence in common. Sameness, not difference, provides the foundation of public life. At the highest level, citizens are equal and equivalent. They are equal before the law, they hold equal rights, they each get one vote. At the more specific level of policy, citizens are governed on the basis of generic categories. They become 'pet owners', 'migrants', 'low-income families' or 'women in the workplace'. Members of these categories are again treated as equivalent to one another. These categories are thin and abstract, saying relatively little about who individual citizens are, what they think or believe, how they act, what they value. These more substantial differences are relegated to the private sphere, where they are both defended and confined – protected against public interference, but also prohibited from being used as the basis of public claims. For instance, liberal thought tells us that we cannot deny others the freedom of religious belief, but also that we cannot invoke our religious beliefs to impinge on the freedom of others. Private freedoms are restricted only at the point where they can be shown to create significant public harm.

This, at least, is the idea in principle. In practice, the universal categories on which liberalism trades are never as inclusive as they sound, and the line between public and private never clear-cut. Part of this is a problem of history. We can recognise, for example, that when the American founding fathers declared that 'all men are created equal', they were referring to white men. It took centuries of (still-unfinished) struggle for this vision of equality to start to include women and non-white people on equal terms. This problem has often been approached as a quest to fully realise the promises of liberalism – to find more universal terms of citizenship, and make public equality and private freedom a reality for all.

A trickier, more fundamental tension surrounds the working of universal categories themselves. Only at their most abstract – pushed to a limit where they hardly mean anything at all – can the categories of liberalism make any strong claim to being widely inclusive. Yet the need to address concrete dilemmas posed by everyday disagreements and competing claims requires liberalism to define these categories in more specific terms. What does it mean to be 'rational'? What sort of 'human dignity' does the law protect? These definitions are always culturally specific, but they often continue to be seen as universal. As a result, the allegedly universal categories of liberalism end up with unacknowledged outsides, while the slippage between universalism and particularity can often work as a disguise for power.

Take reason, for example. Joan Tronto picks up the story of Adam Smith to show how a very specific understanding of reason – as the ability to think in calculative terms about one's own self-interest – emerged out of the Enlightenment-era search for universal human capacities. To highlight the particularity of this understanding, Tronto contrasts it with another form of reasoning, that of 'care'. To think in terms of care, she argues, is to recognise our interests and abilities as entangled with those around us. To shape and be shaped by others in this way makes it difficult to weigh up our own interests, or those of others, in a straightforward, stable way. As a result, while thinking in terms of care can help us assess how to act towards others, such judgements are neither conventionally calculative nor self-interested. Care is a universal human capacity, Tronto argues, and has the potential to play an important role in guiding political judgements. Yet, in terms of dominant understandings of reason, care looks irrational.

In specific dilemmas, some forms of reason are recognised above others. When parents object to schools placing children in lower-achieving classes by claiming to know their child best; when indigenous communities object to income-generating mining or logging projects on spiritual grounds – these claims are often cast as irrational, rather than as alternative versions of reason. At best, diverse forms of reason are accommodated as matters of private belief, but they are curtailed as soon as they are deemed to have public impact. It's no coincidence, suggests Tronto, that in Enlightenment-era Europe the supposedly universal quality of reason was cast in the mould of self-interested calculation. The philosophers and merchants, statesmen and wealthy families who played an outsized role in shaping Enlightenment thought were already invested in this perspective. This vision of reason positioned the wealthy and privileged as the most reasonable of all.[31]

For citizens of liberal states, the ability to lead meaningful lives is often dependent on the ability to inhabit the categories of citizenship. Yet the anthropologist Elizabeth Povinelli stresses that in such efforts some of the richness and complexity of life is always lost. For nearly three decades Povinelli has lived and worked with a group of Aboriginal people living on the north-west coast of Australia's Northern Territory. She notes that for Aboriginal Australians, terms of inclusion always come with a catch. In an era of multiculturalism, the right to a distinctive cultural life is recognised as important, and this is especially true in settler states such as Australia and Canada, which have attempted to atone for historical misdeeds by granting expanded rights to indigenous groups. Cultural identity has become another important category of liberalism. In Australia, Aboriginal people are able to make public claims on the basis of traditional, indigenous culture. They can, for instance, pursue (and sometimes win) court cases against mining projects on the grounds that mining would disturb sacred lands. Yet, in order to do so, Australian authorities expect Aboriginal people to embody a purified form of traditional identity. Any acknowledgement that traditions may change over time, that Aboriginal people may sometimes think in calculative ways about their welfare, or even that Aboriginal people may exercise free choice, can diminish the credibility of appeals to tradition. The result is an inescapable dilemma, where no matter which categories Aboriginal people use to make public claims – whether they invoke culture or rationality – some aspect of their lives ends up falling outside these categories and getting dismissed or suppressed.[32]

This dilemma makes universalism a double-edged sword. To be included under the banner of the universal or the political is to have an innate claim to rights. The moral force of this claim has underwritten some of the biggest steps towards justice in human history – from the ending of slavery to growing notions of the right to water or health, which have helped avoid millions of preventable deaths over the past century. But insofar as the universal categories of liberalism remain grounded in specific cultural contexts, they always have an outside. And to fall outside of these terms of inclusion is to have one's concerns pushed out the political realm and relegated to the private sphere, or to be held personally responsible for one's misfortune or even to be left without rights at all.[33]

If liberal universalism forms the foundation of our political vocabulary, anyone who remains excluded may experience the failure of liberalism as the failure of politics more generally. Meanwhile, people from all sides of the political spectrum have learnt to couch their claims for recognition and power in the language of universalism. People argue that the world they wish to see must be the world for all. The same language that made it possible to think of a common humanity and to argue, across the eighteenth, nineteenth and twentieth centuries, for an ever-expanding understanding of human equality and human rights, has created a situation where it has become difficult to think of politics as anything *but* pregiven and universal. It's therefore exceedingly difficult to recognise the humanity of those who slip through the cracks.

❋

Played out in miniature, Arjun's dilemma is one which takes in the long history of the roots of democracy. But unlike Arendt's forceful advocacy of civic republicanism, unlike Nancy's self-confident trust, Arjun has come through this history conflicted. His frustration at the unwillingness of others to listen – at the stubbornness of neighbourhood gossip and rumour – feeds into decidedly civic republican hopes. He remains a believer in the power of collective deliberation and civic participation to over-come preconceived ideas, and to allow people to develop new understandings grounded in personal relationships. Arendt's account of Eichmann's trial is famous for giving us the phrase 'the banality of evil', but Arendt's full phrase is 'the fearsome, word-and-thought-defying *banality of evil*'.[34] A line can be drawn connecting Arendt's horror at the power of categorisation, bureaucracy and routine to slip below the surface of thought and produce great evil, and Arjun's comment that with the development of the written word, we forgot how to really listen to and understand others.

Despite this, Arjun's upbeat cheerleading of community work is often tinged with resignation – he's come to learn that people rarely listen. In the meeting, he makes a distinctly liberal appeal: 'As tolerant residents – as resilient and tolerant residents – I wonder if we can just manage to wait to come to the park for a couple of hours. Would it be possible for us to just allow them to have their prayers together in the park in the morning, and then simply go back to the park a few hours later and enjoy the afternoon, if we would like?' This tactic gives up on the idea that it's possible to reach some sort of public consensus over the shared use of space, and instead defaults to a notion of universal rights and private morality. There is a tone of 'self-evident' truth to it. *Of course*, Arjun seems to say, *we would have the right to say no – it's our park after all. But since it is ours, might we be able to share it – not out of recognition, but out of toleration? Out of a consent we can always withdraw?* This is a philosophy of equal, but separate, entitlements. To shore it up, Arjun makes another offer to those who are worried that their vision of community is being left out. The summer is coming, and the local council has permitted barbeques in the park. So he proposes a small summer fair – organised by anyone at the meeting interested in helping – complete with a community barbeque. 'I really think this is something we should attempt to launch, because it is going to bring the people together as a community ... Barbeques are very good things for us as neighbours!' Arjun beams at the crowd. Towards the back, a man raises his hand. He's lived in Munich, he explains. There, he laments, 'the Turkish really like having their barbeques ... the parks can become very smoky and unpleasant. It can really go over the top!'

Arjun's smile slips, as several more hands go up.

CHAPTER FIVE

WAITING

What does it mean to be black? As Europeans raided Africa, those they abducted or traded into slavery came from groups who regarded themselves as distinct peoples. Once captured, however, slavers obliterated the varied identities of their captives by imposing a single status: *black slave*. In Europe and the New World, blackness, a status that would previously have been meaningless for the captives, came to be read as the marker for who qualified as human – with access to the rights and responsibilities of citizenship – and who did not.

But things were not so straightforward. Across the Americas and the Caribbean, blood quickly mixed – through rape by slave owners and through the mixing of slave, settler and indigenous populations in plantations, mines or towns. With inheritance, family lineage and political power at stake, it no longer sufficed to define race by physical features alone. In Cuba, the Spanish geographer Esteban Pichardo wrote in 1836 of the presence of many 'negro' or 'mulatto' Cubans 'who are whiter than many of the white race'.[1] In what would become the USA, anxieties over the implications of mixing led to the infamous 'one-drop' rule. Blackness was imagined as much more easily transmitted than whiteness. This belief took on a range of local variations – in some cases having one-eighth black parentage was enough to be designated black, in some cases the threshold was a quarter. In some places, such as the Carolinas, Mobile and New Orleans, people of mixed background were treated almost as a distinct race, and granted certain privileges relative to those considered fully black. Elsewhere people of mixed descent were treated simply as black. In ambiguous situations, race was determined by social convention – where treating someone *as if* they were white or black determined their race for those around them, and where community mobs or courts wielded the power to reassess someone's race and the rights they were entitled to.[2]

The same difficulty in defining racial differences, especially in light of extensive mixing, was prevalent across the colonial world. As with slavery, colonial power and profit depended on maintaining distinctions between colonisers and colonised. Europeans were minorities in most colonial nations, making colonial enterprises dependent on mixed tactics of coercion, collaboration and enticement. Colonial subjects were educated, evangelised and encouraged to identify with colonial powers. They took up administrative positions, married Europeans and had children, blurring the lines of race and identity. In response, difference was reimagined from something written on the body, to something marked by a range of everyday social practices. In French Indochina, anthropologist Ann Laura Stoler gives the example of an 1898 court case in Haiphong – modern-day Vietnam – where Sieur Icard, a French sailor, attempted to intercede on behalf of his son, who had been imprisoned for beating a German mechanic following a dockside dispute. At the time, France's defeat in the Franco-Prussian war remained a source of national frustration. His half-Vietnamese son, Icard argued, had simply been overtaken by patriotic fervour. The judge, however, saw things differently. He argued that Icard's son did not speak enough French and had absorbed too much Vietnamese culture from his mother while his father was away at sea to genuinely harbour such sentiments. He was no French patriot, but a common Vietnamese ruffian.[3] Based on these conclusions, the judge went so far as to cast doubt on whether Icard's son was truly his at all. Rather than biological descent, or physical features marking race, race was cast as a matter of 'moral unity, cultural genealogy, and language' – the absence of which could even put biological descent into doubt.[4] As efforts to sustain slavery and colonialism led to the creation of new social institutions and ways of living, across the world, racial distinctions became increasingly diffuse and subtle.

The fact that racial distinctions took on new force as colonising nations themselves were transitioning to democracy is not incidental. Democracy, founded on a promise of equality and freedom, produced a dilemma for elites and ordinary citizens. Plenty of citizens led relatively unfree lives of menial labour, working not out of choice but to survive. Although democratic states could tolerate some degree of inequality, too much inequality risked undermining their legitimacy. Part of the solution was to pass some of the costs of inequality on to non-citizens who could be exploited cheaply, without the same requirement to ensure their survival or well-being. The opportunities and promises of the new democratic order were shored up by asserting racial difference.[5]

✻

One evening in Kilburn, I joined a friend, Saabira – well known locally, and within certain circles across London, for her anti-racist activism – at an event provocatively entitled 'Is There Room for Black in the Union Jack?' In Britain, 'black' was once widely used by activists to refer to all of the country's non-white migrants. It was a deliberately inclusive term, defined not in terms of skin colour but politics, which pointed to a shared colonial heritage and to overlapping experiences of discrimination and exclusion. Having cut her teeth on activism in the 80s, Saabira had come to think of her identity, as a child of South-Asian migrants, and her politics as *black*. Blackness gave her a place in British history, marking her struggles as part of a broader story that joined together labour organising, anti-fascist movements and the efforts of other minority groups. Under the banner of political blackness, she had met some of her closest friends. To Saabira, the event that evening summoned up this history. It's title, in fact, seemed to be pulled from a famous book, popular within activist circles and published during the heyday of these politics – Paul Gilroy's *There Ain't No Black in the Union Jack*. Chatting outside, Saabira told me how pleased she was that the event's young organisers were still interested in this older language of solidarity.

It didn't take long for Saabira to realise she was mistaken. The organisers had neither heard of the book, nor of the white nationalist chant – prominent at football matches in the 70s and 80s – from which the title came.[6] Instead, they hit on the title because it was a catchy way of asking a question they felt was all around them: *Do you belong here?* And while they were intent on exploring this, they did so with a very different definition of 'black' in mind. Almost all the activists and artists who spoke, as well as most of the audience, were from African or Caribbean backgrounds. The conversation revolved around the experiences and challenges of these communities. Other minorities were positioned at a distance, and their experiences and identities treated as categorically distinct, often in terms of crude stereotypes. Asians, proclaimed one speaker, had figured out the value of education; Jews knew how to take care of their own.

At the pub afterwards, Saabira fumed. She felt things were going in circles. The speakers' insistence on distinct cultural and racial experiences felt as though they had learnt to take people's worse stereotypes – that Afro-Caribbeans and Africans were lazy or uncooperative, that they didn't value education or solidarity – and apply them to themselves, in order to insist on their uniqueness. The idea that different minorities had different experiences was nothing new – people had always known that. The only difference, she argued, was that activists used to understand that these experiences had shared roots, and that they had much more to gain by working together than they did by splitting apart. This sense of common struggle, she lamented, felt increasingly like it had vanished.

Saabira's frustrations came from finding herself suddenly cast outside a movement and identity she had always thought herself a part of, and which she had worked hard to contribute to. But Saabira is not alone. The splintering of broad-based coalitions into increasingly narrow groups, defined in terms of distinctive identities and separate interests, has been noted as a growing trend within British activist communities.[7] Sometimes dubbed 'identity politics', some allegations that activist and minority groups are shutting out others are clearly made in bad faith. University campuses are popular targets, where students have been depicted as coddled and close-minded, quick to call for the firing of any professor who expresses challenging views, or to drive away invited speakers with whom they disagree. Attempts to systematically trace these incidents, however, reveal them to be rare. Those incidents that do occur largely target extreme speakers – the sorts of speakers who would themselves, deny many students their own right not only to have a platform, but to study or hold citizenship, if given the chance.[8] In part, this seems to be a manufactured crisis. Elsewhere, however, there are signs that identity is coming to dominate our political vocabulary.

In America, the scholar and activist Asad Haider recalls his experience in the Black Lives Matter movement at the University of California Santa Cruz, which sprung out of protests against a tuition hike. First, student leaders quickly converged on the argument that the tuition hikes would hit students of colour the hardest. Haider recounts his own puzzlement at this narrower focus, which seemed to imply that 'racially equitable [fee hikes] would be somehow acceptable'.[9] Then meetings got caught up in lengthy debates about language. Protests that 'occupied' university spaces were deemed racist, as this language echoed the occupation of indigenous territory in America by white settlers. Several hours were spent discussing synonyms. Finally, when strategies were challenged as being undemocratic or ineffective, some student leaders quickly accused their critics of racism. All the while, the circle of those involved dwindled.

Haider's experience echoes a story from the writer Barbara Ehrenreich, who writes about inequality in America today. In 2009 she was invited to give a talk in Detroit about post-industrial decline and labour politics. Wanting to take a different approach, she brought along a group of laid-off foundry workers from Fort Wayne, whom she had grown close with. At the event, they talked about their experience of the recession, and how they were trying to win back their lives. 'And then,' recalls Ehrenreich, 'some woman in the room who was an adjunct professor suddenly says, 'I'm tired of listening to white men talk.'[10] Today, Ehrenreich sees this as an increasingly common tendency, where someone's political legitimacy – their right to speak and have their concerns taken seriously – comes not from their experiences or ideas, but first and foremost from the identities they lay claim to. The identities that matter shift from place to place. There are many instances where it's not whiteness, but blackness, or youth, or political belief that are disqualifying, but the idea that identities come first in determining political entitlements is growing. In public forums and collective movements, those who don't share the right identities are often refused entry.

To people like Saabira, this politics of identity and refusal might seem limited and unjust. And yet these politics have not emerged unexpectedly. Rather, they have developed as one response to a long historical experience of waiting, sometimes endlessly, for freedom to arrive. The Australian anthropologist Maree Pardy has argued that 'waiting is universal to the refugee and migrant experience'.[11] The processing and verifying of visa and asylum claims, the struggle to access social security or find a job, reunification with relatives and the slow process of adapting to a brand-new place can make it feel like life has been put on hold for years, if not decades. Yet this idea of waiting – of lives put on hold and stories left suspended – speaks not only to migrants, but to the lives of many excluded groups living in democratic countries today. As markers of difference – of race, gender, sexuality or class – grew increasingly diffuse and subtle, exclusion became increasingly entrenched in the very workings of society. This has made inequality into a stubborn phenomenon. For excluded groups, the fight for equality has also been characterised by a protracted experience of waiting. Today, this long experience of waiting has fostered a deep wariness around the prospects for political cooperation. And so, if we want to understand why the politics of identity and refusal have become widespread, and how we might move beyond it, we first need to understand the history of waiting.

✳

As newborn babies, we start off without any sense of self, or of the world. In fact, we lack awareness of where our bodies stop and where everything else around us begins. We learn these distinctions through empathy, where the glances, gestures, emotions and responses of others hold clues for understanding ourselves, the world around us and how we fit within it. In Chapter Two, we traced how empathy enables us to learn about who we are, and about the nature of the world around us. How does race come into this? The civil rights activist, writer and poet Audre Lorde remembers being a young child on the New York subway:

> My mother spots an almost seat, pushes my little snow-suited body down. On the one side of me a man reading a paper. On the other, a woman in a fur hat starting at me. Her mouth twitches as she stares and then her gaze

drops down, pulling mine with it. Her leather-gloved hand plucks at the line where my new blue snowpants and her sleek fur coat meet. She jerks her coat closer to her. I look. I do not see whatever terrible thing she is seeing on the seat between us – probably a roach. But she has communicated her horror to me. When I look up the woman is still staring at me, her nose holes and eyes huge. And suddenly I realise there is nothing crawling up the seat between us; it is me she doesn't want her coat to touch. The fur brushes past my face as she stands with a shudder and holds on to a strap on the speeding train ... I do not know what I've done. I look at the sides of my snowpants secretly. Is there something on them? Something's going on here I do not understand, but I will never forget it. Her eyes. The flared nostrils. The hate.[12]

As we grow, parts of the world become internal to us, etched into how we think and feel and move. The feminist scholar Sara Ahmed notes that Lorde's story is a story about the boundaries between bodies – one where for the woman on the train, Lorde's own small, black body extends beyond her skin, even beyond her snowsuit.[13] The woman's revulsion is not a response to Lorde as a person, argues Ahmed, but to an idea of blackness that is the product of a whole 'history of association', rehearsed time and time again. In this history, hatred is not a reaction to bodies that are innately different, but a script for how to relate that *produces difference*. Lorde recalls a progression of these scenes: the story hour at the library when they read *Little Black Sambo* and everyone laughed except her; the Catholic school nuns who demanded she un-braid and straighten her hair into a 'more becoming style'; the lunch counter woman who gave her white friend a regular glass and Lorde a paper cup. The cues for this script are written into the everyday life, until the distinctions it marks come to feel naturalised and intuitive.

As we learn to navigate the world, we develop a vocabulary of security and attachment. We learn how to make sense of our experiences, what we are capable of, where we are safe and supported, where we belong. 'I survived the hatred around me,' writes Lorde, 'because my mother made me know, by oblique reference, that no matter what went on at home, outside shouldn't oughta be the way it was. But since it was that way outside, I moved in a fen of unexplained anger that encircled me and spilt out against whomever was closest that shared those hated selves.' Lorde felt she belonged at home, but not in the world outside. Security and attachment play an important role in enabling us to connect with others and to explore and experiment with the world around us, to become proficient in its workings. There is a cruel tension in demanding that some people learn and grow, strive and succeed, in spaces where they are not permitted to belong.

In schools, decades of research have come to reveal that black students are met with lower expectations, placed in lower-achieving classes or streams, and receive less praise and more criticism when compared to white students of similar ability.[14] In the UK, standardised national testing comes with the option of taking an easier or harder paper, where the easier test limits the maximum grade you can achieve. Teachers make the final call on which students are allowed to sit which test, and disproportionately place black Caribbean students in the easier, lower-achieving tier, even when they are performing at the same level as their white peers.[15]

In New Zealand, as students are learning to read, young Maori students start the year at a similar ability level to the rest of their classmates. When asked to estimate how the students will progress over the course of the year, teachers tend to overestimate the progress of every group except for Maori kids. Sure enough, by the end of the year, the Maori students have fallen behind.[16]

In America, work on the impact of teacher perceptions has shown that teachers never simply predict performance, but that predictions change learning outcomes, creating a self-fulfilling prophecy. How teachers view their students shapes the sort of attention, encouragement and support students receive – leading to a meaningful difference in grades or in who makes it to university.[17] The coordinates of belonging that mark out racial differences – the way students speak, dress or carry themselves – play a major role in shaping these mismatched predictions; teachers who share the same racial background as their students tend to predict performance more accurately,[18] making them better able to allocate their attention and care more fairly. To belong at home, but not in the world beyond, is to become illegible to others – to have them impose their story for you.

This same pattern repeats itself over and over – in employment, in healthcare and in public life. Decades of experiments by psychologists and sociologists have shown that writing a non-white-sounding name on an otherwise identical CV will significantly decrease the chance of that applicant getting an interview. In Europe, this pattern persists for those with migrant backgrounds, generation after generation, and in America the same is true for black Americans – no matter how qualified, capable or experienced applicants are.[19] Being pregnant and black or Latina in America means having much higher odds of receiving low-quality care, regardless of income or location.[20] Psychologists have found that black or minority faces are judged as less likeable or more criminal;[21] that having a foreign accent gets you judged as less trustworthy.[22]

In each of these situations, subtle judgements produce results that appear much more overt. The teacher's prejudice can be hard to identify. It may even be wholly unconscious. But it is easier to spot the fact that black or Maori or migrant children disproportionately end up in the lower-performing class. It can be hard to identify why a baby was taken into care but easy to recognise that a mother no longer has her child. As a consequence, patterns which may be a product of prejudice can in fact appear as signs of inferiority. As these signs pile up, difference and inferiority can come to seem like self-evident truths.

As infants, we learn primarily through mimicry. Infants of between two and five months old can distinguish the language of their parents from those of others.[23] By three months, infants seem to show a preference for faces from their own racial group and by six months, infants seem to implicitly categorise people into groups based on physical features, recognising clusters of similarity and difference.[24] These early preferences may be related to the fact that early mimicry relies on infants identifying what around them – people, animals, things – is most 'like me', and therefore most capable of imparting lessons about the world.[25] By the end of our first year, however, when we begin to learn not only through mimicry, but by modelling and responding to the *judgements* of others, these preferences fade – at least for some.

Following the same group of children as they grew up, the American psychologists Phyllis Katz and Jennifer Kofkin found that by the time children reached kindergarten, the preference for one's own skin tone had faded for non-white children, but remained for white ones.[26] Sometime after we begin to internalise the judgements of others, non-white children were coming to view their own features negatively, while white children were learning it was better to be white. In their study, Katz and Kofkin realised that these preferences were rarely being communicated overtly. Parents often hesitated to talk about race. When asked to describe pictures in a book to their children, many parents dodged references to skin tone, referring to characters by gender and other traits instead. This suggests that while we absorb and reproduce judgements about race from an early age, this learning may not take place consciously. Such tacit understandings are harder to recognise, name and transform.

Gestured more than spoken, self-evident more than explained, the script of racial difference is written everywhere and nowhere at once. We don't know that we know it. In the early twentieth century, several American states moved to enshrine the one-drop rule into law, ending the ability for racial status to be decided by convention and consensus. Making this belief explicit, however, also made it easier to challenge. Yet as tropes of racial descent were removed from the realm of implicit, unspoken truths, other markers were created to take their place, in quick succession. In *Stamped from the Beginning*, his winding history of racist thinking in America, the scholar Ibram X. Kendi traces key moments in popular culture during this time, against a background of institutional segregation and inequality.[27] One story he tells is of the boxer Jack Johnson, an emblem of black pride. In 1908 Johnson won the world heavyweight championship. Media coverage of Johnson fixated on his white wife, trading in familiar tropes of hypersexual black men and vulnerable white women. Johnson's victory caused an uproar, prompting the former heavyweight champion Jim Jeffries to emerge from retirement to challenge Johnson. The Johnson/ Jeffries match was about much more than boxing. *The New York Times* wrote that, 'If the black man wins, thousands and thousands of his ignorant brothers will misinterpret his victory as justifying claims to much more than mere physical equality with their white neighbors.' Jeffries was dubbed the 'Great White Hope'. When Johnson did win, there were riots. Shortly after the match Johnson was arrested under a law that forbade 'transporting women across state lines for immoral purposes', for travelling with his white girlfriend – whom he had begun dating following the death of his wife. Shortly after came the nationwide mania around Edgar Rice Burroughs' *Tarzan of the Apes*, which told the story of a white orphan who teaches himself to hunt, grow food and even write, coming to surpass both the apes who raised him and the local Africans – who are depicted as an interchangeable, primitive menace. Next came the explosion of interest in eugenics – which claimed that human traits such as intelligence or morality were inherited, and varied by race. Despite the fact that eugenicists could not prove that any of these key traits were inheritable, eugenicist theories quickly took hold within universities and were used to guide policy in everything from military recruitment to education. When black Americans were excluded from public institutions or channelled into low-quality education, their lack of success was taken as further evidence of deficiency.

Every time a criminal charge was shown to be fabricated, every time a theory was debunked as pseudoscience, there was another counter claim or sensationalist story, another new theory to take its place, crowding the American imagination with images of black difference, black inferiority. Nearly twenty years before Kendi's book, the black British cultural scholar Stuart Hall referred to race as a 'floating signifier', to describe its capacity to continually change its point of reference – in his own time as much as any other.[28] If a black boxer has a white wife, or is arrested on fabricated drug-trafficking charges, that's a sign of the lustful degeneracy shared by all his kind, but if he wins a championship the victory cannot be used to say anything positive about these same people – and anyway, perhaps the true story about black nature lies in *Tarzan* or in the latest unproven theory. In his history, Kendi shows how racist ideas even seeped into the thinking of the leading black champions for equality at the time. He gives the example of the renowned black scholar and activist W. E. B. Du Bois, who masterfully debated some of America's most prominent racist thinkers, yet who also sometimes wrote about race as if it were a matter of fixed, biological difference or of innate traits.[29]

Any single voice, any single instance is debatable, open to challenge. Any single theory can be debunked – it takes effort, of course, but it's possible. But when an idea, a story, a role comes to be restaged over and over, across the spaces and moments of everyday life, it can acquire a more fundamental, incontestable sense of reality. These are stories first learnt through the glances, judgments and gestures of others; stories we acquire unconsciously, woven into our formative knowledge about ourselves and of the world. Racial difference is an idea that precedes and escapes the language we use to discuss it – one which can be voiced in endlessly shifting ways. It is an idea seldom open for debate.

But if the script of our differences is inescapable, what hope is there for change?

❊

On 20 August 1976, in the midst of a sweltering summer, seven workers walked out of the Grunwick photo-processing plant, located just outside Kilburn. The factory was known for its tyrannical management. Workers had to ask permission to use the toilet, and were shamed for doing so, while harsh discipline was meted out in full view of other workers, creating an atmosphere of fear. Wages were low, overtime was compulsory, scheduling was erratic and workers were fired arbitrarily. In a week, workers made between £6 and £7 – the equivalent of £38 to £45 today.[30] Six of the workers who walked out were women. All seven were Asian immigrants. Grunwick seemed to prefer hiring predominantly immigrant workers, particularly women, based on a belief that they were cheaper and more compliant than white British men.

After walking out, the strikers appealed to the British labour movement for support. Getting unions on board, however, was a difficult, slow process. In earlier strikes led by Asian workers, including at Mansfield Hosiery in Loughborough in 1972 and at Imperial Typewriters in Leicester in 1974, the unions to which the strikers belonged refused to support their actions. In both cases, white workers enjoyed better pay, benefits and treatment. The unions were unwilling to challenge this relatively privileged arrangement. They felt the concerns of Asians were opposed to those of their core (white) membership. At Grunwick, the strikers received early backing from the Union of Post Office Workers, who helped bring the factory's mail-order photo business to a standstill. But it took nearly a year of touring factories, shops and offices, making the case to ordinary workers to put pressure on union officials, for the Grunwick strikers to get a commitment from the large national unions. After a surge of mass support in the summer of 1977 failed to win meaningful concessions, national unions unilaterally withdrew backing. They feared that involvement in a more protracted conflict would compromise their political power and support.[31] This withdrawal led the Grunwick strikers to stage a hunger strike outside the headquarters of the powerful Trades Union Congress in 1977, with strike leader Jayaben Desai remarking, 'Support from the TUC is like honey on your elbow: you can see it, you can smell it but you can't taste it!'[32] In the span of a few months, the solidarity Desai and others had spent a year building had splintered – eventually leading to the defeat of the Grunwick strikers.

Over the course of the twentieth century, movements for social justice shifted from fighting for *civic inclusion* to *legal equality*. They shifted from trying to change hearts and minds to seeking to enshrine equality through legal change. The story of this shift, and of the motivations behind it, is reflected in the history of how labour unions grappled with the distinctive needs and demands of minority communities, as well as those of women – a history that played out in similar ways on both sides of the Atlantic. By the time of Grunwick, tension between labour unions and those championing women's and minority rights had been growing for decades. There was a sense of irreconcilable interests. But this was not inevitable.

Before the American civil rights movement reached a cre-
scendo in the 1950s and 60s, there was a century of patient,
often frustrating, activism by black American leaders. This
work, following the end of civil war in 1865, fed into a growing
momentum for change but it was never all of a kind. While the
civil rights movement of the 50s and 60s prioritised fighting for
legal change, many earlier efforts focused on other targets and
strategies. In the 1940s, for instance, black Americans flocked to
labour unions as they moved into cities and industrial jobs. 'Civil
rights unionists' recognised the links between racial and economic exploitation, and developed an ambitious programme
linking the fight for fair work and pay to that for affordable
housing, health, education, social security and suffrage.[33]

Over the course of the 1940s, around half a million black
Americans joined unions affiliated with the powerful Congress
of Industrial Organizations.[34] In the small city of Winston-
Salem, North Carolina, the R. J. Reynolds Tobacco Company
provided most of the jobs. Whites dominated the higher-paying
jobs but the majority of the workforce was black. Following
two years of covert efforts to build support on the shop floor,
Reynolds workers unionised in 1943. Within a year the union
had negotiated a new contract for Reynolds' black workers, with
breakthrough rights around seniority, wage adjustment and the
settlement of grievances. However, the union's greatest impact
was beyond the factory walls. As the historians Robert Korstad
and Nelson Lichtenstein write:

By the summer of 1944 [the new union] had become the
center of an alternative social world that linked black
workers together regardless of job, neighborhood, or
church affiliation. The union hall, only a few blocks from
the Reynolds Building, housed a constant round of meetings, plays, and musical entertainments, as well as classes
in labor history, black history, and current events. Local 22

sponsored softball teams, checker tournaments, sewing circles, and swimming clubs. Its vigorous educational program and well-stocked library introduced many black workers (and a few whites) to a larger radical culture few had glimpsed before. 'You know, at that little library they [the city of Winston-Salem] had for us, you couldn't find any books on Negro history,' remembered Viola Brown. 'They didn't have books by Aptheker, Dubois, or Frederick Douglass. But we had them at our library.'[35]

In their heyday, in the US, UK and elsewhere, the role of unions extended well beyond workplace bargaining. As union activity extended into daily life, everyday matters were wrapped up in a sense of common cause – a feeling that flourishing was a matter of a community striving together. During this time, union life was decidedly civic republican. Beyond the workplace, unions contributed to a surge of political energy where, over the course of the 1940s, the number of registered black voters doubled in the North and quadrupled in the South. Membership of black civic associations – like the National Association for the Advancement of Coloured people – likewise boomed.

In Winston-Salem, the social world centred around the union nurtured a new cohort of black leaders. In the factory, women leaders in low-paid jobs learnt to sit down with male executives and to negotiate, not only for rights but for 'respect'.[36] Beyond the factory, union members challenged the city's traditional, middle-class black leadership, who had long preached an accommodating attitude to segregation. Where traditional leaders insisted the black community needed to be content with the minimal support given to black institutions, and with the lack of organised white violence in the city, the new leaders believed that equality could mean something much more substantial. They had found feelings of substantive dignity in the union.

Civil rights leaders grappled with the potentials and

limitations of such civic republican politics for decades. Born in Marianna, Florida, in 1856, the journalist and activist T. Thomas Fortune played an influential early role in shaping a line of thinking that would eventually come to guide the civil rights movement of the 1950s and 60s.[37] Fortune is a revealing figure in this history, because his thought casts light on a struggle between liberal and civic republican politics in the fight for black equality. Trained in law, Fortune was particularly passionate about inequality, not just between blacks and whites but between Americans in general. Inequality, he believed, was a product of the racial segregation that surrounded many Americans. But it was also a matter of *all* poor Americans being denied opportunities to succeed.

From 1879 onwards, Fortune edited the country's most influential black newspaper – the *New York Age*.[38] In the pages of the *Age*, he championed a range of tactics for pursuing equality. He emphasised participation in the labour movement and building local mutual-aid groups. Fortune believed that unions and mutual-aid groups could work to make equality an everyday reality for blacks and whites alike, as the two groups learnt to participate in the life of the nation side by side. In other words, he believed in building *recognition* between black and white Americans, promoting a distinctively civic republican vision of citizenship, where the full substance of rights would emerge through civic participation. In the Age, Fortune wrote, 'Having been made equal before the law by a spasmodic outburst of goodness, we have got to settle down to that earnest and successful competition which equality of citizenship imposes.'[39]

Fortune's fondness for civic republican politics, however, was tinged with wariness. By his time, legal thinkers had built on the liberal tradition to draw a distinction between 'natural rights', such as the right to vote, hold property or speak freely, and 'social rights' – rights which arose through voluntary association in the private sphere. Natural rights were seen as inalienable, and were guaranteed by the government for all citizens. Social rights were negotiated between citizens and could not be subject to government regulation. Fortune broadly agreed with this distinction. The only issue was that for many thinkers, legislators and jurists of Fortune's time, segregation was seen largely as an issue of social rights. Keeping black students out of white schools, for instance, was seen as an expression of the right to free association, akin to the right to freely worship or to form or join political parties or voluntary associations. For Fortune, segregation entrenched deep forms of inequality that made it impossible for black Americans to participate in public life on an equal basis. Blackness was not a private identity, and so the supposedly 'free' choice not to associate with blacks had systematic, public consequences. Under such circumstances, Fortune believed, attempts to build common cause would inevitably end up with those who already held power becoming dominant.

During his time at the *Age*, Fortune covered a supreme court case that laid the foundation for Jim Crow legislation. In 1876, the sheriff of Crockett County, Tennessee, led a lynch mob into the local prison, where they hauled out and beat four black prisoners, killing one of them. With no charges brought against them locally, the federal government charged the men with depriving their victims of equal protection under the law. In 1883, the supreme court ruled that the federal government's intervention, and the law guaranteeing equal protection, were unconstitutional. Only states had the right to penalise crimes such as murder and assault. Fortune recognised that whatever the benefits of participatory politics, a life dependent on community recognition was a fragile, perilous affair.

Fortune had reservations about unionism for similar reasons. He feared that the force of organised labour could easily be captured by the most powerful within the movement. Fortune was preoccupied with inequality. He saw this as limiting the scope for participating in the forms of civic republican politics he otherwise championed. As such, Fortune emphasised the need for legal reforms that could guarantee a base of equality. Alongside his advocacy of participatory politics, he stressed the need for new laws and court cases that would chip away the foundations of segregation. These legally focused reforms, he believed, were a necessary foundation for a more equal public sphere.

Fortune's fears were prescient – on both sides of the Atlantic. In America, the historian Joshua Freeman notes that while the Second World War is celebrated by the American labour movement as a period of growing confidence, many strikes during this period were in fact 'hate strikes' – protesting black employment or advancement across the nation.[40] Railroad unions went on strike for white-only hiring policies. When strikes failed, railwaymen sometimes turned to terrorism, kidnapping, beating and killing black workers in attempts to deter others from joining the profession.[41] Unions celebrated for embodying the civic republican tradition often built solidarity around commitments to racial exclusion, as was the case for the International Association of Machinists, whose constitution prohibited black membership until 1948.[42] In many cases, union activism was primarily geared towards defending the status and privileges of white jobs, white families and white communities, rather than attempting to represent working-class interests or build solidarity more broadly.[43] Even when there were resounding success stories of unions building community and creating change, as with the tobacco company union branch in Winston-Salem, these projects only worked to shift attitudes for those who engaged with them, often leaving wider patterns unchanged. Summing up these trends in 1935, W. E. B. Du Bois wrote: 'The white worker did not want the Negro in his unions, did not believe in him as a man, dodged the question, and when he appeared at conventions, asked him to organize separately; that is outside the real labor movement.'[44]

The same dynamic played out in the UK following the

Second World War. At that time, facing a dire labour shortage and the need to rebuild, the country made a concerted effort to recruit a migrant workforce from its current and former colonies. As we saw in Chapter One, many new arrivals had learnt to see the UK as the 'motherland', and to imagine migration as a homecoming.[45] The home the new migrants found, however, was a patchwork one. While some Brits rushed to welcome them, others branded them as 'dark strangers' who could never truly be British.[46] The various attitudes migrants faced shaped the lives they were able to build. In Kilburn, older Asian and Caribbean migrants would tell me how only certain landlords were willing to rent to non-whites. It took good connections and a bit of luck to find a place to stay. With a relatively captive market, landlords got away with shoddy conditions, leaving renters to make do with mouldy walls, cold buildings and cramped spaces. The same pattern played out in the labour market. While some employers actively recruited colonial and post-colonial workers, others barred their doors.

As with the distinction between natural and social rights in the America of Fortune's time, these forms of exclusion were defended by successive left- and right-wing governments as a matter of private liberty – as the right of white Brits to associate and do business with whom they pleased.[47] This exclusion had two interlinked consequences. It fed into myths of migrant inferiority. If all you owned was a single suit, slowly going threadbare, if unemployment left young men loitering on street corners or at bus stops, if cramped housing led to more family drama, which bled through thin walls, the consequences of exclusion could easily be mistaken for causes. At the same time, in places like Kilburn, migrants found ways of drawing on common experiences of struggle to build new alliances that could respond to exclusions for which there was no public redress. The idea of blackness that Saabira described – encompassing migrants from the Caribbean, India, China and elsewhere – emerged out of these experiences of shared struggle and support, history and hardship, public exclusion and private belonging.

With limited opportunities, migrant communities grappled with higher rates of unemployment and poverty. This made it possible for employers to dictate conditions for those in work – low pay and long hours were better than nothing.[48] This had consequences for the workforce as a whole. Migrant hires were used to drive down wages and discourage collective bargaining.[49] The briefly successful efforts of the Grunwick strikers to build national support reveals that it was possible to imagine the conditions facing non-white workers as a matter of common cause. More often, however, this was an uphill battle. Many of Grunwick's Asian workers had migrated in the early 70s from former British colonies in East Africa. They arrived to letters in the local paper protesting their arrival.[50] Around Kilburn, as elsewhere, minority workers trying to build common cause had to contend with the fact that they were judged to be a threat before they had any opportunity to speak for themselves. Separate patterns of residence, and different habits and standards of living, nurtured suspicions that migrant workers had no interest or capacity to be a part of collective life or to partake of shared values.

This image followed migrants to the shop floor. For instance, the anthropologist Gillian Evans relates an incident in Bermondsey, south-east London. Local women would take it in turns to clean the common areas of their tower block, scrubbing stairs and landings until they were spotless.[51] When a Jamaican family moved into the block other families grew uneasy, and the women decided not to involve them in the communal cleaning. The mother of the new family, however, noticed this ritual herself and, wanting to fit in, made an attempt of her own. Believing that she was imitating the other residents, she scrubbed the landing and poured her dirty water down the stairs – leaving traces of dirt and increasing the scorn she already faced. The woman telling Evans this story had worked for many years in a nearby biscuit factory. The factory had an informal hierarchy, where the workers who commanded the most respect and had the most say in how things got done were those women who were most respected within the local community – such women were deemed 'decent'. For the lady sharing the story, the seemingly minor incident with the Jamaican woman was proof enough that this 'coloured' woman lacked such decency. Evans's story is one small example of a vicious cycle, which played out across the US and UK in countless ways, where existing prejudices barred people from the sorts of ordinary interactions that may have helped overcome these prejudices and identify shared interests.

Crowded out or browbeaten by the labour movement, minorities in the UK and America looking for justice increasingly turned towards the world of rules, regulations and, above all else, law. Within the American labour movement itself, the conflicting agendas of black and white workers were addressed through increasingly bureaucratic mechanisms such as complaints and grievance procedures. These processes were a compromise. They sometimes resolved individual cases of unfair treatment but avoided addressing the overarching balance of power between white and black workers.[52] Meanwhile, by the time the civil rights movement was in full, era-defining swing in the mid-1950s, legal reform had emerged as the movement's predominant agenda, uniting the efforts of civil rights unionists, black churches and civic associations into a relatively focused drive for change. Filtered through a lineage of civic organisations and thinkers, Fortune's ambivalent attitude towards legal reform had been transformed into a sense of overwhelming urgency. Faced with the seeming impossibility of securing rights by building popular consensus and mutual recognition, civil rights leaders increasingly turned to the law as a guarantee of rights.[53] In the US, these efforts culminated in the Civil Rights

Act of 1964. The act outlawed discrimination based on race, skin tone, religion, sex or national origin. In the UK, a series of laws – on 'race relations', 'sex discrimination', 'disability discrimination' and so on – attempted to do the same, with these disparate laws being consolidated and updated by the 2010 Equality Act.

With legislative changes, difference and inclusion became things to be managed rather than negotiated. Discrimination became a punishable offence. Businesses and civic associations developed policies and processes for managing inclusion on their own terms. Over three decades from 1956 to 1986, the proportion of medium and large employers in the US with personnel offices is estimated to have grown from 28 per cent to 67 per cent.[54] What was once the stuff of contentious public dispute became a matter for corporate managers, government officials and courts. In turn, efforts to secure equality became increasingly corrective rather than proactive. Rules and regulations worked to punish and deter negative behaviour – sexual harassment, hate crime, discriminatory hiring – but did little to address underlying attitudes and prejudices.

This story – where unions failed to negotiate issues of racial difference, leading activists to favour the legal imposition of equality – has been repeated over and over. Many unions resisted not only racial diversity, but the growing presence of women in the workplace, too. Again, this was seen as a challenge of irreconcilable interests. In some cases, the struggles of women and minorities overlapped. Unions were determined to defend a 'breadwinner wage' – where men were paid enough to sustain an average family. This was seen as being undercut by both women and minorities.[55]

Beyond unions, political scientist Theda Skocpol has traced a shift in American civic organisations. Many organisations originally operated on what she calls a 'membership' model – characterised by active participation and leadership from grassroots members. They've since moved to a 'management' model

– where civic organisations fight for legal change rather than fostering political participation. Decision-making has shifted from members to a small cadre of professional staff, while members themselves are increasingly treated merely as supporters. This shift took place within organisations, but also across them, where membership-based organisations have gradually been replaced by advocacy-oriented ones. Skocpol traces this transformation across the latter half of the twentieth century, identifying several causes, but prominent among them are the ways in which older civic associations and forms of organising struggled to deal with growing demands for equality. Associations that struggled to overcome histories of formal or informal segregation according to gender, race or class were outflanked by newer groups with a sharp focus on winning political change, above and beyond building consensus. Meanwhile, attempts to reform older organisations from above by mandating equality and integration often led to them fracturing from within.[56]

In more radical circles, activists found themselves locked in endless debate about the relative urgency of racial versus gendered versus class-based injustices, or over how to respond to those within their own movement who failed to live up to particular standards of inclusion.[57] All this wrangling led to moments of extraordinary political creativity and energy. Often, however, these dynamics led to organisations turning inwards, focusing on modelling justice and inclusion within their own ranks, above and beyond engaging others. Big structural or legal changes often remained on the agenda, but the intermediate level of coalition building, responding to local complexities or changing hearts and minds sometimes dropped out.[58]

❋

What does it mean to be black? It was a chilly spring evening on the Caldwell estate. To ward off the cold while we waited to be let into the nearby community centre, Wyatt suggested that we sit in his car. I shuffled into the back, while his friend and musical producer Jonah took the passenger seat. Wyatt was a man of many talents – rapper, animator, programmer, teacher – and he and I had made a deal of sorts. He was releasing a few tracks and wanted to record an interview to go with them, with Jonah acting as interviewer. I had managed to borrow some high-quality camera equipment and had helped find a space to film the interview, in a Rastafarian-run community centre. In exchange, Wyatt and Jonah agreed to talk to me about their experiences of growing up on the Caldwell estate. Both were Afro-Caribbean, in their mid-twenties, and had lived their whole lives in the area. During this time, the estate changed dramatically. Many older buildings were torn down and rebuilt, bringing in a newer, wealthier and – typically – whiter population. In the car, Wyatt did most of the talking, twisted sideways in the driver's seat, his long braids flicking and swaying as he turned between Jonah and me.

We had got a little off track. Having started by talking about the redevelopment of the Caldwell estate, the conversation detoured into the history of hip hop – a topic Wyatt was particularly passionate about. The link wasn't entirely random. Wyatt argued that the process of the black community gradually being priced out of Kilburn – even as the area was marketed to affluent incomers as vibrant and multicultural, partly on the basis of their presence – was just another instance in a long history of black identity and black possessions being usurped, from slavery, to rap, to Egyptian artefacts. 'Jazz, hip hop, rock and roll, blues – it's been happening for a long time!' In the process, he argued, black history has been one of others speaking for black people, representing them as resilient, violent, creative, lazy or hypersexual – and in doing so, controlling how they were able to live their lives.

'But do you know what? ... here's the thing – hip hop [is]

world music. It started in a small area of … New York. A small area there. So why does everyone feel it innately in their soul – everybody?' He fixed me with a serious stare: 'I think it's powerful because we're the first person – no man on earth predates us. So if everybody comes through us, whatever we feel, or whatever we create—'

Jonah interjected to finish the thought, flashing a grin, 'You actually feel for real!'

Despite this shared human heritage, Wyatt remarked, black art, black ideas, black values resonated with some more than others. Across centuries of conflict and oppression, plenty of people had learnt to respond to black expression not by recognising the humanity it attempted to assert but through an opportunistic lens — asking what it could do for them. Conversely, he confesses, he often feels ill at ease in non-black spaces, with non-black friends, or when he's had non-black girlfriends. This, he argues, is because the capacity to recognise one another is something innate, both biological and spiritual: 'Naturally, I just get an uncomfortable feeling when I follow the masses,' he explains, 'it's just like—'

Curious, I interrupt, 'Well, what makes it uncomfortable?'

Wyatt answers with a single word: 'Melanin.' He waits for a beat, then asks, 'Do you know what that is?'

I'm a bit taken aback, so I respond noncommittally, 'I know it's the pigment in your skin, but that's it.'

'All right. But have you ever heard the saying that God is everywhere? So is melanin.'

He's flatly serious for a second, before cracking a smile that makes all three of us break out into laugher. After this subsides, he continues: 'It's something everywhere in the cosmos – it's what inspires us. And so, you know what, you get this innate feeling that, you know what, this ain't right, fam, this ain't cool. And I know that sounds – that might sound really crazy, swear down, but certain times it has stopped me from doing real stupid things. And sometimes not listening to it has made me do things that have made me end up behind bars, know what I'm saying? And though that sounds crazy—'

Jonah jumps in, 'It's the truth! – that's *absolutely* the truth!'

Wyatt looks at Jonah: 'Because we were talking a while ago, and it's nuts. Like there's this thing that happens, yeah, like I could be walking, yeah, and whenever I sense another black person, I look up. And whenever I look up, they're looking at me! It's crazy!'

The author Toni Morrison once remarked:

> The function, the very serious function of racism ... is distraction. It keeps you from doing your work. It keeps you explaining over and over again, your reason for being. Somebody says you have no language and so you spend 20 years proving that you do. Somebody says your head isn't shaped properly so you have scientists working on the fact that it is. Somebody says that you have no art so you dredge that up. Somebody says that you have no kingdoms and so you dredge that up. *None of that is necessary.* There will always be one more thing.[59]

In 1963, Martin Luther King delivered his era-defining 'I have a dream' speech, where he declared: 'I have a dream that one day this nation will rise up and live out the true meaning of its creed: We hold these truths to be self-evident, that all men are created equal.'[60] By then nearly 100 years had passed since the ending of black slavery in the US, and nearly 200 years had passed since the words he quoted were first set down in the Declaration of Independence. And yet, even after all that time, for King equality remained a distant hope – a promise for another day.

This long experience of waiting has not been faced passively. Rather than simply waiting for life to one day begin, excluded groups have sought out ways of defining their own destinies.

When ideas about difference and inferiority endure, beyond every discredited claim, beyond every challenge, they take on a transcendent quality. They acquire the look of universal truths, written everywhere and nowhere at once. To summon the capacity to resist, or even to simply shrug off such notions, excluded groups have found ways of imagining identities that are similarly transcendent. Where groups have been told they were always lacking, they have learnt to counter: *we were always complete*. The philosopher Patchen Markell describes this as an understanding of identity as 'sovereign' – that is, as 'independent', 'self-determining', singular and whole.[61] This assertion of sovereignty has drawn on, entrenched and transformed the liberal tradition, both in private and in public.

In private, excluded communities have nurtured distinctive identities and ways of living that are not always accessible to those on the outside. They have claimed and cultivated their difference as a means of survival. In the liberal tradition, public life is founded on commonality. Supposedly universal qualities – such as rationality or dignity – are seen as underwriting citizenship. Yet for those who have long been depicted – overtly or covertly – as lacking these universal qualities, the ability to take part in public life has instead relied on a wellspring of private difference. To insist on your humanity when many others deny it requires nurturing the capacity to make this insistence in the first place. And when this denial is voiced in sweeping, seemingly transcendent terms, perhaps any credible insistence to the contrary must find ways of coming to feel similarly transcendent. The scholar and activist bell hooks writes about home for black Americans as a place to 'transcend their tiredness', marked by feelings 'of safety, of arrival'.[62] In family homes and places of worship, among friends and in communities, excluded groups have cultivated their own grounds for belonging, and their own vocabulary of human dignity and worth. This vocabulary has been assembled and animated through deeply familiar habits of thought, feeling and action that give rise to the 'innate feelings' – to use Wyatt's term – emerging from different belongings. Under the surface of all-too-familiar scripts, under the surface of language itself, people have cultivated the ability to think, feel and say something different about themselves.

This difference can become weighty. Experiences of anger and endurance, creativity, struggle and care, grounded in lifetimes of exclusion, can shape radically different perspectives on the world, as well as different ways of connecting. For Wyatt, blackness not only defined a distinctive sense of what it meant to be human, but also the ways he was able to relate to others. Peppered throughout our conversation, Wyatt recounted a history of misunderstandings – where it felt as if the people in his life were never really seeing him for who he really was. Rattling off a string of awkward moments where he felt objectified or misinterpreted when dating white and Asian women, Wyatt contrasts this to his experiences dating black women, where interaction just felt 'normal'. 'It's not strange,' he emphasises 'and it's not scary.'

Meanwhile, in public, excluded groups have continued to fight for rights. Over the course of the twentieth century – and into the twenty-first – they have shifted the liberal grammar of citizenship. Social movements and policymakers have challenged the idea that generic terms of inclusion – such as humanity, rationality or equality before the law – are sufficient for ensuring fairness and justice. They have argued that if equality is to mean anything, it must be understood in relation to the unequal positions occupied by different groups. As a result, they have shifted greater emphasis onto more particular categories of identity – such as race or gender – as a basis for making public claims. These claims remain meaningful, however, only in relation to imagined universal horizons. Poorer or unemployed citizens may be granted access to social security based on the idea that this gives *everyone* a similar freedom in the labour market to make choices informed by more than dire need. Hate-crime laws may protect minority groups based on the idea that *everyone* is entitled to public safety. Indigenous groups are granted autonomy in relation to the idea of a *universal* right to self-determination.

For Wyatt, blackness does not *only* name an inner essence. It also enables him to trace a struggle over representation and profit, where black cultural expression – from the local culture of a gentrifying neighbourhood to rock and roll, or artefacts in the British Museum – has been harnessed to create white wealth and prestige. He argues that it is impossible to calculate what black Brits owe as citizens – how much rent they ought to pay, or whether they ought to open up cultural spaces to others – without first weighing up these debts. He brings up the example of teaching black history in schools, emphasising that this would help provide young black students with a piece of what their white classmates already enjoy in abundance – a sense of an inherited 'birth right'.

The more categories of identity come to name both private wellsprings of selfhood and belonging, as well as the possibilities for public inclusion, the more significant they become. Today, categories of identity have become a powerful shorthand. Labels of ethnicity, race, class or gender are often used to stand in for the humanity of people themselves, for all the possibilities of life. For Wyatt blackness named his ability to connect with others, his creativity, his curiosity. It framed his ability to talk about justice and fairness. For anxious parents in Kilburn – such as Fawzia, whom we met in Chapter Two – ethnic heritage was used as shorthand for everything from the capacity to succeed at school, to the ability to think and act ethically. If children were going astray, it was because they were not Eritrean, or Caribbean or Somali enough. For community groups, identity was shorthand for legitimacy – as Latin American community centres or Irish seniors' centres positioned themselves as representatives of '*the* (Latin, Irish, etc.) community'. For the activists who spoke at the 'Is There Room for Black in the Union Jack?' event, identity represented nothing less than freedom – the ability to live and flourish in a way that felt true to who you were. And, for the college activists described by Haider, identity is used as shorthand both for disadvantage and for the possibility for political action.

As Saabira suggests, this new understanding of identity can be divisive and frustrating. Often such 'identity politics' are also discussed – and criticised – as something decidedly new. Yet across the long history of democracy, and its deferred promise, we can see how claims to identity have always been a cornerstone of liberal politics. Although categories such as rationality or humanity may imply neutrality and universality, they are always constructed in specific ways – mapped onto certain manners, bodies, accents, professions, postcodes – and defined in contrast to others. These categories enable some to claim public inclusion and private belonging. But they deny these possibilities to others.

In this sense, what has shifted is not the importance of identity within liberal democracies, but the *language* of such identity claims. Contemporary laws and politics are often much more explicit about their particularity – they are not trying to address a generic citizen, but specific forms of exclusion, disadvantage or freedom relevant to particular groups. This particularity may lead to fragmentation, defining different terms of citizenship and forms of politics for different groups. But it is also a response to the protracted waiting created by more insistently generic forms of citizenship and politics. Grounded in strategies of resilience and resistance, cultivated across generations, this fragmentation cannot easily be wished away.

These shifts have created a political dilemma. On the one hand, they have enabled excluded citizens to refuse an endless script of difference and inferiority. They have allowed them to claim rights and humanity, increasingly on their own terms. But on the other, they have given rise to an ideal of equality that bypasses the everyday understanding of dominant groups. Excluded groups can cultivate and claim equality by nurturing private belonging and through the top-down force of the law. But by breaking with the need for everyday recognition, this ideal of equality also struggles to identify and tackle the silent, intuitive judgements that form much of the foundation of inequality. It is an ideal of equality that struggles to address a white woman in a fur coat recoiling from a small child in disgust. It is an ideal of equality that will always leave one more thing.

CHAPTER SIX

LOVE AND THE LIMITS OF EQUALITY

The writer James Baldwin was swept up in the swell of the civil rights movement in America: its calls for peace and leaps towards militancy, its infighting, its turmoil and all of its desperate hopes. 'Each of us,' he wrote, towards the end of his life, 'helplessly and forever, contains the other – male in female, female in male, white in black, and black in white. We are part of each other. Many of my countrymen appear to find this fact exceedingly inconvenient and even unfair, and so, very often, do I. But none of us can do anything about it.'[1]

Baldwin lived a conflicted life. As an influential black writer living in America – and later abroad in France – and one who wrote on race, no less, Baldwin and his work were immersed in the civil rights movement. He was often expected to speak for it and in tune with the voices of its leaders. And many were furious. Having seen centuries of oppression unfold with little change, leading black activists and thinkers frequently preached a doctrine of rejection. As we saw in the previous chapter, like so many others, they had become fed up with waiting for their white countrymen to acknowledge their humanity. The only way out of this situation, they argued, was through severing ties with white society and claiming power for oneself. The plans for how to achieve this varied, from the Nation of Islam's blueprint for dividing the USA into separate black and white states, to Marcus Garvey's vision of a return to Africa. Others called for armed insurrection, where black power would claim the United States as its own.

Baldwin's writing crackles with much of this same fury. At times, it is consumed by it. In 1972's *No Name in the Street*, he joined calls for black Americans to rise up in violence against whites – arguing that they ought to recognise coolly and rationally that only insurrection offered hope of true freedom. Yet much of his early writing – and that at the very end of his life – took a more humane, but much more demanding view. As the literary scholar Henry Louis Gates Jr writes, 'If Baldwin had a central political argument, it was that the destinies of black America and white were profoundly and irreversibly intertwined.'[2] For most of his life, Baldwin felt the same fury as his revolutionary counterparts, but he frequently found himself unable to advocate action driven directly by such fury. In part, he feared that this could only produce a monstrous sort of freedom. But, much more than that, he believed that black Americans could never come to see themselves as fully human – as worthy of love and of life – without seeing their humanity reflected in the white gaze that had long denied it. In his short, devastating 1963 book *The Fire Next Time*, he writes:

> All of us know, whether or not we are able to admit it, that mirrors can only lie, that death by drowning is all that awaits one there. It is for this reason that love is so desperately sought and so cunningly avoided. Love takes off the masks that we fear we cannot live without and know we cannot live within. I use the word 'love' here not merely in the personal sense but as a state of being, or a state of grace – not in the infantile American sense of being made happy but in the tough and universal sense of quest and daring and growth.[3]

What prevented Baldwin from ultimately embracing the prospect of violent self-determination was the hollowness that came from being the only one who could define oneself. And what

Baldwin held up as true freedom, and as love, and as grace was the possibility of being recognised as a full moral agent, as truly human in the eyes of others.

As Gates notes, to some of Baldwin's contemporaries, this admission – that one needed the recognition of others, particularly of whites, to be fully human – was tantamount to a deep betrayal of the black American cause. The radical activist Eldridge Cleaver wrote that Baldwin's work demonstrated 'the most gruelling, agonizing, total hatred of the blacks, particularly of himself, and the most shameful, fanatical, fawning, sycophantic love of the whites that one can find in any black American writer of note in our time'. Gates suggests that Baldwin's midcareer turn towards radicalism came from his desperate wish to be accepted by figures like Cleaver, and within the increasingly militant tendencies of black American politics more broadly. Ironically, it seems as if Baldwin's deep desire for recognition caused him to set aside his own expansive vision of human interdependency in the hopes of winning recognition from a more immediate circle of activists, writers and leaders.

Today, many social movements seem to have rejected Baldwin's hopes for recognition in favour of visions of self-determination. The stubbornness of the inequalities and injustices they have fought against, and their refusal to budge, has come to make such hopes seem too costly and too distant to take seriously. In the last chapter, on 'waiting', I looked at how contemporary forms of politics, which seem to stress singular identities over building broader coalitions, are linked to a history of stubborn exclusion. I took the civil rights, feminist and labour rights movements as key examples. These are all broadly left-wing causes, but this refusal to hope and strive alongside others, and this fragmentation into increasingly particular identities, are not simply hallmarks of the left. In the US, the Republican Party has increasingly approached politics as an arena in which there can be no understanding and no compromise between different

groups. Across Europe, a decade of austerity policies following the 2008/2009 global recession transformed welfare systems
into systems for policing the lives of the poor. Over this same
decade, new populist movements have risen to power by presenting majority groups as persecuted victims and attempting
to reassert their dominance. For much of the past half-century,
our major political causes have often been pursued in parallel
rather than in dialogue, and this is true of both the right and the
left. These trends have very different histories, but nonetheless
reflect a similar logic of identity, refusal and self-determination.
Here, too, different groups imagine themselves as sovereign – as
self-sufficient and complete.

Baldwin understood the temptations of self-determination.
Setting out alone, as a black nation, promised a path that was
less fraught, a destination that was less under threat and a life
that was more comfortable, more certain and more just. Yet
such a vision denied the fact that, 'Each of us, helplessly and
forever, contains the other.' Even so, despite Baldwin's fears,
and the fears of many others, we have built our modern politics
around a denial of interdependence, favouring the pursuit of
individual and unalienable rights.

To fully grasp Baldwin's fears requires understanding the
limits of equality. Within liberal democracy, equality remains an
ongoing project. Yet even if there comes a day when equality is
powerfully and fairly guaranteed by law, in a way that accounts for
the different experiences and struggles of citizens, it can still lead
to two pitfalls. The first is the fact that legally imposed equality can
feel hollow, failing to change people's habits or feelings. Insofar as
there may be a mismatch between what the law says about equality and how people truly feel towards one another, prejudices and
resentments may persist within private thoughts and feelings,
perpetuating unequal outcomes in ways which are difficult to
police. As we see today, the result can be an empty equality, which
declares itself triumphant even as it slips through our fingers.

The need for equality to be backed up by a more vital sense of human recognition is partly why some of Baldwin's detractors dreamt of black self-determination.[4] A sovereign nation promised the coupling of public equality with private sentiment in a way that could make equality a robust reality. Here, however, the second pitfall remains. This vision of equality, rooted in both public and private life, relies on a foundation of sameness – in a core equivalence between people that defines shared belonging, recognition and humanity. At its heart, then, equality maintains a certain inescapable opposition to difference. The essences which bind humanity must always be marked in particular terms. Beyond these limits, we always find images of others who appear to be lacking in these essences. Baldwin experienced this first hand. As a gay man, he drew the ire of black nationalists like Cleaver not only for his ideas but for his sexuality. He embodied something that cut against the vision of black masculinity that Cleaver and others had worked to build up as a foundation for black liberation. Especially when the sense of being part of a common world forms the foundation of politics, differences that don't fit neatly within dominant images of identity can come to be seen as especially threatening.

In his writing and thought, Baldwin attempted to chart a way beyond these pitfalls. This he found in his commitment to interdependence and, with it, love. Baldwin recognised that interdependence carried with it a profound risk. To open oneself up to others was to put the question of your humanity at risk. Yet instead of refusing this risk, he asks what would it mean to live in a world where this risk was taken on evenly – by all citizens attempting to live and define themselves in light of one another. He points the way towards an ethic of political love – one defined, as he put it, not by simple happiness or affection but by 'quest and daring and growth'.

❄

In 1967 the American supreme court declared that prohibitions on interracial marriage were unconstitutional. This move foretold a slow but sweeping change in public opinion. Nearly a decade earlier, in 1958, a mere 4 per cent of Americans approved of marriages between black and white Americans. In the year following the legalisation of interracial marriage, this proportion had risen, but still comprised a small minority of the population, at 20 per cent. In fact, it wasn't until 1997 that a majority of Americans polled by Gallup voiced support for interracial marriage. This has continued to grow, and in 2013, a full 87 per cent of Americans were in support.

In a much earlier 1869 court case, the Georgia supreme court rejected the legalisation of mixed-race marriage. In their judgement, the justices confidently declared that 'moral or social equality between the different races [...] does not in fact exist, and never can ... and no human law can produce it'.[5] And yet, despite the self-assurance of the justices, attitudes *have* changed, and it seems as if 'human law' has played a key part in this. In fact, the legalisation of interracial marriage in the US is often presented as one of the most powerful illustrations of the ability of laws to change everyday attitudes. Shortly before her death, Mildred Loving – who, alongside her husband Richard, was responsible for the famous Loving v. Virginia supreme court case – reflected on the importance of this change: 'I am proud that Richard's and my name is on a court case that can help reinforce the love, the commitment, the fairness, and the family that so many people, black or white, young or old, gay or straight seek in life.'

This is a story of social change deeply rooted in the liberal tradition, where legal change leads to social change, until equality is both a 'social' and a 'moral' fact. The Georgia supreme court justices of 1968, the story goes, were caught up in the dominant white American culture of their time, which they couldn't see beyond. But laws have the power to transform the world and, with it, people's perspectives. As the state guarantees the ability to exercise new rights, these practices come to look normal and are taken for granted. The pattern of other lives, once strange and disconcerting, becomes more like our own.

That, at least, is the story we often tell. Yet today, this ideal of equality rings increasingly false. This is a double disenchantment. For members of excluded groups – for women whose ideas are undermined at work, for black youngsters who grow up navigating harassment from the police, or from LGBT couples who face simmering hostility in public – the idea of legal equality can feel pretty thin. The law proclaims them equal, but everyday experience says otherwise. Meanwhile, those who are *not* the targets of equality legislation have often come to feel a sort of deep disorientation and even a sense of disenfranchisement, living in the shadow of such laws. This, too, leads to a sort of thinness: when equality is imposed from on high, rather than something evident in the background of your life, it can feel artificial.

The gap between legal equality and everyday feelings, judgements and values can be detected even among those who profess egalitarian principles. The dating website OkCupid periodically publishes statistical glimpses into the behaviour of its users. This data provides a rare insight into both the stated preferences and actual behaviour of huge numbers of people. Revealingly, in a five-year analysis of attitudes and behaviours around interracial dating, OkCupid found that while people had become much more vocally supportive of interracial dating between 2009 and 2014, these overt attitudes did little to predict actual behaviour. Regardless of their own racial backgrounds, the average lonely heart on OkCupid seemed to apply a penalty to black singles, while those of almost all backgrounds showed a marked preference for white men or women. By and large minorities were much more supportive of the idea of interracial dating than white users. However, each minority group also demonstrated a distinct pattern of preference, favouring some groups over others. Based on these preferences, users avoided messaging others from different racial backgrounds. They also tended to rank them as less attractive. All of this while continuing to claim that they had no objections to being in a mixed-race relationship.[6] This same finding has been confirmed by several other studies of online dating over the past decade.[7] Principle and practice, then, are clearly two very different things.

It is not only romantic preference that works this way. Scholars of exclusion – be this racism, sexism or homophobia – tend to emphasise three forms of discrimination. There is overt discrimination, where people discriminate against a particular group, explicitly and consciously. Then there is cultural discrimination, where discrimination is woven into the workings of language, media and practice – into the story of Tarzan or theories of eugenics. Here, people who draw on these elements of culture may act in discriminatory ways without necessarily being conscious of doing so. And then there is structural discrimination, where the rules of institutions or the arrangement of the physical world generate unequal outcomes. For instance, the rules guiding police searches may end up with the police disproportionately targeting non-white people. These forms of discrimination often reinforce one another. Cultural tropes about foreigners as docile, conniving or unsophisticated can prompt employers to pass over qualified minority candidates, while the lack of minorities in positions of leadership can help reinforce these cultural tropes.

In the language of liberal citizenship each individual is the bearer of their own humanity, and so of their own conduct and choices. This language has made it possible to build legal protections against overt discrimination, but has also made it harder to name and unpick cultural and structural discrimination. Often, these latter forms of discrimination can't be pinned on any one actor, while nonetheless potentially influencing anyone. The result is what sociologist Eduardo Bonilla-Silva dubs 'racism without racists'. Bonilla-Silva has spent his career documenting forms of instinctive discrimination – attitudes towards intelligence, attractiveness, trustworthiness, relatability – that emerge in the behaviours of people who often express explicit attitudes to the contrary.[8] Similar patterns have been found regarding gender – where, for instance, the Spanish psychologist Juan Díaz-Morales notes a trend among Spanish youth who have learnt to profess 'abstract egalitarianism', while continuing to behave in sexist ways.[9] Today, the foundations of exclusion lie not in what can be easily challenged in public, but in the understandings of the world people acquire through empathic experience. Abstract commitments to equality, even when approached with genuine conviction, are often not enough to recognise or prevent discrimination.

Beyond the quiet, private endurance of discrimination, another hazard remains. Even if we were able, one day, to overcome prejudice, even if we could reach a state of meaningful equality, we may end up with little common purpose. The struggle for equality has, in effect, been founded on an insistence that our humanity cannot be hostage to the fickle recognition of others. Humanity – and the rights, responsibilities and freedoms that flow from it – has been imagined and asserted as innate. Yet, because of this insistence, this liberal vision of equality also struggles to then say what we may owe to others. Collective action becomes reliant on attempts to calculate relative privilege and disadvantage. In situations where disadvantage and privilege resist easy calculation, or where there is need for more than a simple balancing of the books, it can be difficult to justify action.

Take questions of reparations, or climate change. In places such as the US, UK or France, scholars and activists are revealing how present disadvantages facing historically excluded populations, at home or in former colonies, are the product of long historical legacies. These past conditions continue to shape unequal life chances today. As just one example, the economist Utsa Patnaik recently calculated that British colonialism led to the expropriation of an estimated US$45 trillion from India between 1765 and 1938. Goods and money that would have otherwise stayed in the Indian economy were siphoned off, into British hands, through aggressive taxation and manipulative trade policies.[10] Despite claims that British rule benefited India, for much of this same period the British oversaw a stagnation in Indian per-capita incomes. Even during periods of famine, which claimed millions of lives, the British maintained an economy oriented towards export and profit.[11] In the face of these sorts of historical reckonings, the idea of reparations – redistributive policies to counterbalance these past harms – is gaining ground within activist circles, but remains highly controversial among the public at large.[12] Part of the challenge comes from some members of the public resisting the idea that they have been comparatively privileged. But another part comes from a challenge of historical accounting. Even if present privileges could somehow be added up, they are unlikely to come close to the cost of historical wrongs or turn out precisely equal to present disadvantage. Anyway, the harms of colonialism extended well beyond the economic realm. As we have seen, colonial orders often laid the foundation of modern-day images of inferiority. It is tricky to imagine how such images might be dismantled through economic means alone.

A similar challenge surrounds climate change, where action is needed now so as to mitigate consequences for future generations. As with reparations, those in the present are asked to bear costs that they did not fully incur, and to invest in change for the sake of distant others. More broadly, to address these challenges people may have to give something of themselves that does not boil down to privilege alone – their time and energy, their attention and commitment. These are challenges that require people to embrace living in a world not simply of their own choosing, but shaped in relation to others. They require public action not simply on the basis of calculation, but animated by collective values. This sense of collective commitment is something the liberal logic of equality cannot achieve alone.

For nearly the first 200 years of America's history, interracial marriage was illegal. In many states, laws prohibiting interracial marriage predate the founding of the United States itself. Often these rules came into being as a part of the broader laws permitting human slavery. The connection was no coincidence: to think of someone as a partner in a relationship was anathema to thinking of them as mere property. Part of the denial of black equality involved denying that black Americans were capable of taking part in loving relationships.

Thomas Jefferson, who came to advocate for the abolition of slavery, while continuing to believe that blacks were inferior, once wrote: 'Among the blacks there is misery enough, God knows, but no poetry. Love is the peculiar oestrum of the poet. Their love is ardent, but it kindles the senses only, not the imagination.'[13] Jefferson paints black people as unable to master their passions and transform sensual feelings into a deeper love. By extension, he suggests they are incapable of having deep relationships, producing art, taking part in politics or living meaningful lives. For Jefferson, the ability to love was a fundamental qualifier for true humanity – one which he saw black people as lacking.

The forces which draw us towards others and forge our most deeply felt connections are funny things. We say that 'love is blind' or that we were 'struck by compassion', because such statements reflect the truth of our hearts. Many of our most compelling connections feel unpredictable, indescribable or deeply personal in how they move us. And yet, on a collective level, love, compassion, care, friendship and the other bonds we forge are highly patterned – as the OkCupid data and other studies of interracial marriage make clear. These patterns are deeply implicated in the possibilities for justice in society.

We are public beings and love is a public matter. When we see someone for the first time, we try to form a picture of what they might be like. We guess at what they are thinking, at how we might interact – often in quick, unconscious ways. These mental snapshots draw on a collective body of images and associations. Whether we find someone attractive or companionable, intelligent or bull-headed, this is never *only* a personal judgement. It is also one coloured by shared culture. A striking illustration of this comes from the journalist Esther Honig. In 2014, Honig sent the same photo of herself to graphic designers from twenty-five different countries, simply asking them to edit the photo to 'make me look beautiful'. The wide variation in images, which range from sallow and pale, to plump and swarthy, sometimes with accessories such as a pearl necklace or a hijab added in, serve as a powerful illustration of how culture shapes our preferences.[14] Culture provides us with a familiar set of scripts for thinking about all those we don't yet know. It traces the contours of all the relationships we have not yet formed.

Throughout history, philosophers and political thinkers have explored the link between the forms of interpersonal love that might develop between people, and the sorts of bonds needed to hold a society together. Many arrived at a similar conclusion: granting citizens equal *status* is not enough. For a society to flourish, citizens must cultivate ways of caring for one another. Aristotle dedicates a significant proportion of his *Nicomachean Ethics* to the ancient Greek concept of *philia*, translated both as love and friendship. Aristotle identifies friendship as a more powerful bond than justice. To Aristotle, acting justly was about refraining from harming others, whereas *philia* involved actively valuing others for their capacity to act as moral beings.[15] In more modern language, we might say that *philia* – friendship and love – allows us to recognise each other's humanity.

Without this, justice is possible, but it can become a begrudging, disconnected justice, where citizens act fairly towards one another merely because they acknowledge they ought to. If this standard of behaviour is all that ties citizens together, they are unlikely to engage in shared projects or to truly feel attached to one another. Today, we are realising that without deeper bonds between citizens, weariness, resentment and disconnection can set in to such a degree that they can come to threaten principles of justice themselves. For Aristotle, part of the answer to this problem comes from valuing love as a vital political force.

Latter-day thinkers have also explored the political importance of love and friendship. One key idea, developed by thinkers such as the American psychologist George Herbert Mead, the Canadian philosopher Charles Taylor, and the German philosophers Georg Hegel and Axel Honneth is that of 'recognition'.[16] In different ways, they have argued that recognition forms one of our most important needs. To be recognised is to see an image of ourselves, as someone valued, reflected in how others act towards us. This doesn't mean we expect others to see us exactly as we see ourselves, but rather that we have a deep desire to be considered worthy of understanding, love and belonging. When attempting to understand ourselves – who we are, what about our lives is worthwhile – we often look for answers in the eyes of others. And so, to be recognised by others is both to have our humanity affirmed, and to be offered a place within society.

Thinkers on recognition show it takes numerous forms. Recognition can emerge between people, through the ways in which they act and react towards one another. Recognition can also come from the common norms, values and symbols that circulate within a given society. There are certain standards of what 'good' or 'acceptable' people look like and do. Those who do not meet these standards may come to develop a deep sense of exclusion and hurt. Yet the inability to meet collective standards of goodness often has less to do with personal fault than it does with how these standards are coded and with how accessible they are. And, as we have seen, even attempts to define standards of human value in broad, inclusive terms almost inevitably produces an outside – something that falls beyond them.

These two forms of recognition have a complex relationship. It's impossible to fully prise apart the public language that defines specific images of human value, and the ways in which people relate to one another face to face. We make sense of one another through shared language. At the same time, our close relationships have the capacity to exceed the confines of this language – to attune us to one another in ways that language only partly captures. As they do so, these relationships can become what enables us to take part in wider society. When we fight for public recognition, our close relationships can remind us that we deserve love and care – even when this is denied by society at large.

The philosopher Jean-Luc Nancy writes that love entails abandoning oneself to another, in order to become more fully human. He quotes Hegel to claim that such love entails 'having in another the moment of one's subsistence'.[17] For Nancy, love 'shatters' the illusion that we are complete or self-sufficient apart from one another. We are always formed by and dependent on those around us – so that 'being cannot be anything but being-with-one-another'.[18] Nancy writes of a range of loves: of interpersonal love and spiritual love, of the love found in art and of love in community and in politics. These experiences, he argues, are united by a practice of allowing ourselves to become something more than what we currently are, by giving something of ourselves away, while holding ourselves open to someone or something else. They involve entrusting others with our sense of who we are as they entrust us with the same. This dependency is not a trap, but a collaboration, where people sculpt each other into something new, together. Nancy's work resonates with feminist thinking on the ethics of care, which highlights the qualities that make interdependency work. For such thinkers, care is a practice of committed, skilful attention, responsiveness and responsibility, directed towards others.[19] To care for others means always trying to understand the particularities of other lives and experiences, and acting with regard to these.

Drawing these ideas together, we can arrive at an understanding of something like *political love*. This isn't love as we might understand it in a romantic or familial sense – although, like these forms of love, it involves feeling and commitment. Political love can be understood as a commitment to pursuing political change based on a recognition of a fundamental human interdependency, and to acting in ways that extend this interdependency. This involves vulnerability and trust. Political love marks those moments where we not only entrust our fate – the design of our cities, or our sense of national identity – into the hands of others, but when we do so never fully knowing where this will lead. Rather than approaching politics by asking, 'What is right for me?', political love commits to politics as a shared project, asking, 'What might we accomplish, together?' Such collective projects may not always fit personal priorities. Perhaps taxes are too high, or the local school system is becoming overburdened. Yet, in acts of political love, our commitment to the collective draws us out beyond ourselves, making such projects personally compelling. Politics may be contested, but not as a battle, or an exercise in accounting between millions of individuals – rather as a constant give and take, asking, 'What is best for us, together?' Likewise, political love trusts that some form of understanding and recognition will emerge through the process of collaboration, and that this recognition need not be perfect or complete for it to count. We don't have to be the same as others to work and grow alongside them.

Whether we can recognise certain people as deserving of care, or as capable of caring, is a political matter. Abstract, principled commitments – to equality, to justice, to fairness – may carry us a certain distance, but they are also often incapable of fully guiding the ways in which we act towards one another. We may believe prisoners deserve second chances, only to balk at the prospect of working with an ex-con; we may celebrate diverse communities, while continuing to mostly spend time and form bonds with people from similar backgrounds to our own. In these moments, our openly held convictions run up against pregiven cultural scripts that tug us in different directions. As they add up, these moments have very real impact in determining who is able to access opportunities, who gets to feel safe and secure, or who is able to lead a worthwhile life.

Getting beyond cultural scripts is no easy matter. We may feel confident that the brooding, hooded young man is threatening, that migrants have no desire to take part in public life or that people living beyond the major cities have few opinions worth taking seriously. But these judgements almost always emerge *before* we engage with such people. How might things develop differently if we approached the young man *as if* he were kind-hearted, or the migrant community *as if* we had much to learn from one another? What sort of story might these acts of loving trust, rather than suspicious judgement, set in motion instead?

When it comes to love, however, the limits of our principles of equality, and indeed of the legal system, become starkly apparent. There is something about equality that sits uneasily with love and care. We do not form our friendships or meet our partners by giving everyone around us an 'equal' chance; we exercise choice and preference. More than this, love and care require difference. They involve a process of connecting across different perspectives. This difference draws us out of ourselves, helping us become more than what we are. The bonds we build with others do not treat these others as generic equals. This is true whether in our love for the work of an actor or an author whom we have never met, or in our love for our friends and family.

The law becomes powerless when it comes to love. If our ability to love is shaped publicly, then surely public bodies ought to be able to shape this, to ensure a more caring society for all? This simply isn't possible. Practically, we are far from understanding how friendship or intimacy develop in a way that would allow lawmakers to intervene and guide their growth. Morally, to have the law regulate human relations at this intimate level would be incredibly oppressive. It's hard to imagine anyone, anywhere on the political spectrum, who would consent to such an intervention in their personal lives.

How, then, can we kindle political love, without turning it into a dark reflection of itself?

❋

It can be hard for some people to imagine Kilburn as a place full of love. During the time of the Irish Troubles, Kilburn's large Irish community became entangled in the struggle. Stoked by fear of Irish republican violence, some Londoners came to see Kilburn as a place where you were likely to be jumped, beaten or even bombed. Meanwhile, for the Irish residents of Kilburn themselves, life in the neighbourhood was coloured by the anti-Irish sentiment that seemed to emanate from everyone from the police to drunken visitors to the neighbourhood, who would show up, looking for a fight. By the time the Troubles ended, the neighbourhood was struggling from years of neglect.

I arrived in Kilburn many years later, at a time when the Irish population had dwindled and Kilburn had grown increasingly diverse. But the stories I was told of the area echoed the upheaval of the past. I heard stories of the relentless back-and-forth shootings and stabbings between youth from rival estates, of bricks being thrown out of windows at passers-by, and of grandparents mugged on their own doorstep. These incidents echoed an even older past, where the first Caribbean migrants to arrive in the area in the 50s and 60s had their windows smashed in or were chased down the street by children hurling stones.

On the Caldwell estate, where I lived, the streets were marked by the bloody history of a 'gang'[20] rivalry that continued into the present day. Graffiti and murals commemorating those killed, on purpose and by accident, marked street corners. The splintered remains of kicked-in doors, discarded syringes and broken bottles, and the sudden scream of police sirens in the night, spoke of continuing tensions, and their costs.

But this was a conflict without clear lines. At a local youth club where I volunteered, young men were often introduced to visions of gang conflict not by their peers but by the police – who treated them like recruits in waiting, subjecting them to constant scrutiny and frequent rough, demeaning searches. Or else it came from teachers, quick to dismiss them as thugs when they spoke out in class. Treated like criminals anyway, some began to experiment with what life on the streets had to offer. They began drug dealing, hustling stolen goods or cultivating reputations as local toughs. Meanwhile, others engaged in experimentation of a different sort. Frustrated with the high costs and claustrophobic horizons of street life, they sought new ways of living. Drawing on the vocabulary of the street, they branched into fashion, music or fitness, hoping to forge new identities away from the violence. Others still made their peace with poorly paid shift work in retail, construction or hospitality, but kept their old friends around to provide the sense of esteem these jobs denied. These young men turned to the street as a resource for moving beyond violence and drug dealing, blurring the lines between involved and uninvolved, between street and straight.

To the press, the local council or indeed many residents, however, this complexity vanished. For many, there was little to be gained from talking to the young men and women out on the street. Teachers, charities and residents wanted to help them, but their visions of what would help were top down rather than collaborative. One local parent, whose wife was mugged, became a determined advocate for school reform, convinced that better education would save future generations from a lifetime of crime. Others, spooked by the sights and sounds of late-night confrontations and sullen youth lurking in public spaces, embraced law and order, campaigning for better police protection. Local charities staged employment workshops and funded arts spaces, hoping to divert restless energies. Everyone had their own solution; few of these solutions started from the experiences and lives of young men and women themselves. Most solutions involved doing something *to* or *for* these youth, rather than *with* them. They were a problem to be solved.

If you looked closely, however, there were exceptions – people who approached things differently. They were hard to spot precisely because, unlike more vocal community groups, government officials or media commentators, they shied away from claiming they were offering 'solutions'. And yet, these were the figures whose presence made a real difference. Here, away from the gaze of council officials or reporters out for a headline, in small run-down spaces or tucked away in living rooms, you could see something like love.

For many years Arlene had run a café on the estate, hidden in the basement of a community centre. Beloved for her Caribbean cooking, the café attracted a range of locals, from older men arranged around games of dominoes, to families popping in after church wearing their Sunday best. Sometimes, among groups of school friends or young mothers meeting up for a chat, the younger clientele also included those known locally as drug dealers or toughs. The line was never a clear one. A young man with street ties might have used the café as a space away from the street, to meet up with other friends, while others took advantage of the café's seeming normality to arrange drug deals or deflect scrutiny.

Over time, the police began showing up with increasing frequency, typically not in response to any call-out or complaint, but simply as part of patrolling, hoping that they would catch someone with something illegal in their pocket. Increasingly frustrated with these visits, the manager of the community centre instituted a strict sign-in policy, leading to a sharp drop in patronage across all ages. The young bristled at the surveillance of the police and the sign-in policy, but their absence, and the control and exclusion signalled by the sign-in policy, clearly mattered to others as well. Arlene, for her part, was incensed.

She was far from oblivious as to who some of her regulars were and what they got up to. And she knew full well where their activities could lead, and just how much they might come to cost. For years in her tower block, she had grown used to the sounds of aggressive confrontations, police sirens and doors being kicked in. She knew the stories from families and friends of children, now in jail or dead. Once, she watched a young man being chased by the police sprint along the outdoor corridor by her flat, only to jump the railing at the end and fall to his death. For years afterwards, she was haunted by the image of a falling body outside her kitchen window, or of the same body lying broken in the grass of the park below.

Even so, Arlene remained insistent that her café remained a space open to everyone. However much she disapproved of what some people got up to, however much the actions of others had cost her, no good would come of driving them away. To do so would deny that these young men and women were someone's son, someone's friend, someone's partner. It would relegate them even further to the streets, rather than welcome them into a space where they could embrace their other selves. The café was a place for local gossip or for joking with elders. People asked around for help with childcare, planned parties or picked up information about jobs. Even today, when the café is no more, many residents of the Caldwell remember it fondly. In these reminiscences, the café comes to life as a space where lives were lived in common. However fragile these shared bonds of care were, Arlene refused to limit the space available to them.

Mia, too, was no good at keeping her distance. A former documentary journalist for the BBC with mixed Polynesian-German roots, she had more recently been working freelance, taking video jobs alongside running training workshops and other odds and ends of work. At the heart of the Caldwell, funded as part of the area's ongoing regeneration, a creative hub had been set up as a space for artists, freelancers and entrepreneurs to work, host events and (at least in principle) give something back to the local community. First with a community radio station in which she was involved, and later in her own 'studio' in a corner of the hub, Mia was a regular presence. And it was through her that a group of friends from the Caldwell streets also came to find a home.

Things kicked off when Jack, who ran the community radio station, stopped a gathering of friends on the street with a mic in his hand, hoping to get interviews for a radio show on life on the estate. The group he ran into were more than happy to talk, but for over an hour they pilloried the creative hub, asking where this seemingly alien presence had come from and why it seemed like so few locals were benefiting from it. Quite a few of the hub's tenants got defensive, but Jack and Mia saw an opportunity to do something different. They invited the group to host their own radio show. Led by brothers Damon and Troy, the show began with a rush of enthusiasm, but soon lost momentum. It was enough, however, to get Damon, Troy and some of their friends to start hanging around the hub more frequently.

This group of friends all had their own histories. Several had spent time in jail. A few had been implicated in violent attacks. Most of them looked tough and intimidating to many of the creatives and freelancers in the hub, who were not always happy with their newly established presence. Mia was different: she could often be found trading jokes with the group, or chatting with Damon and Troy until the small hours of the morning. Eternally cheerful, and frequently found running late with armfuls of video equipment and an overflowing handbag, Mia sometimes cut a strange figure among the younger, predominantly black and male crowd she had fallen in with. And yet it was also readily apparent that many of them trusted and respected her. A non-drinker herself, she could nonetheless be found keeping the peace at local parties, just as she might turn up at family dinners or for a chat in the park. Over time, Mia became a go-to source for advice on how to earn a living, an outlet for gossip about the street community or a trusted confidant for heart-to-hearts about relationships, about living with violence, about dilemmas, doubts and dreams.

Within these friendships, and within time spent around the hub, other changes took root. Damon trained as an apprentice tradesman, eventually working his way up to be second in charge at a small company. Troy, who had once enjoyed some success as a rapper on the local scene, not only returned to the studio but started thinking about how he might use music as a tool for education – eventually collaborating with a local theatre, running workshops for younger students. Others started designing and selling clothing, got back with partners or simply worked to give up dealing drugs. Not everything changed, and when things did, these changes didn't always stick. And yet it was clear that between these friends and around the hub, a new sort of space was emerging – one where the chances, the sense of what was possible, shifted.

These changes were never the result of a direct push, from Mia or from anyone else. And yet, they all seemed to implicate her. Work was a question that Damon and Mia turned over repeatedly in their late-night chats. Was there such a thing as a respectable job if you were from the hood, and people would look down on you just for how you looked or spoke? What did it mean to try to leave the streets behind when family and friends had been hurt and killed? These questions never resolved perfectly, but they resolved well enough for Damon to commit to a new job as a tradesman. As he progressed, there were other moments of doubt, but each time, they were talked through together. When Troy decided he wanted to get back into music, Mia helped him to secure an empty space in the hub and to refit it as a recording studio. With others she swapped business tips, passed on leads for jobs, helped mediate arguments with partners or simply chatted.

The transformations that developed from these exchanges were rarely directly intended. Rather they emerged bit by bit, collaboratively and indirectly. Change flowed from conversations about the meaning of work and dignity, or about relationship troubles, the outfitting of a recording studio or feedback on the design of a jacket. In this process, Mia too changed. Today, having learnt that she has a knack for helping to open doors, she has begun to run film-making workshops – not for would-be journalists, but as a tool of empowerment, helping others to find a voice. Just as others put their trust in her, to discover something new about themselves, she put her trust in them.

Arlene and Mia's ability to produce small but meaningful changes on the Caldwell came from an attitude of political love. They didn't see the youth around them as a problem to be solved, but as people to share their life with. When charities and community groups started with the idea that local youth were a problem, they almost always ended up getting nowhere. Youth would instinctively stay away from projects and services that subtly suggested they needed fixing. Contrived arts workshops or preachy skills-training courses were met with laughter and scorn. On those occasions when they did engage, they often failed to connect with workshop leaders, job coaches or support workers, whom they saw as representing a professional, corporate world that had no space for them. This revealed a paradox:

those who did not set out to solve problems were often the best at solving problems.

This paradox can be understood in terms of the tension between political equality and political love. Equality seeks to accomplish goals, whether promoting freedom or combating injustice, by eliminating difference. If individuals or groups are understood as unequal, this is in terms of some crucial difference: income, respect, opportunities granted. This isn't to say that advocates of equality think that difference is a bad thing. Rather, the argument is that difference ought to be a product of freely made choices, rather than something that shapes or constrains our relations with others, especially when this leads to unequal outcomes. There are always forms of otherness that equality sets itself against. On the Caldwell, volunteers and activists saw youth unemployment, attitudes and behaviour as problems to overcome. In most of these cases, their aim was to make these youth more like themselves: employed, law-abiding and well behaved in public spaces.

We have run into the limits of what equality has to offer. Ideals of equality are wearing thin for those they are meant to empower, as well as those who struggle to believe in an equality that does not resonate with their everyday experience. Political love offers a radically different approach to questions of how we might live together. While visions of equality see otherness as a problem to be overcome – something to be flattened out – love sees otherness as an invitation to become something more than we already are. It's an act of faith in others, posing the question 'What might we be together?' In our communities, in politics, we can act with love, approaching others with the belief that we can do more and be happier, together, than we are apart.

The potential in others may not always be apparent. At first glance they may appear unknowable, disorienting, even threatening. Our joint histories may speak mostly of division and conflict. Political love requires suspending these judgements and anxieties. It requires trust that this potential will emerge if we act as though it were there all along. It requires a sense of commitment that can maintain connections, even as understanding and cooperation unfold messily. And it requires humility: this potential may not always come to fruition in a satisfying way. Just as our friends or family sometimes let us down, so too may those in our political community. The trick, as with strong friendships or families, is wanting to persevere, guided by a belief that even in difficult moments we are, or can be, better together. And, although this belief can be cultivated by each of us individually, as we will see in the final chapter, we don't have to try to build it alone. The ways in which we construct public spaces and resources play a powerful role in allowing such love to blossom, or in stunting its growth.

For James Baldwin, love was an act of faith in others. Faced with the stubborn racism of life in the United States, as well as the mounting bitterness of many peers in the civil rights movement, this was a faith that was hard to maintain. Sometimes Baldwin wavered. But, ultimately, he saw little hope for life beyond such faith – and beyond the love it could produce. Writing of the human capacity to overcome, and come together, he declared:

> It is a mighty heritage, it is the human heritage, and it is all there is to trust ... Generations do not cease to be born, and we are responsible to them because we are the only witnesses they have. The sea rises, the light fails, lovers cling to each other, and children cling to us. The moment we cease to hold each other, the moment we break faith with one another, the sea engulfs us and the light goes out.[21]

PART III

WEAVING

CHAPTER SEVEN

ENCHANTMENTS

By early March, when the UK government had begun to react in earnest, the outbreak already seemed out of control. Over the following year, and spilling into the next, the deadly virus would bring life to a standstill in communities across the UK, creating a protracted state of anxiety and uncertainty. It would end up causing billions of pounds of economic damage, leading to hundreds of thousands of deaths and leaving behind deep scars.

This story may sound familiar. The events in question, however, took place in 2001, when Britain experienced an outbreak of foot-and-mouth disease among livestock – a virus that previously hadn't been seen since 1967. The challenge in managing the outbreak came not only from the disease itself, but from the disagreements between different experts on how to diagnose and track the disease, and on how to react.[1] Vets diagnosed and traced the virus by the outbreak of symptoms, laboratory scientists through blood samples and antibody tests, and epidemiologists by producing mathematical models, which simulated contact between farms and animals to calculate the chances of spread. Each of these perspectives had their limits: the symptoms of foot-and-mouth disease rarely showed in some species; antibody tests relied on someone actually administering the test; and epidemiology relied on making correct assumptions about the behaviour of humans, livestock and viruses within mathematical models. Officials also had to evaluate between several different epidemiological models, each with their own assumptions and blind spots.[2] For instance, one model was produced by a team at Imperial College London, led by Dr Neil Ferguson – who later played a major role in advising the British government in the Covid-19 pandemic. The Imperial model treated all animals (goats, sheep, cows, etc.) interchangeably, assuming their likelihood of catching and transmitting the disease was the same. It did not incorporate live data on where infections were present, instead focusing on estimating rates and patterns of spread. Notably, however, all models insisted on their own objectivity, their own truthfulness – with the authors of one model declaring that their mathematical approach was 'just like real life'.[3]

Each of these perspectives also pointed towards different courses of action. Initially, the UK government based its policy on an epidemiological model developed by government scientists. In late March, however, as the outbreak continued to spread, the government switched to relying on the Imperial model, which offered much more pessimistic predictions. Politics played a major role in this choice. Imperial's predictions were reported in the press, upping the public pressure for a more decisive response, and they had a direct line to Prime Minister Tony Blair. Adopting the Imperial model led policymakers towards a programme of large-scale culling. Six million animals were slaughtered. The total economic cost to the country – from the dead livestock as well as the halting of travel, trade and ordinary life – was estimated at £8 billion. A couple of years later, a government-commissioned review found that most of the killing had been unnecessary.[4]

Nearly twenty years on, the questions of science and truth, knowledge and authority that surrounded the outbreak of foot-and-mouth disease have exploded in scope and significance. Globally, misinformation influences how citizens think about matters of public importance. International surveys find that almost everywhere, citizens tend to overestimate rates of murder and terrorism, the proportion of immigrants in the population, the proportion of immigrants among those in jail and the rates of teenage pregnancy. But they underestimate the prevalence of other risks, like obesity, cancer and heart disease. Although there is no credible evidence to suggest vaccines cause autism, in most countries less than half the population actually trusts that they are safe, in this regard.[5] Meanwhile, disinformation widens political divisions. In the US, supporters and leaders of the two major parties routinely disagree over questions of reality – from who won the 2020 election, to whether school shootings and other national tragedies even occurred. Among climate scientists, there is a strong consensus around the reality of man-made climate change: a 2016 study comparing various surveys of climate scientists estimated the level of agreement as between 90 and 100 per cent.[6] But across Europe, only around a third of citizens believe that 'the vast majority of scientists agree that climate change is happening and that human activity is causing it'.[7] In the UK, although public concern about climate change has grown rapidly, understanding of what needs to be done seems to have gone down. Polls from 2019 and 2021 show that, over this time, Brits have become worse at identifying effective personal actions they can take – increasingly overestimating the impact of less effective actions such as recycling, while underestimating the impact of more powerful choices such as having fewer children or going car-free.[8]

Meanwhile, in the midst of the Covid-19 pandemic, high levels of scepticism over face masks, vaccinations, lockdowns and other preventative measures hampered the ability of democratic nations to combat the virus, costing countless lives. Even after months of gradual improvement, figures from April and May 2021 found that only 44 per cent of US Republicans were willing to get a vaccine (or had already done so). Meanwhile, a study of seven EU countries, including Germany, France and Sweden, found the percentage of citizens saying they were willing to be vaccinated ranged between 44 per cent and 66 per cent.[9] With scientists warning that stopping the spread of Covid-19 will require a large majority of citizens to be vaccinated, this hesitancy, if it remains, is likely to play a role in prolonging the pandemic for years to come. As the case of foot-and-mouth disease shows, tensions and uncertainties around truth and knowledge are not confined to the general public but can be found among elected leaders and between rival groups of experts as well. Disorienting and dividing citizens and decision-makers at every level, it's clear that the current confusion around truth and reality poses a major challenge to democracy. It's much less clear what can be done about it.

Part of this intractability comes from how these issues are understood and discussed. The Covid-19 pandemic is instructive. People around the world have been asked to trust policymakers, even as leaders make costly errors or impose restrictions that come with heavy burdens. They have been asked to trust scientific knowledge, even as expert advice changes, and the media is flooded with a deluge of confusing, even contradictory, information. And they have been asked to trust one another, as the capacity to stay safe has relied upon the actions of others. Yet, at the same time, the predominant language in the public conversation has downplayed the importance of trust in favour of a language of objectivity. Truths are absolute and indisputable, and they ought to be innately recognisable and compelling to any reasonable citizen. Strikingly, even public voices who frame themselves as pushing back against received wisdom – activists questioning the necessity or fairness of lockdowns, or sceptics voicing doubt over vaccines – have often resorted to this same objective language, insisting that only one truth exists.

Here, again, an anthropological perspective comes in handy. It reminds us that even this notion of objectivity is distinctly cultural – that there are plenty of other ways of imagining what knowledge is or does, and that different concepts of knowledge create different possibilities, while closing down others.

This language of objectivity can work to deepen divides. If what's at stake is not simply a matter of trust – which, after all, can be built – but a failure to grasp 'the truth', working across divides begins to look daunting. First, it requires our opponents to recognise the error of their ways and correct themselves. Only then can people begin to cooperate. This impulse to build public life around singular truths can carry a dark logic seeking to eliminate, or exclude, any form of difference that complicates these public truths. Historically, these impulses helped lead to the creation of residential schools in Canada and the US, and the 'stolen generation' in Australia. In both cases, indigenous children were forcibly taken from their parents and communities to be re-educated. Frequently violent and abusive, this systematic abduction of children was driven by the belief that indigenous culture was incompatible with the rational world view required for democratic citizenship.[10]

Yet if the maintenance of singular truths remains impossible without attempting to eradicate difference then navigating plurality nonetheless remains challenging. When it comes to politics, an openness to all truths can prove divisive and paralysing, undermining the capacity to act. As the history of foot-and-mouth in the UK shows, even experts make competing claims to truth, and the ability to weigh up these claims can have life-or-death consequences.

How we understand the nature of public knowledge – and how we act on it – matters. It informs our capacity to live with others in general. If someone, vying for our attention and support, claims that migrants are taking jobs, that the police discriminate against minorities or that a rival political party is corrupt, how do we assess and respond to these claims? In fact, questions of how we understand different forms of expertise, and how we understand unfamiliar others, are connected at their roots by two different understandings of what knowledge is. This goes back to the liberal and civic republican traditions. In the liberal tradition, the essence of truth is always out there, universal and unchanging, whether people recognise it or not. In the civic republican tradition, truth – at least any truth that is connected to political questions of how best to live – is understood as a collective accomplishment. The product of shared traditions and efforts, it is open for negotiation. Each of these images of truth carries different ways of knowing. If truth is singular and fixed, it can be named and represented in clear terms – as rules, laws or mathematical formulae. If truth is plural and dynamic, with different forms of truth emerging in relation to experience, then truth is grounded not only in representations but also in empathic bodily knowledge, leaving truths ephemeral, difficult to communicate or debate. Today, our explicit understanding of what knowledge is draws heavily on the liberal notion of knowledge. Yet, covertly, both conceptions of knowledge circulate – and clash.

Over the past three chapters, we explored liberalism and civic republicanism as distinct political traditions. We saw how each offered important tools for living with difference, marked by certain potentials and constraints. Liberalism creates universal notions of commonality, which form the conceptual foundations of citizenship and projects pushing for equality, even among vast groups of anonymous strangers. Rather than holding excluded groups hostage to public attitudes – which often serve to reproduce such exclusion – liberalism provides a top-down guarantee of equality, in the form of state law, rules and regulations. Today, even as forms of inequality remain, this vision of essential human equality remains an important horizon for activists and reformers.

Meanwhile, civic republicanism provides a deeper sense of connection and solidarity that transforms even the allegedly 'private' thoughts that liberalism remains unable to touch, but which often become the foundations of publicly damaging forms of inequality. In doing so, it provides a way of building common cause that doesn't rely simply on eliminating differences, and which responds to the ways abstract notions of equality often feel thin and artificially imposed. One important lesson from this exploration is that the potentials and limits of liberalism and civic republicanism reflect each other in important ways – the shortcomings of each tradition are answered by the other. Historically, however, different visions of human nature and political life has frequently led scholars, activists and politicians alike to treat the two traditions as opposing alternatives.

In these final three chapters, I want to reverse this perspective and look at what we can learn from those who have attempted to hold these traditions in productive tension with one another. What, for instance, might it mean to treat the two conceptions of truth associated with liberalism and republicanism – truth as universal and fixed versus truth as particular and fluid – as complementary, rather than opposed?

※

Poking my head around the door, I found Imran with his back turned, intoning in a deep voice, his hands raised solemnly. I quickly realised he was leading *Jum'ah* prayers – the midday Friday prayer performed by most Muslims and considered the most important of the week. Across from Imran in the small front room, a group of a dozen men and women mirrored his motions. Imran stood not far from the entrance. Not wanting to distract the worshippers, I did my best to quietly slip my shoes off and move across the carpeted front room to an even tinier kitchen out the back. Having become familiar with the space over the past few months, I made myself a cup of tea and set up at a rickety table with my notebook, fleshing out my research notes until Imran finished and came over to say hi.

This unusual space was known somewhat enigmatically as The Door. As I would later learn, this name was borrowed from an old Persian poem attributed to Abū Sa'īd Abī al-Khayr, which reads:

Come again, please, come again
Whoever you are.
Religious, infidel, heretic or pagan.
Even if you promised a hundred times
Of hopelessness and frustration.
And a hundred times you broke your promise,
This door is not the door
Of hopelessness and frustration.
This door is open for everybody.
Come, come as you are.[11]

Run by a shifting band of young, largely Muslim volunteers, The Door was a unique hybrid. In many ways, it was a distinctly Muslim space, hosting prayers, lectures, courses and events focusing on facets of Islam. Within its Muslim guises, however, it was fiercely non-denominational, making a point of approaching Islam from different perspectives. Keeping with this diversity, many of The Door's frequent visitors would joke about their own uneven adherence to Islamic practices, or else speak more sombrely and honestly about their feelings of frustration, doubt or uncertainty. Some came for a sense of community, some to volunteer, others to learn about a faith they had not yet committed to. All were welcome.

But The Door stretched beyond a focus on Islam, offering a range of events open to all. Run by volunteers and a couple of low-paid part-timers, the centre came perilously close to closing more than once during my time in Kilburn. But it also experienced periods of sustained, vibrant energy. During these stretches, a typical month at The Door might include a handful of courses on calligraphy, permaculture or the Quran. There would be film nights, book clubs, yoga or martial arts, as well as meetings or events organised by other local groups who arranged to borrow the space. At another location, volunteers organised a weekly soup kitchen and food bank, sometimes serving upwards of a hundred people. And on one Friday or Saturday evening there was an open-mic night, where performers came from across London. With most events open to all, this eclectic mix of offerings drew an equally eclectic mix of attendees. Whether organising religious services, or events aimed at a wider community, those who ran the centre seemed to hold fiercely to an ethic of openness – a determination to be welcoming.

Imran and I had planned to meet for a chat about his involvement in The Door, where he had come to play a prominent role, especially on the religious side of things. Imran, however, had a more pressing concern: lunch. He opened the invitation up to those in his small congregation, some of whom texted other friends to join, and soon we headed out for fried chicken as a small group – a special Friday treat. A few people broke off, heading to other commitments, and Imran jokingly chided them that they were missing out on the *barakat* – the blessing – of a shared meal.

This was late in April 2015, barely a week before the 2015 British general election. In a bid for re-election, and hoping to quell dissent within his own Conservative Party, Prime Minister David Cameron had committed to holding a referendum on Britain's membership of the EU. This gambit led to a flood of public debate around questions of borders and migration, national identity and connection, which seeped into daily conversation. The debate, however, seemed to be dominated not by Cameron, but by Nigel Farage – a well-heeled commodities trader with a talent for mockery, who had come to head the UK Independence Party, or UKIP. Hailed as a man of the people who told candid truths, almost everyone had an opinion on Farage – good or bad – including Imran.

Once we settled into our meal, the conversation turned to the election. He didn't intend to vote, Imran declared – and then was abruptly cut off as others rushed in to agree. Everyone was fed up, it seemed. After some of the annoyance had been vented, Imran resumed his thought. He didn't intend to vote, he clarified, but if he did it would be for UKIP. He said that the idea of getting out of Europe was important – that the UK had lost control of its borders.

Surprised, I jokingly asked Imran if he was hoping to get his parents deported. He was the son of first-generation migrants from Egypt, and he had spoken about the sort of hostility they had faced as new arrivals, struggling to be accepted. This struggle had shaped Imran's own upbringing. His parents coped with feeling out of place by doubling down on a sense of traditional identity. This was a familiar story among many of the young Muslims who frequented The Door – where the traditionalism of their parents felt increasingly alienating against the backdrop of their own British upbringing. For Imran and others, childhood was characterised not only by religion and family, but experiences on London streets, council estates and schools that pulled them in different directions – by football, schoolyard taunts, shisha cafés, Dizzee Rascal, *Call of Duty*, school gossip, crushes, Disney, raves, playing in bands, experimenting with fashion … Imran himself sometimes hinted that he had had his share of criminal misadventures as a teenager, before simultaneously discovering martial arts and arriving at his own understanding of religion – one that felt much more resonant, more alive.

By 2015, Imran had come to live his life by global coordinates. His friends, from The Door and elsewhere, hailed from across the world. He had become an expert in Indonesian martial arts and took immense pride in his work as a PE teacher at a highly diverse school, where he relished helping his students – each with their own backgrounds and challenges – develop a sense of personal worth. Imran's comment about UKIP, then, was startling not only because it seemed to echo the discrimination his parents faced, but also because throughout his life, and especially in his work with The Door, he was steadfastly committed to openness and connection.

I quickly discovered I was nearly alone in my surprise. Within our group of eight or so, all of us from migrant backgrounds, there was only one other person who expressed disbelief, while everyone else rushed to back Imran up. This chorus of assent enabled Imran to elaborate. He had no patience for prejudice, or lazy stereotypes, he stressed, but he also strongly believed that immigration needed to be controlled. The fundamental issue, he argued, was the loss of a common moral purpose. When earlier generations migrated from the countries of the British Commonwealth, they were united by a shared identity and destiny. Being from the Commonwealth made immigrants believe they were part of a bigger project, that they had a place in British society – making it easier for settled Brits to accept them as well. In contrast, Imran continued, migrants arriving today – from all around the world – largely came for personal gain, resulting in different communities keeping to themselves and focusing on their own benefit, even at the expense of others. Putting on a mock-scandalised voice, Imran quipped, 'These Muslims who want nothing to do with us are taking over the high street!' The group dissolved into laughter and a flurry of other impersonations; everyone had heard similar lines from strangers passing by The Door. Voice tight with laughter himself, Imran doubled down, attempting to strike a half-sincere tone, 'But for real – *I* don't know what they're up to in that *other* masjid [mosque] up that way!'

Imran's involvement with The Door, characterised by an ethic of openness, and his apprehension around immigration, characterised by a suspicion of newcomers, may seem to present a paradox. It may be tempting to paint these sorts of views as irrational and incoherent. Imran's comments on immigration and on Farage foreshadow the 2016 Brexit vote, where a slender majority voted to leave the European Union in one of the biggest upheavals of modern British politics. During the referendum, those on the 'leave' side made controlling migration a central pillar of their campaign, often using rhetoric that suggested Brits were fed up with migration not only from the EU, but globally. Although only an estimated 30 per cent of Kilburn's residents voted to leave,[12] the huge level of diversity in the area means that plenty of these leave votes likely came from people with migrant backgrounds – making complex attitudes like Imran's far from uncommon.

To criticise these sorts of attitudes as contradictory or irrational risks missing the point. Charges of irrationality were a mainstay of the 'remain' campaign. Remain campaigners brandished economic projections, assiduously fact-checked opponents and challenged the emotionally charged rhetoric of the leave campaign as lacking substance. Remain lost. Here, again, an anthropological perspective is helpful, focusing not on how others may be wrong, but on how they may be right. How, then, might the forms of openness and closure Imran champions fit together?

※

For centuries, education and reason have been seen as cornerstones of a fair society and functioning democracy. The capacity to make informed, reasoned decisions has been understood as crucial for effective public deliberation and the exercise of private freedoms. In public politics, education has been treated as an especially important safeguard against the corruptions of power and against popular rule descending into tyranny. Thomas Jefferson made the point two years after the American

Declaration of Independence that, 'illuminat[ing] ... the minds of the people at large' provided the 'most effectual' means of keeping the powerful in check and keeping tyranny at bay.[13] In 1905, the influential British writer G. K. Chesterton wrote about the importance of popular education in maintaining a level playing field in public life, drily quipping that, 'Without education we are in a horrible and deadly danger of taking educated people seriously.'[14] And following the Second World War, the concept of 'critical thinking' gained new force as the ideal foundation for public deliberation, as thinkers rallied against the nationalist myths that gave such deadly force to fascism.[15]

Education and reasoning have been seen as fundamental to private freedom even by some of history's great champions of liberty. The English philosopher and politician John Stuart Mill wrote, in his famous treatise *On Liberty*, that education was one of 'the most sacred duties' of parents, and of the state.[16] The French diplomat and writer Alexis de Tocqueville likewise noted in his landmark meditation on *Democracy in America* that without education, citizens risked losing sight of the 'close connection which exists between the private fortune of each of them and the prosperity of all', and in the process risked acting in ways that ultimately undermined their capacity to 'remain their own masters'.[17] Today, driven by such ideals, whistle-blowers like Chelsea Manning and Edward Snowden have taken dramatic risks to disclose concealed information, placing the value of an informed public above their own life and liberty.

This vision of an educated, rational public trades on visions of knowledge associated with both the civic republican and liberal traditions, but firmly subordinates the first to the second. Good citizens are distinguished by their capacity to reason and deliberate, but the truth is understood as something that is objectively discoverable, not something they create. Or, put differently, knowledge and reason are seen as the *foundation* of politics, not a *product* of it.

This vision of objective knowledge is opposed to two other concepts: *subjectivity* and *error*. Citizens are expected to understand and deliberate over the world around them in impersonal terms – in terms that do not rely on context or personal experience to make sense. This means abstracting beyond local particulars to produce forms of information that are representative. A citizen wanting to sound the alarm about air pollution is likely to have more luck if, instead of complaining about their own difficulty breathing, they are able to produce figures measuring the level of pollutants in the air. Likewise, a biologist wanting to show that a new disease is killing trees will do so not by describing thousands of individual trees in minute, idiosyncratic detail, but by identifying something they have in common – perhaps a patch of rot – and then counting how many trees share this commonality. The claims citizens make are expected not simply to be abstract but, crucially, to be reproducible as well. Given a certain set of premises and, perhaps, access to the same base of evidence, other citizens ought to be able to reach identical conclusions about the world by following the same logical or investigative steps. Knowledge that is not sufficiently abstract is seen as subjective, and knowledge that is not reproducible is seen as erroneous.

How does this ideal play out? When commentators say that we are living in a 'post-truth' era, they draw an implicit contrast to a past era where objectivity reigned supreme. For many, the solution to our current disputes over public knowledge – over fake news and 'alternative facts' – is to reinvest in education, work harder to promote critical reasoning and, hopefully, reignite the torch of objectivity. Yet a closer look at the intertwined histories of democracy and science, as well as a look at how citizens make democratic decisions, points to a more complex picture.

The ideal of objectivity faces three challenges. The first has to do with complexity. Even in the earliest days of democracy, thinkers such as Jefferson expressed anxiety over levels of public understanding. Since then, the scope of human knowledge and the complexity of the everyday world has exploded. We live lives heavily dependent on technologies and systems – from smartphones to traffic controls, to industrial agriculture – any one of which could take a lifetime of learning to really understand. Already, during the Industrial Revolution, the dramatic expansion of the natural sciences struck a decisive blow to the idea that citizens – even the most exceptionally talented ones – could establish some sort of meaningful grasp over the breadth of human knowledge.[18] This idea crumbled over the course of the nineteenth century, so that, as the historian and philosopher of science Sheila Jasanoff writes:

> By the beginning of the twentieth century, belief in an open public sphere weakened in the face of rising social complexity and reliance on expertise. Some saw the delegation of political power to technocrats as essential and inevitable ... others as pernicious and excessive ... Calls arose on both sides of the Atlantic to limit expert influence in order to safeguard people's right to design and deliberate on their own futures. Skeptics countered by asking whether the idea of an informed public, the sine qua non of functioning democracies, any longer made sense.[19]

As the twentieth century continued, accelerating scientific development compounded this problem. When Hannah Arendt set out to rethink the civic republican tradition for the modern age in her 1958 book *The Human Condition*, her starting point was the launch of Sputnik and the breathtaking progress of modern science that led up to it. She fretted over 'the fact that the "truths" of the modern scientific world view, though they can be demonstrated in mathematical formulas and proved technologically, will no longer lend themselves to normal expression in speech and thought'. This had major implications for political life, she argued as 'we, who are earth-bound creatures and have begun to act as though we were dwellers of the universe, will forever be unable to understand, that is, to think and speak about the things which nevertheless we are able to do'.[20]

Arendt was not only concerned that science was growing increasingly incomprehensible to most citizens, and therefore harder to engage with politically. She was also critical of how the language of expertise closed down debate by asserting a single, fixed point of view. Complexity and singularity reinforce one another. To communicate increasingly specialised knowledge, experts must distil things down, often obscuring the complexities and uncertainties that may exist for them. When collaborating with political leaders or the public at large, experts may be drawn to present their understandings and methods as more fixed and certain than they really are – as in the case of the epidemiologists during the British foot-and-mouth disease outbreak, who insisted that their models were 'just like real life', even as they generated conflicting conclusions.

A second challenge has to do with how political judgements are made. In the ideal of a reasonable public, it is legitimate for citizens to hold different political values and preferences, but this variation is understood as rooted in a common capacity for reason. Yet political scientists are increasingly finding that even for those adept at reasoning, political judgements tend to be based on considerations of values, identity and connection, above and beyond more abstract, calculative reasoning.

In a series of experiments in America, the lawyer and psychologist Dan Kahan has explored the relationship between knowledge, identities and political beliefs. In one study, Kahan and his collaborators started off by giving volunteers a series of problems that measured participants' ability to reason mathematically. They then gave participants one of two versions of the same maths problem. In the first version, participants had to figure out whether a rash cream being tested was effective or not, based on the relative number of people who got better or worse when given the cream or given a placebo. In the second problem, participants had to figure out whether banning concealed handguns was linked to an increase or decrease in crime, based on crime figures from cities that had and hadn't implemented the ban. In both problems, they varied the right answer so that sometimes the cream or the ban was effective and sometimes it wasn't. The thinking required to get both problems right was identical – both required participants to calculate proportions and compare them. But mathematical ability only predicted success in the rash cream puzzle, whereas holding political beliefs aligned with the correct conclusion predicted success in the handgun puzzle. In other words, even good mathematicians approached puzzles with political implications as questions of conviction.[21]

The same goes for education. In another study, Kahan and his team found that scientific literacy did not predict attitudes towards climate change. In fact, those with stronger scientific literacy were slightly *more* likely to be climate sceptics. On either side of the debate, stronger scientific literacy was associated with stronger conviction. What did predict attitudes was, again, political belief. People appeared to start from their existing convictions, and then drew on these to marshal a range of evidence to argue for or against the reality of climate change.[22] In a third experiment, Kahan and his colleagues found that people watching the same video of a protest remembered the behaviour of the protestors differently – whether they acted threateningly – based on what they were told the protest was about, and how this cause fitted within their own political beliefs.[23]

Political beliefs not only frequently override abstract reasoning, but reflect a distinctive social logic of their own. The election of Donald Trump gave psychologists Michael Barber and Jeremy Pope a unique opportunity to explore political reasoning. A one-time Democrat, Trump has exhibited a willingness to cherry-pick his political ideas, based on what will win support. Barber and Pope took advantage of this to design a test, where they gave participants examples of both liberal and conservative policies championed at some point by Trump. They found that a significant proportion of Republicans judged these polices not based on their content, but on the fact that they came from Trump.[24] Barber and Pope's experiment fits with a much wider pattern of voters from across the political spectrum judging policies not based on content, but on political tribe and the personality of leaders.[25]

These forms of thinking, driven by value, connection and identity, not only seem to constrain more abstract reasoning, but also to reduce our motivation to engage in such reasoning. A team of social psychologists from Winnipeg in Canada and Illinois in the US found that a majority of people were willing to give up a chance to win money if it meant not having to hear opposing views on issues such as gay marriage, elections, marijuana, climate change, guns and abortion.[26]

These patterns should not come as a surprise. The world gains its reality through everyday experiences which entangle empathy and symbolic reasoning. Knowledge is not free-floating but is often a part of belonging. If faced with a political question, if asked to reflect on how our world is and what we hope it to become, we pursue these questions through worldly ways of thinking.

The first of these challenges is *practical*. It is a time-management problem: how, given the staggering complexity of the modern world, can citizens be equipped with the right knowledge and critical-reasoning skills to be able to make well-informed decisions? This challenge is daunting, but it may be surmountable. Western culture has built up a strong belief in the ability to overcome practical challenges with technical solutions – and educators and policymakers continue to search for ways to ensure education systems can engage with the complexity of the modern world. The second challenge is *institutional*. It emerges not simply from psychology but from the specific way in which psychology interacts with politics as an institution for organising human life. This challenge appears more stubborn. Addressing it requires reshaping the institution of democratic politics itself, in ways which may not always be desirable. One way in which governments have responded to complex challenges is by de-politicising them, shifting decision-making power away from the public towards powerful groups of experts – regulatory agencies and advisory committees, consultants and bureaucrats – who offer stronger claims towards objective knowledge. This response, however, not only constricts genuine democracy, but risks feeding into the same public attitudes it tries to offset, as members of the public become increasingly sceptical of expertise without transparency or accountability. There is a third challenge to the ideal of objectivity, however, which may be even more fundamental. This has to do with the *nature* of knowledge itself.

Within the ideal of objectivity, knowledge produced by scientists and other experts is understood as corresponding to the natural world. The problem with this idea is that our only way of experiencing or understanding the natural world involves *mediation*, and mediation is always political. Thinking back to Chapter One, we know that what our eyes see may not be the only way to see the world – that there may be hidden colours or patterns visible only in UV light. More than this, we know that these perspectives are often mutually exclusive: we can see the patterns that emerge under UV light, or the colours that emerge within daylight, but not both at once. The tools that enable us to see the world in a certain way – from the lenses and nerves in our eyes, to the names we give to distinct colours, to UV light bulbs or the equations that describe the wavelengths of light – can be understood as *mediators*.

Recognising that knowledge is mediated challenges the idea

that knowledge can simply 'fit' the natural world. Instead, it suggests that all knowledge – even scientific knowledge – entails plural, partial perspectives. In turn this draws knowledge and politics close, as without a single, all-encompassing standpoint from which to understand the world, we are forced to choose and commit to particular perspectives, and their implications. The ideal of objectivity has been a powerful cultural myth in Western history. The notion of plural, mediated knowledge can be hard to grasp, or accept. Yet there are many scientists who not only embrace this idea, but take it as the basis of scientific advancement.

Take the history of research into micro-organisms – bacteria, viruses and the like. Early systems for classifying species, such as those pioneered by sixteenth-century Swedish naturalist Carl Linnaeus, relied on characteristics like form or function to group beings into distinct species and sub-species. Biologists, however, found that many micro-organisms refuse to retain their traits – changing form, function and even genetic make-up either within their lifetime or across generations.[27] This made it tricky to understand them within the frame of modern science, but it also contributed to an evolution of these frames.

The development of modern methods of isolating and growing micro-organisms in the lab, led by figures such as Robert Koch and Louis Pasteur, stabilised the situation somewhat. Suddenly, we had gained a way of looking at micro-organisms that appeared more consistent, and which could be fitted into the standard approach to experimentation. Yet, to this day, micro-organisms remain slippery – especially when let out of the lab and back into natural environments. Modern technologies have helped reveal the full extent of this slipperiness, showing, for instance, that many micro-organisms possess a patchwork of genetic material, seemingly taken from other species – challenging our idea of what a species is. Others have built on this understanding to explore the critical role bacteria and gene-transfer may have played in the making of human-ity.[28] Despite these challenges to the prevailing way of thinking, scientists continue to make new discoveries operating on the assumption that micro-organisms (or any organisms, really) are separate, and distinctly categorisable.[29] At the same time, other important discoveries have been propelled by rejecting the idea that organisms, large or small, are distinct entities. Taken in relation to one another, both perspectives are understood not as fixed facts but 'as if' propositions. There is something important to be gained by approaching each perspective *as if* it were true, and recognising that acting in this way is more productive than resolving the truth one way or another. Science can advance in certain ways by treating species as distinct categories, and it can advance in other ways by suspending this idea and letting the boundaries blur.

Many scientists understand the scientific process in these pragmatic terms, holding to theories and models only insofar as these take them to useful or interesting places, and searching for alternative perspectives when they do not. Yet the myth of objectivity is powerful. Others go to great lengths to deny the ways in which knowledge is mediated – to insist on objectivity and attempt to escape the entanglement of science with perspective and politics.

Politics, however, has a way of catching up with you. The historians of science Lorraine Daston and Peter Galison trace one such attempt among makers of scientific atlases in Britain, France and Germany from the late 1600s into the early 1900s. They focus especially on medical atlases – compendiums of organs and joints, muscles and nerves, painstakingly drawn, etched or, later, photographed, to be used as references for aspiring doctors and a curious public. These images were often made from cadavers by artists supervised by medical experts.

In depicting the body, atlas makers faced a dilemma – not unlike the one facing biologists studying micro-organisms

– over how to represent the parts of the human body. Daston and Galison trace shifts between competing visions of objectivity and accuracy. Earlier atlases, from the eighteenth and early nineteenth century, they note, reflect competition between subtly different visions of representativeness, based on images being 'typical', 'characteristic', 'ideal' or 'average'. 'Typical' images, for instance, were taken as templates – original models from which all variations could hypothetically be derived. 'Ideal' images were seen as perfect examples, which may or may not have counterparts in nature, while 'characteristic' images were based on actual specimens considered to be exemplary. Anxious about how each of these frames relied on their own choices, atlas makers in the late nineteenth century embraced a vision of mechanical objectivity. Images were based on actual photographs or X-rays, and presented with virtually no interpretation to specify whether they were representative or abnormal. In some cases, atlases even superimposed multiple images on top of one another, to present readers with a sort of composite from which they could draw their own conclusions.

This attempt to avoid the responsibility of interpretation rarely panned out. When images of the human body were used as forensic evidence in court, irate doctors took to the stand to highlight how even photographs and X-rays could tell different stories depending on how they were produced – puncturing the atlas makers' claims to neutrality. Denying the politics of interpretation not only proved impossible, it was often unhelpful. Efforts to disguise the inevitable interpretation that went into selecting and composing images left viewers without any bearings for making sense of what they were seeing. Attempts to present pure objectivity did not so much serve to generate knowledge, as to close it down.

Another way of describing knowledge as mediated is to say that all knowledge is based on *relationships*. We see a particular shade of green because of the relationships between the lenses and receptors in our eyes, our optical nerves leading to the brain, the brain itself, and the cultural concepts which direct and habituate our perception. Change one of these components and you will end up with different knowledge. Likewise, a scientist can come to know something about bacteria by establishing a relationship between a sample in a Petri dish, her microscope and the scientific concepts she has to hand. Members of the public, meanwhile, may know things about bacteria by establishing a relationship with the scientist herself – through a TV interview, say – treating her as one more link in a network of mediators that make knowledge possible.

And, just like the partial perspectives they afford, it is always possible to establish different relationships and know the world otherwise. Our scientist can come to know one thing about bacteria by establishing a relationship between it and a sterile Petri dish, and an entirely different thing by tracing its relationships in the wild. We might choose to learn about bacteria from scientists, YouTubers or by conducting our own experiments. Relational knowledge is inescapably plural: even when faced with a common truth, each of us comes to know this truth in different ways. At the same time, this doesn't do away with our ability to assess knowledge. Rather, in these terms, the reliability of knowledge is based on the ability of relations to hold together. For instance, what is seen in the microscope is linked to what is reported by the press and shown on TV. As the philosopher of science Bruno Latour puts it: 'Facts remain robust only when they are supported by a common culture, by institutions that can be trusted, by a more or less decent public life, by more or less reliable media.'[30]

This changes how we might approach public knowledge. Just as with other people, we can form relationships with mediators, and the knowledge they facilitate, in a variety of ways. We can approach mediators with suspicion or trust, curiosity or indifference. We can approach knowledge as practical and useful, or value it for its own sake, no matter the use. How we under-stand knowledge and how we relate to mediators goes hand in hand. If, for instance, we value curiosity, we may be likely to privilege mediators that enable exploration. If we value trust, we may prefer to draw on mediators that appear authoritative. The ideal of objectivity puts particular emphasis on one type of relationship, where knowledge is something all citizens *possess*. Yet many other possibilities exist. If all knowledge is relational, then what sorts of relationships make for a healthy democracy?

❋

When Fareed first got involved with The Door, he was at his wits' end. Just like Imran, he had grown up experiencing a version of Islam from his parents that felt out of touch with his own life. Once away at university, he attempted to get involved with student faith groups, hoping to find a community of other young people who shared his anxieties and frustrations.

What he found instead was a turf war. Different campus Islamic societies, representing different denominations and schools of thought, sniped over whose interpretation was correct or who could attract the most members, while insist-ing on their own rigid interpretations of things. As he put it, 'Even there, it was like, "This is supposed to be a community," but it was more about telling you what being Muslim had to mean. They didn't understand that people could be in any way different.' Frustrated, for a long while Fareed shunned anything that looked like organised Islam while focusing on his budding career as a poet and multimedia artist. Years later, and only after a significant amount of coaxing from his wife, Fareed visited The Door for the first time, to take part in an open-mic night. Wondering what to perform, he struck upon the idea that the conflict he'd witnessed between campus Islamic societies felt like a gang war. He composed a rap, with each verse delivered from the perspective of a different school of Islam, mirroring the violent rivalries and outlandish boasts found among certain rappers. To his surprise, rather than scandalising the Muslims in the audience, his performance went down brilliantly.

This marked the start of Fareed's involvement in The Door. Still wary of organised religion, Fareed was drawn towards the community of artists and musicians that gravitated around the centre. Soon he decided to set up a philosophy discussion group. Discussing philosophy provided Fareed with a way of grappling with some of the unresolved questions he had around faith and belief, without either committing to or rejecting a religious framework. When Khadiija, who was managing The Door, decided to take a year off, Fareed was asked if he might take over in her stead. During the year he ran the centre, Fareed curated a lively programme of events, listening to attendees and helping them organise things in line with their interests. He also played a key role in involving non-Muslim community groups, inviting a range of local organisations to borrow or book the space. Fareed promoted these externally organised gatherings within The Door's own community, leading to a growing crossover in attendance. Helping organise different events also helped reconcile some of his own frustrations with religion. Organising prayers, or religious talks with others, helped open perspectives on faith and belonging that felt less stifling or divisive than what he had known.

Fareed's story reaffirms the notion that knowledge is mediated, and that mediators matter. Growing up, Fareed's understanding of Islam was first mediated by his traditionally minded parents, then by the confrontational, self-assured students he met at university. For Fareed, and for others with similar histories, these sorts of relations shaped an understanding of Islam as rigid, narrow and out of step with the rest of their lives and the diversity around them. Conversely, as a space and as a community, The Door also played a mediating role. By holding different experiences, events, groups and personal histories together in the same space, and as a loose collective, the centre promoted an understanding of Islam as something much more worldly, plural and open.

This mediating role was made especially clear by Khadiija, where she contrasted The Door to her experience of other Muslim institutions. Born to Jamaican Christian parents, Khadiija discovered Islam for herself and converted along with her best friend. She remarked that it was strange that she had grown up just across the road from a mosque, yet knew very little about Islam for most of her childhood. 'No one invited us [...] And that troubles me [...] that's why I think there's a need to have a place where you can just walk in off the street and be who you are.' The issue, she suggested, was that organisations with too much certainty as to what Islam entails will struggle to recognise or accommodate people who are searching and uncertain but still want to have some sort of relationship to Islam. Laughing about the stuffy-seeming mosque near her childhood home, she asks, 'Can you imagine what would happen if you had a blonde girl in leggings walk up?' Sitting on the carpet, with her legs folded, she lunged forward in imitation of a rugby tackle: 'You'd have bearded men diving on her before she ever made it to the door! "Nooo! Unclean! Haram!"'

In contrast to these other institutions, Khadiija believed that The Door worked as a space where Islam could be encountered from various perspectives. During her time managing The Door, Khadiija had become fond of repeating a saying, riffing on al-Khayr's poem – 'come as you are to Islam as it is' – which gradually became a sort of unofficial slogan for the space. Crucially, this slogan did not reject Islam as a fixed, knowable thing – it did not promote an 'anything goes' interpretation. Yet it did suggest that anyone could find a way of relating to Islam – and that The Door was a space that could mediate this link.[31] In turn, this allowed those involved with The Door to hold on to the idea that they were all on a similar journey, towards a shared destination, no matter their differences in the present.

One of the most famous anthropological accounts of witchcraft comes from the British anthropologist E. E. Evans-Pritchard in his 1937 volume about the Azande people.[32] Marked by a history as conquering warriors that distributed them across north-central Africa, today the Azande live primarily as small-scale farmers. Witchcraft, Evans-Pritchard reveals, is a central force in the Azande world. In the wake of illness, accident or misfortune, suspicions and accusations of witchcraft are commonplace. The Azande recognise other causes that play a role in these events – the impact of disease in causing illness, or the work of termites in causing a granary to collapse. Yet to them, such explanations, on their own, are insufficient. Allegations of witchcraft are often brought in as a further explanation, precisely because what needs accounting for is not physical cause and effect, but the ethical significance of such events. Thinking about witchcraft opens a line of ethical inquiry into seemingly settled matters – sure, the termites caused the granary to weaken and, so, collapse, but why did this happen at the exact moment when a particular individual was beneath it? Were there forms of ill intent or ill feeling that may have contributed towards this? As the anthropologist Webb Keane notes, these beliefs allow the Azande to explain – or attempt to explain – more, not less, of the world.[33] Questions of witchcraft often do not reach definitive answers, but asking such questions opens new domains of searching. This allows the Azande to approach various events that seem random or indifferent to human influence and probe them as diagnostics of good social relations. In turn, this active searching becomes part of what gives witchcraft its reality.

In these accusations, certainty and uncertainty reinforce one another. Certainty that witchcraft exists as a force in the world animates a process of ethical searching that shapes how people relate to one another. And this active, uncertain searching invests witchcraft with reality, making it something that can speak to a range of everyday situations and experiences. For Khadiija, Imran, Fareed and their friends, a similar play between fixed facts and open searching characterises their exploration of faith at The Door. In different ways, before coming to The Door, they had been confronted with an image of Islam as a fixed, absolute truth. But this rigidity left them little space to inhabit it on their own terms. At The Door, however, they did not dispense with this idea of fixed truth, but repositioned it in relation to forms of exploration.

Bruno Latour draws a distinction between 'matters of fact' and 'matters of concern'. Matters of fact pertain to what is taken as fixed and given about the world, and matters of concern pertain to what is open, uncertain and negotiable. Latour cut his teeth carrying out anthropological research, spending his time following scientists around as they did their work. Azande witchcraft, religious belief at The Door and the work of scientists are three very different things. But Latour's work highlights important commonalities. All three approach matters of fact and matters of concern in relation to one another. Scientists do not sit around in labs talking about what they already know. They experiment and explore to discover what they don't yet know. This active searching, however, necessarily relies on given knowledge – on the reliable working of instruments, on established concepts and methods, on data and analysis coming from other scientists. Science, for scientists, is made possible not by certainty or uncertainty, but by a dynamic movement between the two, where exploration is anchored by fixed truths and fixed truths are revised by exploration.

This dynamic back and forth between fixity and fluidity stands in marked contrast to how the public is exhorted to approach scientific knowledge – or, indeed, to the ways in which young Muslims at The Door experienced Islam in other contexts. In both cases, truth is presented as a stand-alone matter of fact. The result is a sense of alienation – a feeling that certain truths are, at best, irrelevant to the experiences and dilemmas of daily life and, at worst, an active barrier to understanding and acting on the world. These responses are not products of facts themselves; they are generated from how we relate to them. Both for the public response to scientific knowledge versus that of scientists themselves, and for the different responses to Islam within and beyond The Door, the facts in question remain the same. In other words, it's not fixed understandings of truth per se that drive alienation, but the ways fixity is or is not brought into relation with open-ended exploration.

Conversely, we can understand the link between matters of fact and matters of concern as a process of *enchantment*. Simply put, enchantment approaches knowledge as always containing a dimension of mystery. This sense of mystery emerges from the capacity of established knowledge to point towards domains of exploration and action. Politics, argues Hannah Arendt, relies on such a step into the unknown. Arendt associates politics with the possibility of what she calls 'natality' – of bringing something new into the world. The pursuit of change always involves risk and uncertainty. It is a way of acting that relies inescapably on other actors in the world, and which cannot be predicted in advance. She writes: 'It is in the nature of beginning that something new is started which cannot be expected from whatever may have happened before. This character of startling unexpectedness is inherent in all beginnings.'[34]

Although this may sound grandiose, the anthropologist Cheryl Mattingly reads Arendt's notion of natality as a part of ordinary life. Between 1997 and 2011, Mattingly spent her time following a group of nearly fifty African American families living in Los Angles, raising children with chronic illnesses or disabilities. She traces how families step into the unknown whenever they navigate everyday dilemmas: should a physically vulnerable, wheelchair-bound child be allowed to join a soccer team? How should parents divide their time between their children with medical needs and those without? How should you respond after your brother was killed in a gang feud? When answers are given by experts in advance, they almost always end up fitting badly. People don't need definitive answers, but forms of knowledge that contain space for exploration and experimentation – 'moral laboratories' that enable 'experiments in hope and possibility'.[35]

Enchantment sounds fanciful. But by opening spaces for exploration and action, it is decidedly practical. Indeed, the very fact that enchantment has come to sound fantastical is a product of the same cultural history that shaped the ideal of objectivity. The anthropologist Talal Asad traces how, in ancient Greece, the idea of myth 'never [meant] a symbolic story that has to be deciphered – or for that matter, a false one'.[36] Tellers of myth and their audiences were expected to possess a capacity for reason, but this ancient notion of reason did not distinguish between emotion, evidence and logic. Reason was reason, and knowledge was knowledge, insofar as they were effective in the world. The separation of myth, or other forms of story, from 'reality' came first from the Greek Sophists, but only really took hold as a notion in the modern era. The quest for a singular knowledge involved attempts to identify and separate different components of knowledge – emotion, opinion, observation – into different domains, to distil truth to its essence. Evidence became the stuff of science; reason that of politics and philosophy; emotion the stuff of psychology, and so on. Paradoxically, in trying to purify knowledge, modern Western culture ended up fragmenting it, delineating different forms of knowledge whose claims never quite added up.[37] It highlighted the very terms by which universal claims to truth might be challenged, anticipating the divides we face today.

Asad's account of ancient myth helps reveal the power of enchantment. What was striking about ancient myth was its capacity to mediate between different forms of knowing. It was something of a cultural Swiss army knife: myth could be used to impart settled knowledge but also to ask questions about the workings of the natural world, weigh up questions of politics and morality, or bring people together. By treating these different forms of knowledge as parts of the same whole, these different perspectives were able to inflect and make claims on one another. What modern expertise often lacks is this connectedness – this capacity to create different sorts of relations and sustain different ways of knowing. What is needed, in other words, is to build public knowledge by weaving more fixed facts together with possibilities for exploration and action.

Fortunately, there is already a rich counter-tradition in the history of democracy that approaches knowledge this way. In her monumental history of the United States titled *These Truths*, the historian Jill Lepore looks at the central claims of the Declaration of Independence. For Lepore, statements like, 'We hold these truths to be self-evident, that all men are created equal,' (or, in Thomas Jefferson's rough draft 'We hold these truths to be sacred & undeniable ...') were not meant to set out something taken for granted, but to mark an ideal horizon to work towards. Lepore presents an American approach to 'truth' as a process of ongoing inquiry and experimentation. She points to figures across American history who hold to uncritical and heavy-handed visions of universalism, more interested in imposing consensus by force than in genuinely redressing inequities and grappling with difference. Yet she also points to others who treat the 'truths' of equality, rights and freedom not as given facts, but as something to be discovered.

In a similar way, the literary and political theorist Amanda Anderson writes about a tradition of 'bleak liberalism'. In this tradition, liberal ideals are recognised as imperfect fits for a messier world. For the bleak liberals she describes, imposing these ideals heavy-handedly would be self-defeating. Nonetheless, these ideals, impossible as they may be, retain value as guiding principles within the world, while experience can always serve as the basis for updating them. Yet when we look at liberalism this way it takes on a distinctly civic republican hue. When we think of liberalism as invested not with blithe self-confidence, but with hope, curiosity and doubt, then what we end up with is not pure liberalism, but a productive tension between liberal and republican orientations to truth.

As with grand claims to truth and knowledge, so too with politics. If, as Arendt tells us, all politics requires a leap into the unknown, then enchantment is something that animates rather than diminishes politics. Critics of contemporary politics are fond of criticising the personal, emotive tone of political debate. But making politics personal and emotional can help open up forms of thinking, knowing, acting and exploring that are so often closed down. A striking example comes from a team of anthropologists based at the London School of Economics, investigating responses to the Covid-19 pandemic. Early in the UK vaccination drive, experts began to note that some minority communities were especially sceptical of vaccines. For many in such communities, the LSE team found, what made the difference was not more insistence of the facts about vaccine safety, but a different way of relating to vaccination. Vaccination centres were set up in temples and mosques, community workers hosted events to listen to and acknowledge fears, and community 'ambassadors' used social media to celebrate getting their jabs. In a post-truth era, against the assiduous fact-checking and insistence on reason championed by those holding to the ideal of objectivity, it is those who invoke the possibility of a more expansive political world who carry the day.

Although the view was somewhat uncommon, Imran was far from the only person with a migrant background in Kilburn drawn to Farage. On a sunny summer day, I found myself chatting to Ray – a child of Caribbean migrants now in his forties and a well-known figure on the Caldwell estate – as he insistently tried to explain why he felt so many people were drawn to the controversial politician. 'He seems like he is the type of guy you could sit down and have a pint at the pub with. You could just talk – you know what I'm saying?'

CHAPTER EIGHT

REWRITING HISTORY

On a frosty November night, I joined Simon and Evelyn to attend an 'Irish music night' at the Duchy – a pub near the Caldwell – alongside some of their friends. Both in their sixties, Simon and Evelyn had lived in the area for over three decades, occupying the same council flat, eventually coming to run the residents' association for their complex. They spoke of feeling a strong sense of community and connection from living in Kilburn – much of which they associated with the dwindling Irish community there.

Today, the most visible traces of Kilburn's Irish history are the names on the street signs – Kylemore Road, Glengall Road. But for many decades, Kilburn was known as a predominantly Irish neighbourhood, and even after the area grew more diverse following the Second World War, the Irish remained a significant part of Kilburn's mix. Older Irish residents tell me about how the neighbourhood was known by their parents or grandparents as the place Irish migrants headed for first, travelling to Kilburn straight from Paddington station. In this era, where the Irish were seen as essential labour for an industrialising nation, and in heavily racial terms – as innately 'degenerate', prone to crime and disorder – Kilburn was often the nearest place within reach of central London where Irish migrants were welcomed. Over time, people came to view Kilburn as a microcosm of Ireland transplanted to London. By the time the Troubles broke out, Kilburn was so closely associated with Irish life that it became the only site of a loyalist paramilitary bombing on English soil.

Simon moved from Ireland to Kilburn, but during his time in the area he had witnessed this sense of Irish identity diminish. Residents dispersed across London and community hubs closed. Evelyn described the music night as a self-conscious attempt to 'bring together' and 'revive' the local Irish community and suggested that I might be interested in coming along. At the start of the night, Simon explained the deep sense of belonging connected to his Irish identity. 'I'm not a spiritual person,' he remarked, 'but it's quite a spiritual feeling when I go back.'

As the performer, perched on a stool in the corner, launched somewhat unexpectedly into a rendition of 'Folsom Prison Blues', I scanned the crowd: most were older, and the majority clearly white. But there were a number of others as well – a few Afro-Caribbeans and several others who looked South-east Asian. Among the white majority, judging by the accents and the handful of people I knew, no more than half seemed to be Irish. Evelyn was American. The organiser, another Simon, was not Irish himself and was married to a Polish woman. She had brought along other Polish friends. Glancing around the room, I nudged Simon to get his attention over the music:

'What percentage of the people in here do you reckon are Irish?'

'Hm?' he shouted, taking a moment to process, amid the noise, 'Oh ninety-eight, ninety-nine per cent, for sure. This whole pub. Totally Irish.'

I looked at him, a bit baffled: 'I think there's a lot of people from elsewhere in the world.'

'Ah, they're all related.' Simon shrugged. 'Ninety-nine per cent Irish or related! It's all about the same.'

Later that night Simon and Evelyn talked me through the roots of this 'Irish' community. Evelyn explained that in October 1974, two pubs in Guildford, Surrey, were bombed by the

Provisional IRA. In December, six members of a local Kilburn family, the Maguires, were arrested – including their two teenage children, plus a family friend. They were collectively imprisoned for supplying the IRA with the materials to make the bombs. The youngest, a fourteen-year-old, served four years, while Mr and Mrs Maguire spent fourteen years in prison. In 1991, the convictions were overturned, after a constant trickle of pressure and accumulating proof that the evidence against them was forged or altered. While they were in jail, a group of activists, neighbours and friends came together to campaign against their imprisonment. Later, this same group campaigned against injustices carried out by the British army in Northern Ireland. In the process, the Kilburn Irish community grew, drawing in people from elsewhere around the world – such as Evelyn – brought together by a sense of common cause. To Simon, solidarity and familiarity worked to make these new members effectively Irish themselves.

The Maguires lived a sort of double life. They were locals – familiar faces who came back to drink at the Duchy after their release. But they also existed as a story of prejudice and injustice that mobilised people across the UK and Ireland who championed their cause and lobbied for an appeal. As their story travelled, it tangled with others. After the Second World War, when Caribbean and Asian migrants arrived in Kilburn in larger numbers, they found themselves facing a similar struggle to the Irish. Many landlords, employers and communities closed their doors to the new arrivals. Irish residents recognised this treatment, marked by British colonial rule and ongoing discrimination, and the shared story provided the basis for a sense of solidarity and for the cultivation of networks of support between older Irish residents and newer migrants.[1] During my time in Kilburn, I would sometimes hear non-white residents characterise the neighbourhood as a home for excluded peoples and talk, in part, about the struggles faced by the Irish as proof.

In 1983, the historian and political scientist Benedict Anderson released a landmark book, *Imagined Communities*. Born in Kunming, China, to parents from Ireland and the UK, Anderson's family moved to the US in 1941, and then later to Ireland, to escape the Japanese invasion of China during the Second World War. In Ireland, Anderson grew up amid simmering ethnic conflict. The local Catholic boys targeted him and his siblings, presuming they were English and Protestants. These early experiences helped shape a lifelong fascination with ethnicity, politics and nationalism.[2] In *Imagined Communities* Anderson started with the question: what was it about nations that commanded such fierce loyalty? As his title suggests, Anderson argued that nations were 'imagined communities'. His use of 'imagination', however, was not meant to convey thinness, but to point to the way powerful loyalties could form among groups of strangers who relied on symbolic connections to bind them together. Anderson explored how storytelling, from poetry to the daily news, worked to bind people together and to build commitments to nations. In doing so, he emphasised how such nation-building stories were often universal *and* particular. They were universal, because new technologies of communication allowed for stories to be told and transmitted in identical ways across large, anonymous groups. These technologies also helped create a sense of shared rhythm to daily life – newspapers, say, allowed the public to 'experience' national events simultaneously. Yet these stories were also particular in their capacity to evoke highly personal emotions in their audiences. For Anderson, welding these individual emotions to a universal frame created a sense of 'deep, horizontal comradeship'.[3]

Ever since *Imagined Communities*, there has been a flurry of work that focused on this central insight, looking at how shared narratives bind nations together. And yet, as many countries have grown more diverse, the shared stories and strong emotional attachments that Anderson and his successors saw appear to be fraying. Difference, not only in ethnic backgrounds, but in the ways in which we live our lives or consume media, leads to a multiplication in the stories we use to make sense of our world, and shrinkage in how much of this is shared with others. If part of what was at stake for Anderson in national identities was their ability to motivate people to care for strangers, even to make significant sacrifices on their behalf, then this may seem to be under threat. Indeed, this is the risk scholars highlight when they note that growing diversity is often linked to citizens coming to favour narrower, less inclusive welfare and social assistance policies.[4] It seems as though the less we are able to see others as linked by common stories, the less we are willing to do on their behalf. The mounting challenge posed by issues such as climate change or global inequality can make the struggle to preserve national welfare systems look relatively small or easy in comparison. But together, these challenges beg an increasingly urgent question: is it possible to tell uniting stories in a plural world?

Of course, searching for stories that unite us is not the only way of living in a world of growing diversity. It may not be the fairest or most desirable. The dominant way we are learning to tell stories in relation to the plurality all around us is by telling *more* stories, letting a thousand flowers bloom. In some cases, this has been a result of growing personal choice and increasingly accessible technology. People have felt both increasingly compelled and increasingly able to tell their own stories to distinct audiences. In other cases, however, this has been a hard-won victory, where members of excluded groups have fought for media representation.

Recognising other voices is important. Yet doing so has a fragmenting effect, creating different collections of stories, often tied to different networks of communication that operate in parallel – a sort of 'separate but equal' situation. It plays into the idea that we owe little to one another – that we are each the authors of our own tales, which need not reference each other.

It's not just advocates for minority voices who champion a right to self-definition: white nationalist leaders and groups, from Richard Spencer in the US, to the European ethno-nationalist movement Generation Identity, often concede that different groups are entitled to their own distinct stories, culture and heritage, which they can shape for themselves.[5] They then leverage this claim to call for minority populations to be expelled from majority-white countries.

Beyond the risk of reinforcing nationalist logic, a further challenge in insisting on telling our own distinct stories, is that we may overlook the common elements, or bigger forces, that shape different stories in similar ways. In Chapter Five, when Saabira voiced frustration over the loss of the notion of political blackness in the UK – which brought together a range of backgrounds under the banner of blackness – this is what she lamented. Political blackness argued there were common drivers to racial inequality, and that these commonalities mattered as much or more than experiences of specific communities.

In these concerns, Saabira is far from alone.[6] Scholars and activists across the democratic world are pointing to the increasing difficulty in crafting broader stories that knit people together across their differences in order to drive collective change. This has led certain commentators, such as the political scientist Mark Lilla or the psychologist Jonathan Haidt, to link calls for more diverse stories and spaces directly or indirectly to the decline of liberal democracy and the growth of radical nationalism.[7] The implication of these sorts of arguments seems to be that in order to rebuild a politics of common cause, and to resist the worst peddlers of division and conflict, everyone needs to return to universal, overarching narratives and stop worrying so much about difference.

As we have seen, however, the stories we tell can be a matter of life and death. Particularly within liberal democracies, public stories define the possibilities for citizenship and connection.

Historically, the insistence on shared narratives has favoured dominant groups, while making it difficult to imagine and communicate alternatives. While there may be a need to build common politics, there is also an urgent need to do so in a way that contains different stories, different experiences of struggle and joy, different feelings of identity, rather than simply waving these away as politically inconvenient in the way commentators like Haidt or Lilia do.

Fortunately, we do not need to treat the choice between unity and inclusiveness as either/or. Instead, there are ways of telling stories that hold these possibilities in productive tension. This approach to storytelling resists the idea that every group or individual ought to be the sole author of their own story, or the idea that when faced with the limitations of previous stories the only way forward is to start anew. Rather, this is a way of storytelling that starts with the world in which we live and attempts to rewrite stories we inherit – with all their flaws and limitations – not only to revitalise them, but to weave them together. This is a sort of storytelling that starts with familiar understandings, categories, relationships and narratives, gets under the skin of these familiar elements and transforms them from within.

There are three key lessons for this sort of storytelling. The first is that the way in which stories are framed affects what can be done with them. The second lesson is that stories are physical – that to be credible, stories need to play out in the world around us, in the opportunities we have or the ways we live. Believable stories are those backed up by forms of infrastructure that are woven into our everyday lives. Stories that lack this physical dimension may feel like impositions from uninterested elites, writing scripts for others. Finally, and perhaps most crucially, no story can be all-encompassing on its own – even those that claim to span the globe or include all humankind. As a result, stories that are both inclusive and unifying rely on translation – on stories being able to take on different lives in different communities, to be told in different ways while still retaining a connection to one another. Translation is not always easy, but it is vital to building common ground.

※

The years of struggle between self-styled republicans, who wanted Northern Ireland to break from the UK and join Ireland, and loyalists who wanted to remain part of the UK, are seen as a period when group identities became more rigid and divided. The conflict is frequently depicted as a bitter, violent confrontation between religious tribes, with Irish Catholics mostly supporting the republican side, and Protestants the loyalist one. But under the surface, the Troubles prompted small, everyday reworkings of these identities.

Just as activism enabled Kilburn's Irish residents to imagine a more expansive sense of Irish ethnicity, community involvement allowed women in Northern Ireland to challenge gender stereotypes. In Belfast, the political scientist Melanie Hoewer interviewed women about their experiences of the Troubles. During the conflict, many men ended up in prison or as fugitives. The absence of men caused hardship for communities more broadly: families grappled with lost income; local businesses struggled to operate; the police withdrew protection. Faced with these challenges, many women took up roles as community leaders. A Catholic woman named Eilish explained:

> We started changing the social fabric we women did ...
> There were our little victories, they were not big victories
> demonstrating all the women's strength, but there were
> practical victories and they made women who hadn't been
> involved previously think, 'OK, we can do that.' [...] We
> weren't just looking after nationalists, it was women. It

was women and we were quite open to work with women from the [Protestant] Shankill [area of Belfast], because their needs were just as great as the women's needs here … It shows that the Republican Movement was much wider than the IRA.[8]

While the Republican struggle was most prominently defined by militancy and by a cohort of largely male leaders, Hoewer describes how women quietly forged their own vision. They took the well-established values of the Irish republican movement such as 'caring for your own people' or 'justice' and tied these to matters of daily survival, care between neighbours and women's rights. Hoewer notes that these women did not necessarily identify with the broader women's rights movement, often seeing it as an 'outside' imposition, disconnected from the reality of their lives and associated with British rule. Nonetheless, they came to take up many of the same principles as this movement once they were able to frame them within a republican identity. As they did so, writes Hoewer, activists began to refer to 'caring for the people in the community' as a 'natural thing' […] and as a form of being spiritually connected to [their] ethnic identity […] to their way of being Irish'.[9] Framing women's rights as part of the Irish republican struggle also helped make these issues compelling for others, as Eilish explains, with regard to a campaign she helped run against domestic violence: 'Every time we did find out that men were beating their wives we went into all the pubs and clubs and handed their names in and demanded "don't serve them, because every time you serve them a pint, she is getting a punch" […] Although it was small progress you were aware that you made changes, and we actually did make significant changes in the system.'[10]

For the activists Hoewer interviews, Irish ethnicity and republicanism provided a frame for thinking about and acting on feminist principles in familiar, local terms that spoke to the everyday struggle for survival. Even as women and their communities converged on similar principles to the feminist movement, and even as some women came to call themselves feminists through this experience, having immediately relatable frames helped make these principles and labels compelling.

In Kilburn, the ability to tell new, transformative or inclusive stories within the fames of well-established narratives wasn't only present within the Irish community. It was on display at many of the events held at The Door. At open-mic nights, performers would confront a range of themes, from doubt to drug use. On one night, a turbaned woman with a husky voice and an acoustic guitar sang a haunting trio of songs that simmered with lust. Many of these themes were ones The Door's more religiously committed attendees might have balked at, or found unsavoury. Yet the open-mic MCs had a knack for helping these performances resonate for Muslims and non-Muslims alike. Following the singer's performance, for example, the female MC led the room in applause, exclaiming, 'It makes me want to get married!' After each performance, MCs would hold a short, chatty interview with the performer and take a few audience questions. This opened up other perspectives – an audience member pointed out how erotic desire was a strong theme in Sufi poetry, used to convey a longing for connection with Allah. Many of the attendees, and sometimes the MCs themselves, would admit that these things never fitted together perfectly – there were, of course, crucial differences between lust and spiritual longing. Yet by folding understanding of one partly within the other, these differences were not divisive – but rather a basis of conversation and a shared sense of exploration.[11]

Framing stories in familiar terms makes them accessible to wider audiences, but not all frames are equal. The anthropologist Webb Keane talks about how ideas and things have *affordances* – a term he borrows from the psychologist James Gibson. For Keane, affordances are the capacities for thought and action contained within an idea or thing. A chair facilitates sitting down, just as a pair of scissors facilitates cutting. These objects can be put to other uses, of course, but some of these will be more challenging than others – and some possibilities will be outright impossible.

Similarly, our shared categories make certain possibilities easier to imagine than others. For instance, back in Northern Ireland, Hoewer is careful to note that women varied in their attitudes towards the challenges they faced. While those involved at the community level were more likely to highlight and challenge gender discrimination, those involved in more militant groups such as the IRA were likely to downplay gender issues in favour of a story of comradeship. In many ways, the idea of Irish republicanism – especially in the context of a large militant movement – relied on a range of related concepts that limited its inclusiveness. It conjured the idea of a united people, motivated above all else by the desire for independence. Likewise, it strongly suggested that those who opposed independence were fundamentally different – on the opposite side of a seemingly irreconcilable divide that made violence necessary. Although it was possible to use ideas of Irish republicanism to think and talk about gender inequality or about forms of community building that crossed religious divides, these projects risked clashing with visions of internal unity and external division that republicanism frequently traded in.

In 2013 the Northern Irish City of Derry celebrated its four-hundredth birthday. Over the last half-century, Derry – Londonderry to some – had been riven by violence. The decades-long Troubles were sparked by a clash during a Derry parade, and the harrowing events of Bloody Sunday – when the British army gunned down peaceful protesters – took place there. Even after the Troubles had subsided, Derry was a place of divided identities, marked by bloody history. How, then, to celebrate the city in a way that didn't simply serve to fan the embers?

Part of the answer lay in art. In the run-up to its fourth cen-
tennial Derry had bid to become the first UK City of Culture,
and used the attention and support this attracted to stage a
series of grand public events. Among those involved was Frank
Cottrell-Boyce, a children's book author and screenwriter.
Digging through Derry's past, Cottrell-Boyce searched for
a way to retell its story in a way that moved beyond the long
shadow of the Troubles without ringing false. This he found in
the figure of Saint Columba, also known as Colmcille. As one
of the earliest Christian missionaries to Ireland, Colmcille pre-
ceded the Protestant–Catholic split in the Church. During his
travels he founded a monastery at the site of present-day Derry,
giving the city its original Irish name – Doire *Colmcille*. Later
in his life, he entered a self-imposed exile in Scotland to atone
for a series of bloody battles in which he had become caught
up. There Colmcille founded a monastery on the island of Iona
from which he and his monks worked to transcribe hundreds of
volumes of books by hand, which then made their way across
the Christian world. These labours transformed Iona into an
early centre of literacy and, centuries later, contributed to the
start of the European Renaissance. Cottrell-Boyce used the life
of the saint to reimagine Derry as a place of knowledge and
wisdom, radiating its influence into the world and shielding
Europe from the ignorance of the Dark Ages. Funnily enough,
despite Colmcille's efforts in spreading literacy, his own story
had largely been preserved within an oral tradition, marked by
a history of appropriation, embellishment and adaptation. This
varied oral repertoire provided a rich set of resources for adapting Colmcille's story once more, to reimagine history in the
present.[12] As part of the sweeping celebrations Cottrell-Boyce
renamed city streets with words pulled from the life of Colmcille, floated a giant dragon down the River Foyle and gathered
stories from local residents. In the process, he helped rewrite
the history of Derry. The festivities provided residents with a

renewed language of commonality – one that can increasingly be heard in the language of activist groups or seen in museum exhibits. Today, when talking about why he's a storyteller, Cottrell-Boyce has become fond of quoting Colmcille himself: 'Life is a story. Death is a story. Everything is just a story. So we must find the most enduring story.'[13]

※

Not everyone in Derry was happy with the City of Culture celebrations. Growing inequality and decades of neglect form part of Derry's modern-day woes. The loss of industry and the deterioration of older buildings created a patchwork of derelict areas. Many residents struggled to find and keep employment. Critics worried that the event served to pump money into well-to-do areas, rather than truly investing in Derry's future or those who needed it the most.[14]

For others, enduring feelings of injustice prompted deeper ambivalence towards the celebrations. Some felt they were premature. In 1972, the British government released the Widgery Report into the events of Bloody Sunday, which laid the blame for the deaths that occurred on the protestors. Years of careful work by activists gradually uncovered the political motivations behind this narrative, where in conversation with Lord Widgery, the then prime minister and chancellor explicitly discussed the importance of the report as part of a 'propaganda war' in the ongoing conflict.[15] In June 2010, just a month before Derry was named the inaugural UK City of Culture, the findings of a new inquiry, the Saville Report, cut through decades of official silence. A staggering five thousand pages long, the report dissected the event and its aftermath in minute detail. It found the protestors innocent, placing responsibility with the British paratroopers who fired on them without warning, and who later lied to cover their guilt. For those who had spent decades pursuing justice – such as John Kelly, whose brother Michael had been killed – the report opened the possibility of finally bringing charges against the British military. For many years, Kelly worked and volunteered for the Museum of Free Derry, telling his story of what had transpired and campaigning for justice. Kelly took part in the City of Culture celebrations, but, for him, things were not yet resolved. There was still justice to be served.[16]

This tension points to the second lesson: stories are written in the world around us. Stories are told not only in words and images, but through the behaviour of others and in the patterns of our environment. The homes we live in, the jobs we do, the sorts of people we interact with – all this and more shapes which sorts of stories are likely to be credible and compelling to us. This is a point I have returned to throughout this book, but it has important implications for how stories might be rewritten. If we are trying to weave stories that may work to bring people together, then it is important that these stories echo and resonate across everyday life. Within liberal democracy, the validity and weight of different stories is often thought to be determined through debate and dialogue. But set against the subtle, ordinary ways in which stories are reproduced within daily life, such efforts risk becoming hopelessly abstract and detached. Meanwhile, if more divisive stories remain stubbornly entrenched, we may want to look at the ways in which these too are being silently retold. This points towards alternative ideas as to what counts as persuasion, where persuasion too must be a worldly act. 'Talk is cheap', the adage goes, but to tell stories in more everyday ways requires resources and commitment. A failure to appreciate this will leave those working to change engrained narratives fighting against the tide.

In many cases stories that dominate the media or public debate tend to be widely believed. In fact, there's a growing body of research that points to the key role of government and popular media in shaping popular opinion. For instance, studies in the UK have shown how the language of parliamentary debates around benefits, or the popular media around immigration, seems to get ahead of public opinion – expressing views and sentiments that prompt adjustments in personal and collective attitudes.[17] It might be tempting to conclude, then, that powerful institutions shape our collective narratives. But things are not so simple. Rather than assuming that powerful players are unconstrained in their ability to shape opinion, I would argue that the narratives that stick are those that resonate with a wider set of existing physical and social relations, and offer a way of making sense of them. In other words, there is a back-and-forth between the sorts of stories it is possible to tell convincingly and the world they pertain to – with the affordances of each shaping and constraining the other. This becomes especially evident in cases where top-down storytelling fails.

In the mid-2000s, the Israeli-born anthropologist Nitzan Shoshan spent a year and a half getting to know the angry young men and women who made up Berlin's extreme right-wing community. Shoshan's account of these young lives begins with a story modern-day Germany tells about itself. Following German reunification after the cold war, leaders had to confront a dilemma around national identity. On the one hand, there was the need for a renewed story of collective identity, to unite the former East and West and help navigate questions such as who qualified for citizenship or what sort of role Germany was to play on the world stage. On the other hand, there was a need to reconcile this story with a wariness around nationalism as the force that had led to the horrors of the Second World War. What emerged, as a result, was an image of Germany as an industrious, innovative, open-minded nation. Virtuous citizens were seen as embodying economic success, multicultural open-mindedness and a rejection of the nationalist past.

As Shoshan grew familiar with Berlin's radical nationalists, he came to a striking realisation. As he put it: 'Racism and xeno-phobic nationalism were deep and widespread, yet awareness of formal politics was, for lack of a better word, astoundingly rudimentary – several of my informants, for example, could not correctly name Germany's chancellor at the time. Only a handful had participated in organized political groups or attended demonstrations.'[18] Nationalists could not agree over who the 'good' and 'bad' foreigners were or why outsiders were supposedly so threatening. They frequently acted in ways that contradicted their professed views. What many young right-wingers shared, however, was an upbringing – working-class or simply destitute, few educational qualifications, volatile home environments marked by abuse or domestic strife, a history of low-level criminal activity and a tendency to rely on state ben-efits or drift in and out of employment. What Shoshan came to realise was that nationalist views were often a response to the ways in which the circumstances of birth and chance wrote certain people out of the German national story. Some people could never really be good citizens – they were at best a problem to be solved. Embracing nationalism was one way of contesting this story. But it was also a way of giving shape to the feelings of frustration and abandonment that youth not only felt, but saw mapped onto their everyday environment – in the form of iden-tical blocks of grey, crumbling state housing and dead-end jobs. Nationalist youth may not have been ideologically coherent, but their beliefs were nonetheless united by feelings of anger and vulnerability.

If feelings of frustration and abandonment are linked with extreme views, however, this link is never simply given. A useful contrast comes from another anthropologist working in Germany, Felix Ringel. Ringel lived and worked in Hoyerswerda, a town in the south-east of Germany, known as Germany's fastest-shrinking city. Since the reunification of the former East and West Germany, the population of Hoyerswerda has been dwindling, despite the trillions that have been invested to help improve life in the former Communist East and encourage people to stay. In some instances, this decline has crystallised sharp resentment. In 1991, for instance, a wave of violent attacks targeting immigrant workers and refugees shocked Germany, forcing citizens and leaders to grapple with the possibility that right-wing nationalism, reminiscent of the Nazi era, was alive and well in the newly unified nation. In 2008, when he was living in Hoyerswerda, Ringel found groups of neo-Nazis promoting a similar story, talking about the 'planned Volksdeath' (*geplanter Volkstod*) of the German people, epitomised by Hoyerswerda's decline.

Ringel's interest, however, was in how people living in Hoyerswerda were able to create a sense of the future that cut against such narratives of decline. He traced how the ability to tell alternative stories about Hoyerswerda's future relied on marshalling different physical elements in the present. So, for instance, in a talk at a seniors' education institute, a former hydrologist set out a vision for Hoyerswerda as a green-industry hub, crisscrossed by waterways that would make it into the 'Lusatian Venice'. To bring this narrative to life, he began his talk in the last Ice Age and traced the history of Hoyerswerda's waterways and industry, describing a long historical arc of change that was far from over. Another resident, Helfried, a former mining engineer, took Ringel on a tour of the surrounding countryside, where a series of man-made lakes and reforested land were being transformed into a new 'natural' tourist destination. Helfried linked these developments to the history of industrialisation over the past hundred years, again tracing an ongoing, unresolved history. Notably, for many residents, the ability to imagine a liveable future in Hoyerswerda was closely intertwined with their participation in various civic associations. These acted as hubs of connection, creativity and belonging, in ways which could make the town feel both liveable and durable. In Ringel's account, people were able to imagine alternative narratives about the future by focusing on the potentials of their everyday material and social worlds and spinning new stories from these elements.

When worldly realities and abstract narratives fail to hold together, stories fall apart. But, as in Hoyerswerda, everyday worlds are also rich with elements for composing new stories. Political life can be seen as an effort to hold worldly stories together. Politics not only involves grappling over how resources should be distributed or how institutions should operate, but also, crucially, involves crafting stories for how citizens should make sense of the world they face. Inequality, for instance, can be presented as a product of the state or of the market, the fault of migrants or of billionaires. Citizens can respond to inequality with acceptance, anger or resentment, based on how they relate to these narratives. Yet this work of spinning stories and contesting how they hold together is not just a matter for national politics – it is the stuff of everyday life.

On Tuesday evenings, in Kilburn, I would volunteer at a youth club on the Caldwell estate. Tuesdays were for football, which took place in a battered old gymnasium at the back of the club. In the small space, matches were quick, loud and rough – thick with shouted cursing and covert contact – providing an outlet for pent-up frustration. On the sidelines, waiting for teams to rotate, or before or after sessions, I would hear stories from young people about the way they were treated at school or at home. For instance, Ollie, who was fifteen, stocky and surly, would hint at his volatile relationship with his parents – their refusal to sign school forms, things shouted, objects thrown. But he also talked about the resigned attitudes of his teachers. Once, before a session, out of sight in the youth team's office, he produced a maths test from his bag, showing off the A he had received. He had been studying hard and was clearly proud – though reluctant to admit this outright. Both his teacher and parents, he admitted woundedly, had brushed the result off as a fluke. A week later, when I asked him about a subsequent test, he glared angrily at me: 'What's the point of that bullshit anyway?'

Ollie's capacity to understand himself – as a success or a failure, as striving or doomed – depended intensely on those around him. In this he wasn't alone. Ollie's anger was not only related to his difficult home life, but to a broader pattern in how youth on the Caldwell were treated. From apathetic teachers to hostile police, it often seemed as if their futures had already been written for them. It took months of me living on the Caldwell to realise how claustrophobic this could feel. Young people talked about the aggressive use of stop-and-search tactics by the police, where sometimes they had been stopped multiple times a day – as if the police were certain they were already criminals and were simply looking for proof. I heard stories from a family who lived for months without a front door after the police had battered theirs down in an early-morning raid. I talked to teaching assistants who fumed at the indifference of more senior teachers, who were quick to write off any child who showed even a flash of disruptive behaviour as a lost cause.

These experiences were often drawn together by young people to come to conclusions about how and what they could do and where they belonged. Following a workshop organised to inform locals of their rights in dealing with police, I spoke with Damon, who questioned whether you could talk about people on the Caldwell as having rights in any meaningful sense:

> Even if you feel British, if you look foreign you are treated like a foreigner […] You get trouble at school sometimes cuz they think you don't fit in. And you've got the police stopping and searching people on the street, because you look different, or you act different, right? So that's just another way of telling people they ain't really British. And then, did you know, if you go to jail for over two years they

take away your passport? They can just take it from you if you end up in jail like that? So how British are you?![19]

Damon's perspective is especially valuable, because as we saw in Chapter Six, he was someone who had been entangled with street life and had managed to break away from this. Despite the changes in his life, he remained acutely aware of what it meant to be young and black on the Caldwell. In connecting the dots between schools, policing and citizenship law, he deftly unpacked why Brits from migrant backgrounds may find it hard to believe that they're really being given the same chances as other citizens. On other occasions, Damon would talk about how street life offered a refuge from the web of suspicion, scorn and low expectations that could envelop life on the Caldwell. Getting into fights with youth from rival areas or finding ways to earn your own money through drugs became a way of asserting a sense of defiant pride.

For Damon, stepping beyond the streets did not mean breaking with the Caldwell, but drawing on its possibilities to assemble a different sort of story. When he met Mia through the creative hub on the Caldwell, the fact that the hub had gradually become a local institution – a space used for birthday celebrations, informal chats or carnival parties – and the fact that Mia was already well known locally helped him to trust her. Later, when he made the leap into looking for a legitimate, long-term job, it was Sarah, who helped manage the hub, who helped him find an opportunity. He had experienced his share of dead-end jobs and pointless training programmes before, and made it clear that he was trusting in Mia and Sarah that this would be different. As he progressed with his training, he began to understand that stepping away from making money on the streets didn't have to mean stepping away from the people he had cared about – the people who helped him build up his sense of dignity. He could still trade in local gossip, hold court at parties or supply the drinks on a night out, just as before. Whatever teachers or the police may have insisted, 'street' and 'straight' weren't two separate worlds after all. All this served to shape Damon's sense of belonging and the sorts of stories he felt able to tell about himself. 'London's all I know,' he once remarked, chatting with a group of friends, 'but also I feel like I don't like it. It takes something out of you.' Someone else – a DJ at the community radio station – chimed in, talking about how some cities were once very different entities, owned in common by their inhabitants. 'I don't feel like I own London,' Damon retorted, 'but I feel like I own Kilburn.'

※

The third lesson is translation. Translation, however, can be a tricky business, as I learnt first-hand on an August morning in 2015.

The weather wasn't helping. What started out as a blue, sunny day had turned oppressive, as the wispy clouds merged into a uniform, off-white blanket. There was a constant drizzle, but it was still warm and muggy, making the idea of pulling on a waterproof feel deeply undesirable. It was clear that most people passing by just wanted to do their shopping and head off, and as people passed by you could see many of them tried to avoid eye contact. I remember thinking that this is how street preachers must feel.

I was out with an environmentalist group who had travelled out of Kilburn to nearby Willesden Market. The group had been given a free stall by the market manager who, like them, was apprehensive about climate change and sympathetic to their mission of raising awareness. The group had some experience running stalls promoting their campaigns – at summer fetes or cultural events – but Willesden Market was a different beast. A hub of cheap goods and everyday commerce, it was a decidedly practical place. For the environmentalists I was with, this made the prospect of running a stall there both daunting and appealing. After all, they were convinced that climate change ought to be an everyday concern – so why not make the case for action in an everyday space? The group decided to give the stall a try, and I was invited to join in and help.

It was a slow, awkward affair. Our main goal was to get people to write to their MPs, demanding action. We had a stack of pre-typed letters, ready to sign and send off, or a guide for composing your own. Optimistically, the group hoped to even sign up a few new members. Jill, one of the group's leaders, explained to me that the best way to accomplish these tasks was to give others the space to express their own thoughts. She suggested trying the somewhat leading phrase: 'I think climate change is a problem for everyone, don't you?' or else announcing, 'We have letters people can sign to their MPs, but what do *you* think about climate change?'

To help accomplish this, I'd attempt to wave down passers-by, sometimes using Jill's questions, sometimes simply asking if they had a moment to talk about climate change. Mostly this was met with looks of studied indifference or quick glances of disdain. Sometimes people would deliver a quick rejoinder, while continuing to walk on by: 'Nonsense', 'God will provide'. Even though I was there as an anthropologist – to learn first-hand from the experience – the steady stream of dismissal felt bruising, and I was grateful when it became my turn to stand behind the stall while someone else took over the job of trying to flag shoppers down.

Despite this difficulty, several people did engage – one every handful of minutes – responding to our concerns from a variety of perspectives. A man from Uganda asked, 'So what does this mean? You want to see more trees? Fewer trees?' Left to field the question, I hesitated for a moment – the letter the group had drafted mostly focused on reducing greenhouse gas emissions as the most urgent priority, but planting trees seemed obviously helpful. Should I explain all this? I stumbled over an answer: 'Well trees are just a part of it, but yeah, more. More trees and less deforestation would certainly help change things. More trees!' The man beamed and signed a copy of the letter without really reading it – while explaining to me how he cultivated fast-growing eucalyptus on his 26-acre plot back in Uganda. With pride, he told me about how he had sold cuttings for growing new trees to various international projects, including ones backed by the EU and UN. From his 20,000 trees, he explained, over a million others must have grown by now. So he was all for more trees!

Another man, from Barbados, stopped by. 'There,' he explained, 'we talk about climate change everyday!' He went on to explain how people now took it very seriously, because they could see the worsening effects of hurricanes, year on year. Although, he added, this had been going on for a long time before, without much of a reaction. Over the past century, as the Cuban sugar cane industry grew and came to undercut the local Bajan one, people had to cut down many sugar fields, replacing these with timber, and this, he explained, had long been making things worse. Again, I felt at a loss. The replacement of sugar cane with trees didn't sound to me like a cause of climate change as I understood it. If anything, it sounded like a positive development ('More trees!'). To him, however, the demise of the sugar cane industry and worsening hurricanes in the present were clearly linked. Remembering Jill's instructions, I bit my tongue. He signed a letter, wished us luck and headed on his way.

Sometimes diversity of perspectives could become a challenge. Campaigners in the group frequently commented on how hard it was to foster interest and understanding around environmental issues. In October, a different team from the group journeyed to a large branch of the bank Barclays to protest

their funding of fracking projects. Fracking, or hydraulic fracturing, is a controversial method for extracting hard-to-acquire
oil and gas by pumping pressurised water and other chemicals
underground, pushing these fuels into easier-to-reach places.
Scientists and activists have highlighted the tendency of fracking projects to heavily contaminate groundwater and to cause
seismic instability. Both have also objected to fracking on the
more straightforward basis that the urgency of climate change
means that *all* fossil fuel extraction ought to be halted as soon
as possible. Fracking can be a complex issue, and prior to the
protest, group members debated whether to frame the issue
more in terms of local environmental damage or the wider issue
of climate change. In the end, they decided simply to ensure
the protest was attention-grabbing and to hand out information
leaflets, in the hope that people would pass their own judgements and act accordingly.

At the protest, Jan, a social worker in her forties, originally
from Australia, had come up with a catchy slogan: 'Barclays is
investing in fracking, that's not retail banking!' sometimes following this with a rhetorical 'now is it?' I quizzed her – did she
think that most passers-by knew what fracking was? She found it
doubtful: 'Probably not, but what you've got to do is grab their
attention with something that's going to stick in their head, and
then they will go away and work out for themselves what it's
all about.' Yet even this simple goal – to appeal to a range of
perspectives by delivering a minimal, catchy message – could be
thwarted by difference. Jan had brought along a friend, a woman
her age who worked as a local teacher. After being rebuffed by
a man who looked to be Middle Eastern – who shot our group
a sceptical look – Jan's friend remarked to us: 'I don't think he
understands what retail banking is. A lot of the people around
here, they probably don't understand what's going on. It makes
it really hard to get them to wake up – they're just being taken
advantage of by the big powers, and they don't even understand,

you know?' After a beat, she added, for emphasis, 'You got to learn English!'

Jan responded in kind: 'This area is very diverse. It does make it hard to campaign sometimes. You're always like "Oy, you!" and you're never sure if they get it, you know?'

Over the past few centuries, the world has grown steadily more interconnected – driven first by colonialism, and more recently by developments in technology and new forms of global migration. We have also grown more attuned to ecological connections that have always existed. Nonetheless, politics – and especially democratic politics – has primarily been understood as an affair taking place within individual countries. Increasingly, however, there are issues – such as climate change, the global movement of refugees, food security, disease or the complex supply chains used to produce goods – that demand a global perspective. Part of the anxiety and frustration surrounding these issues is often that our ethical and political imaginations are too narrow. As a result, campaigners, educators and politicians have often pushed for the cultivation of broader perspectives, able to take in the scope of these challenges. The modern environmentalist movement, for example, is often traced back to the moment in 1968 where we took the first colour photograph of the earth from the moon – literally providing a global perspective on the planet and provoking new ways of thinking about planetary connection and interdependency.

And yet, this push for encompassing, big-picture perspectives stumbles over difference. In the worst instances, this has led campaigners to flatten diverse experiences of history, pain and particularity in their efforts to impose an all-encompassing narrative on things. Take Roger Hallam, the co-founder of the global climate activist network Extinction Rebellion. Hallam has argued that the importance placed on commemorating the Holocaust made it difficult to address other past and present-day tragedies, and has brushed off requests that Extinction

Rebellion grapple with questions of racial inequality linked both to climate change and potential sustainability policies.[20]

When the Canadian-born climate scientist Katharine Hayhoe arrived in Lubbock, Texas, to start a new job, all her experience was with the big-picture questions of climate change. Her research models the impact of various greenhouse gases on patterns of change, often at a global level. This expertise led her to work for the US government, the National Academy of Sciences and as an expert reviewer for the Intergovernmental Panel on Climate Change. However, locally, she struggled to get those around her to take her work seriously. To her, the evidence for human-driven climate change was irrefutable. But many Texans weren't so sure.

Dr Hayhoe's big revelation came when she was invited to talk to a local church group about her work as a scientist. During her talk, she pleaded with the audience to take climate change seriously. This fell flat. In the questions, however, she was asked what motivated her research. She responded by discussing her upbringing in an evangelical Christian household, and how faith motivated her work. Suddenly the room transformed, and she found herself in the middle of an animated discussion around the question of responsible stewardship over creation and the role science could play in this. Rephrased in familiar, religious terms, she found her claims suddenly taken up with enthusiasm.

Since then, Dr Hayhoe has gone on to become a prominent public communicator around climate change. Only, oftentimes, she doesn't call it that. *Climate change*, as she sees it, is a term that the public has come to understand as representing a particular political agenda. It is broad, contentious and too abstract to feel relevant to the choices people make in their daily lives. Instead, she tailors her message to those she's speaking with. With churchgoers, she talks about faith and care, dominion and stewardship. With parents she talks about their kids. With younger audiences she explores hopes for the future and how these tie into natural systems. And, with professionals, she will frequently reframe the problem to centre their own expertise. By privileging these more familiar frames and categories, she tries to make it clear that these, too, are ways of thinking and talking about climate change.

Dr Hayhoe's insight is that climate change is a useful label for scientists and policymakers. The ordinary citizens she spoke with, however, often felt much more compelled when the set of political, economic, ecological and social challenges collectively called 'climate change' were broken apart and put back together under the banner of concerns that resonated more strongly with personal lives. Dr Hayhoe, then, is a rare sort of figure, and one we are desperately lacking today – a translator. There is a well-known feminist slogan, that the personal is political. In her outreach work, Dr Hayhoe works to make the political personal. In doing so, she makes environmental activism accessible to a wider range of people beyond those whose lives already predispose them towards taking on such concerns.

Translation remains aligned with the representational politics of liberalism, allowing people to negotiate common issues through stories and symbols, without having to know one another face to face. Yet it transforms liberal politics in three important ways. Firstly, it helps bring these representational politics back down to earth. The very idea of translation holds on to the idea that certain issues or ideas matter to all of us, but it rejects the idea that there is a single universal language in which to express such concerns. It pays attention to the nuances of everyday life and allows them to inflect our understanding without abandoning the hope of establishing common ground.

Secondly, translation tempers the universalising logic of liberalism. Totalising images of humanity, or of collective group identity, always have their outsides, and when they are conceived as singular, to fall outside of them is to fall beyond humanity. Translation breaks this singularity. We can see multiple images of humanity in relation to one another. For instance, we might recognise logic, care, sympathy, evidence-based inferences and belief, all as forms of 'reason', expanding the grounds by which citizens may make claims on the state and one another, without dispensing with the idea that citizenship flows from a collective core. Third, then, in doing so, translation expands the scope of the political. For those who don't believe that the imposition of equality through law and force has brought about meaningful transformation, as well as for those who feel such impositions are heavy-handed and misguided, translation can open up space that singularity closes down.

Translation is vital, but it is rarely easy. Back at the anti-fracking protest outside Barclays, Tessa, a younger black woman, hit on a new strategy. Unusually for a Saturday, the bank was closed. Playing on this, she worked up a few new slogans to try over the megaphone. 'Barclays aren't open, they're away fracking!' she declared, indignantly. 'The bank's closed, the cash-point's broken, and Barclays are busy putting their customers' money into fracking!'

We were not the only ones gathered at the entrance of the bank. Over the course of the protest, would-be customers arrived, only to be met with the unexpected closure. Intermittently, a few lingered, seemingly at a loss. To my surprise, Tessa's new slogan drew some of these perplexed passers-by. Fitting with Jan's stereotype, many were not very fluent in English. But they came over, and Tessa and Jan attempted to explain the protest. It was clear that not everything from their explanation landed, but it was also clear that the small crowd did pick up on some sense of social and environmental wrongdoing, prompting indignation of their own. Their irritation with the closure seemed to create sympathy with the protesters and helped them pick up on their broader message. Brandishing a clipboard, Tessa got several signatures for her anti-fracking petition before people moved on with their day.

With the environmental group, as with so many others in Kilburn, translation was touch and go. At times it worked in powerful or unexpected ways, bringing people together despite their differences. In fact, almost every core member of the environmental group had their own idiosyncratic understanding of climate change or 'the environment'. But the group had learnt to let these different perspectives bloom in relation to one another. Despite the notable difference between members – one a homeopath, another much more interested in urban gardening, the group's co-leader, Jill, an old-school socialist who linked environmentalism with issues around inequality, and so on – they shared a common commitment. Translation demanded both effort and a conscientiousness that was not always easy to maintain. As Jill once explained to me, reflecting on her years as a campaigner, it was one thing to know what worked to include others on paper. But it was another to actually act this way when you were 'switched on' – when you were driven by your own passion or anger, or nerves, or exhaustion – and still remember to give others space– to let their voices and views come out and to hold yours back until the point where both could be woven together. As with the frustration voiced by Jan and her schoolteacher friend around the diversity in Kilburn, sometimes the need for this effort and vigilance could be a turn-off and could even feel like a barrier to effective change.

Translation shares this quality with the approaches to storytelling explored in this chapter. Working to find familiar but effective framings, ensuring they have a material dimension and translating them to hold different audiences and perspectives in relation are all slow, costly strategies, requiring both time and physical resources. Part of the appeal of sticking to taken-for-granted, abstract, singular stories is that it's easy. Such stories require less effort to imagine, to tell and uphold. The solution of liberal modernity to growing diversity over the past several centuries has been to prioritise these broad, encompassing and cheap

ways of holding people together. It has been to reach for univer-
sals that might unite strangers and allow for exchange between
them in the absence of committed, personal relationships.

We've seen the ways in which such universalising, grand narratives are untenable. Yet it is hard to tell stories in the plural
– it is slow, demanding and challenging. To commit to this
sort of storytelling, then, we need a different way of thinking
about what is valuable – what is worthwhile in terms of time
and resources. This different approach to value cannot come
from storytelling or from the liberal tradition alone. In the final
chapter, we will explore how a rethinking of republicanism,
again in tension with liberalism rather than on its own, can lead
us to new ways of valuing one another and the bonds that might
bring us together.

CHAPTER NINE

NEW REPUBLICS

Megan Phelps-Roper was five when she first started protesting.[1] At that age, she couldn't read the sign she was clutching, but she worked out what it said later: 'Gays are worthy of death'. From the day she was born, Megan belonged to the Westboro Baptist Church, which was led by her charismatic grandfather, Fred Phelps, with Megan's mother, Shirley Phelps-Roper, as his right hand. Believing that America was spiritually corrupt and deserving of divine punishment, the church made it its mission to expose corruption and celebrate punishment through public demonstrations. Following school shootings, church members would show up with signs reading 'Pray for more dead children'. They would target other places of worship with signs such as 'God hates Jews', or stage aggressive protests at the funerals of dead soldiers, or of victims of HIV/AIDS. This self-righteous public vitriol quickly became notorious, leading to the BBC documentarian Louis Theroux describing them as 'the most hated family in America'.

Recalling her childhood, Megan contrasted the venom of their public protests to the warmth and care of their private lives. For Megan and her siblings, belief in Westboro's radical doctrines was cultivated, not imposed. Megan describes a world of loving relatives, a caring community and of patient, reasoned discussion in family meetings and bible study. Strong family relationships not only provided a secure foundation for church members to take on the world, but also served to connect feelings of religious righteousness with those of familial love. Reflecting on her early relationship with her mother, soon after beginning to join church protests, Megan writes:

> This was the same era in which I sat just to her left during church, when she belted out the hymns so high and so loud that it hurt my ears. I discovered that to protect myself from the sonic onslaught, I could stick a finger into my left ear, press myself into my mother's side, and listen to her sing from *inside her body*. It was so soothing, the warmth and the vibrations and the feeling of her arm holding me close as I tucked into her. I didn't know then that this special place at her side would always be mine. That as her eldest daughter, I would become to her what she had become to her father – and as that relationship had defined my mother, so this one would define me. *For I was tender and only beloved in the sight of my mother.*[2]

For Megan and her family, protests formed a part of this intimate, passionate atmosphere. Conviction and care made church members seemingly unshakable in their beliefs. Quoting Scripture and standing tall, they would almost always leave their public demonstrations with a sense of triumph. Online, too, Megan had taken to Twitter as a crusader for the church, goading and sparring with the church's many detractors – confident in her own righteousness.

Early on, I wrote that there is a familiar story that we tell about difference: that it always carries a threat. This story stems from the dilemmas of living with others in a finite world. In our communities – whether face to face or anonymous and 'imagined' – we are held together by particular symbolic, practical and physical resources. We craft categories that define our humanity or our shared background and tell stories that bring these categories to life, giving them emotional heft and pull.

We cultivate orientations towards others, which connect us and hold us apart; we maintain polite indifference towards strangers on the train; grow accustomed to unfamiliar languages until they are mundane; or learn to actively appreciate the sounds, smells or tastes of particular cultures. We encounter others in parks or libraries; we take part in community festivals; or we build organisations that enable us to cooperate in new ways. Together, we can think of these symbolic, practical and physical resources as a diversity commons – a collectively accessible pool of resources that enables us to live with difference.

As we have seen, the capacity of these resources to connect us with one another depends on the ways they are joined together. The credibility of a story, for instance, depends on how it provides a script for action, and on the material realities that underpin it. At the same time, when these resources are subject to conflicting demands, their potential can erode. The Westboro Baptist Church provides a handy example. Its members reject public stories about equality and tolerance and, in doing so, expose these as flimsier than they claim to be – revealing that democracies can leave plenty of space for hate. Their beliefs impact the ways others are treated in public, denying them equal dignity. These same beliefs have also been asserted in order to limit the legal protection of equality. At the US Supreme court, members of the church have successfully defended their right to harass others, in the name of free speech. And they take up public resources, creating costs for other citizens. Their protests take over public parks, draw on police protection and force others – such as synagogues and funeral homes – to invest in greater security. This is where the familiar story about difference comes in, suggesting that when different groups make claims on collective resources, they are locked into a zero-sum game – a situation where one party's gain is another party's loss.

Although the Westboro Baptist Church is an extreme example, our story about difference and conflict tells us that some form of loss occurs every time our collective resources are subject to diverse claims. In Chapter Four, some residents of Kilburn expressed this belief in relation to an Eid event, or even barbeques, in a local park. These, too, were imagined as crowding out other possibilities. Even more subtly, this story animates those all-too-familiar instances where people are abused for being different in public – for speaking an unfamiliar language, wearing a headscarf, holding hands with a same-sex partner. These innocuous markers of difference are often seen as diminishing wider possibilities: 'Soon it will be illegal to even *say* you're English!' 'Soon marriage will have lost its meaning.' Making matters trickier, people insist on their own sense of irreconcilable difference.[3] Anti-abortion activists insist on a different definition of 'life' than that implied by pro-choice policies. Citizens guided by faith, or political conviction, carry their own truths, where people may *not* be morally equal, but may be defined by their adherence to various doctrines. And, as with Wyatt's vision of blackness as a spiritual essence – which we explored in Chapter Five – even without organised faith or politics, people often inhabit their own universes. These are real to them, and cannot be relativised as mere 'belief', equal to all other positions. These moments of confrontation and genuine, weighty difference can reinforce the familiar, zero-sum story.

This pessimistic accounting can lead towards dramatic conclusions. In 1968, the biologist Garrett Hardin coined what would become one of the most influential ideas of the modern era – 'the tragedy of the commons'.[4] Concerned about the growing human population, Hardin imagined a pasture where different herders would take their animals to graze. For each herder, it made rational sense to allow their livestock to graze as much as possible. Yet if everyone followed this strategy, the field would become overgrazed and barren and the farmers would be collectively ruined. Even knowing this risk, however, the herders would still likely overgraze, Hardin argued. For each individual to hold back would be to give some other herder an advantage over them. For Hardin, the pasture was a metaphor for our planet, where he believed that, left to their own devices, people would deplete it to the point of ruin. A few years later, Hardin drew on this argument to justify closed-border migration policies and sharp limits to humanitarian aid.[5] The earth, he argued, could only sustain a given number of people at a healthy, comfortable standard. To try to bring the global population up to this standard would result in resource depletion. As such, wealthier countries were for the most part justified in shutting their borders or refusing to share their resources more widely. It was tragic, Hardin argued, that prosperity would not be available to all, and that some were born in well-off places and others into poverty, but nonetheless, a failure to close borders could only lead to ruin. It was necessary.

Where Hardin called for closed borders to preserve prosperity, others took his logic further, applying it to resources that held groups together more generally. In the same year as Hardin's intervention, the English politician Enoch Powell made his infamous speech – which we explored in Chapter Two, where he railed against migrants crowding white British citizens out of schools and neighbourhoods. Seven months after his speech had thrown the UK into upheaval, he followed up on his claims:

> The West Indian or Asian does not, by being born in England, become an Englishman. In law he becomes a United Kingdom citizen by birth; in fact he is a West Indian or an Asian still. Unless he be one of the small minority [...] he will by the very nature of things have lost one country without gaining another, lost one nationality without acquiring a new one. Time is running against us and them.[6]

For Powell, the loss of identity worked both ways. Except for a 'small minority', who might adapt, identity was determined by heritage, not by living together. Migration diminished both migrants and the societies they travelled to, exposing each to forms of difference that clashed with their vision of the world. Today, Powell's claim is echoed by nationalists of all stripes, from India's BJP party to Germany's AFD, who yearn for a world of culturally homogenous nation states. For Hardin, the only solution to the tragedy of the commons was enclosure, where open access to the commons was replaced by either government or private control. Powell and other nationalists echo this conclusion, arguing that the only way to preserve collective cultural and political resources is banishing those who may erode them. Yet even within national borders, threats remain. Groups like the Westboro Baptist Church – where citizens themselves[7] assert irreconcilable differences, and in doing so, diminish collective resources – illustrate the limits of enclosure as a solution, even for those who embrace it. Excluding all those who make competing claims on collective resources is not only practically impossible – it is fundamentally incompatible with preserving the right of democratic citizens to differ and disagree.

Hardin's bleak predictions, alongside our zero-sum view of the commons, continue to be enormously influential today. Yet this is not the only story that can be told. In the late 1950s, before Hardin's predictions had gained notoriety, Elinor Ostrom was living in Los Angeles, growing increasingly bored with being a lawyer's wife. To keep herself occupied, she took a course in public administration at UCLA and enjoyed it so much she went on to do a master's, and then a PhD, graduating in 1964. Where Hardin started with grand philosophical pronouncements about human fallibility and earthly finitude, Ostrom began by looking at how people grappled with 'collective action dilemmas' in real life. Committed to paying attention to local particularities, first in California and later ranging across the world, what Ostrom came to realise was that the tragedy of the commons was a possibility, but it was far from inevitable. From studies of fragile Swiss mountain pastures to open-water fishing in Turkey, to traditions of forestry management in Japan, Ostrom gathered stories of people successfully stewarding and preserving what she called 'common-pool resources'. Along the way, she divorced, remarried, founded one of the most influential political science labs in the world with her new husband Vincent, and in 2009 became the first woman to win the Nobel Prize in Economics.

Ostrom's research offers a different way of thinking about our 'diversity commons' – not as strained and stretched by difference, but as something people from different backgrounds can work together to sustain. Drawing on this work, we can identify four key principles that are especially important for the stewardship of diversity commons: *joint commitment, versatility, boundedness* and *nesting*.[8]

※

The men showed up late, at a time when the streets were virtually empty, save for the occasional night owl, winding their way home. They seemed to be aware of the CCTV cameras that dotted the Kilburn High Road, taking care not to reveal their faces. Moving quickly, they stuffed their target into the back of a van and drove off. It was only when morning came that their activity became apparent, and Len received the news.

The bench had been abducted.

Len was the coordinator of a small, scrappy community group, Kilburn Ageing Together, better known by its initials as KAT. At first glance, KAT might look like a relatively ordinary older people's organisation, running movie nights or meet-ups at cafés. It had just about enough money to employ Len part-time, maintain a simple website and print and distribute the occasional leaflet – with both website and publications looking like they hailed from a much earlier time in computing. This relatively unassuming presence, however, hid the fact that KAT was one of the most influential, and mischievous, community organisations in Kilburn.

The Kilburn High Road was an unfailing source of grief for residents. Even those who loved the neighbourhood, who couldn't imagine living anywhere else, often griped about the High Road. The pavements were dirty, and obstructed by unscrupulous, aggressive traders who colonised spaces meant for walking. While people jostled on the pavement, cars did the same on the road, which retained its Roman-era designation as a major road leading out of London, despite the fact that it only had one lane running in each direction. When human congestion met vehicular congestion, accidents frequently followed. It seemed like every month there was a new report of pedestrians or cyclists sustaining severe injuries. The shops were often shabby and never had quite what you wanted. If you did like a place, this was a sure sign that it would be closed in three months. The only establishments that truly managed to endure were loan shops, betting shops and pawnbrokers – all three of which had proliferated in unusually high numbers. Meanwhile, anything that might serve as a possible public space had fallen into disrepair or been effectively privatised. A 'public square' consisted of three low planters with benches, typically layered with pigeon droppings, installed besides a tall blue fence which concealed Kilburn's struggling outdoor market. A building that was once Europe's largest cinema, built in imitation of the Empire State Building, had now become an unfriendly megachurch – after a failed bid to secure it as a community centre – while Kilburn's famous music venues, where big-name acts in the 60s and 70s had often cut their teeth, had all been shut down.

Following the pattern of the streets themselves, these complaints branched outwards from the High Road, to the smashed-up bus stop one street away, the needles found in a park bush, or nearby crumbling buildings. Underlying this kaleidoscope of complaints seemed to be a sense from people that their neighbourhood wasn't really theirs – that the danger, dereliction and impermanence made many of the neighbourhood's most public places feel unwelcoming. These complaints were typically voiced with a sense of resignation. If it wasn't one thing, it was another. What could you do?

KAT, however, was not resigned. As a group it had come to champion the quietly radical idea of 'ageing in place' – that growing old need not mean withdrawing from society. If ageing required change, members believed, then why couldn't it be places that changed to accommodate the elderly, rather than the other way around? In practice, what this meant was that members of KAT were seasoned campaigners fighting for small, but crucial, local changes. Pedestrian crossings that offered more time to cross, letting people know how much time they had left. More benches. Home visits from podiatrists to help people clip their nails – which, as you aged, could become impossible and immobilising. Bus stops moved to avoid steep drops off the kerb. Through campaigning and fundraising, through public events and private negotiations, KAT reshaped Kilburn's public realm, piece by piece.

KAT, however, endeavoured not only to transform the physical form of the neighbourhood, but also people's perceptions and experiences of it. Perhaps it had to. Its work met with a good deal of resistance. During my time in Kilburn, KAT developed a project they titled 'Bench to Bench'. Looking to tackle isolation, help older people build new connections and restore accessibility to Kilburn, the project mapped the benches in the area, lobbied for new ones and mapped ten walks that threaded between benches, to help older residents navigate the neighbourhood with regular breaks. It was through this work that I came to learn, to my amusement, that benches were controversial. When Len and his collaborators lobbied the council or raised funds to install new benches, they often courted backlash. Concerned residents fretted that benches would attract the homeless, or street drinkers. Parents worried about drug use, shopkeepers feared they would lead to loitering and vandalism. When KAT prevailed, its opponents would sometimes take matters into their own hands. In addition to the abduction, Len told me of another bench that looked like it had been hacked to bits with an axe. In other cases, simple indifference was enough to undermine their efforts – benches broke through rot and neglect.

'Bench to Bench', however, was more than an exercise in map making. During the winter of 2014, I set out with Len as he attempted to map benches and test potential routes. Along the way we stopped and chatted with shopkeepers, café owners or cemetery groundskeepers, picking up titbits of local history, learning who would allow walkers to use the toilet without a purchase, and explaining the project as we went. As we did, we tweaked our maps, incorporating our findings – an unmapped pedestrian crossing, a friendly café, some historic homes that would make for a good story.

In spring, Len began to organise 'test walks', which evolved into regular, organised outings. The fact that the walks were shared played a vital role. It wasn't simply that others provided company, but that being together turned the walks into something of a collective achievement. More able-bodied participants pushed those in wheelchairs or offered a steadying arm when dealing with steps. Walkers would point out little architectural details or share stories associated with certain areas. If we arrived at benches as a larger group, people would take turns sitting and standing to give everyone the opportunity to recharge. Participants invited friends or helped each other plan bus routes, ensuring they arrived at the start on time. Often, others would be drawn into this sense of collective accomplishment as well. Once, upon reaching a set of benches in a park, we found a group of daytime drinkers already there, enjoying the sunshine. Our group hesitated, unsure of how to approach, but before anyone could decide what to do, one of the men rallied his friends to free up the benches for us. That day, Len and I were both pushing wheelchairs, and as we swapped places with the previous group, their momentary ringleader grinned broadly at me: 'I was a carer once, now you're a carer, we're all— You're doing good work!'

KAT's efforts at urban reform remained controversial. Yet when faced with resistance Len and his collaborators strove to generate the same sense of recognition and collective accomplishment as that day in the park. They invited naysayers to KAT meetings or worked with local artists to highlight the mobility challenges of older residents. They would take the time to meet shop owners or residents, stressing the difference that benches or accessible toilets could make for older people, but also negotiating solutions – to see if there was another location for a bench, bus stop or pedestrian crossing that would help allay their misgivings.

The philosopher Margaret Gilbert refers to this sort of shared endeavour, where capabilities or goals become dependent on one another, as 'joint commitments'.[9] For Gilbert such commitments attune us to one another and intertwine our interests. Joint commitments work to motivate collective endeavours, but they also emerge from them. This suggests that when cultivating understandings across difference, the journey matters as much as the destination. Gilbert approaches joint commitments descriptively – that is to say, she sees them as the foundations of social life, and at the heart of what makes us human.

Another philosopher, Donna Haraway, argues, however, that much of our trouble starts because we don't recognise the basic fact of interdependence. In Western democracies, much of our political and ethical imagination, she says, is structured by a fantasy of freedom and mastery. Ethics and politics are about taking hold of our destinies, and determining our lives and the shape of the world. It's from this fantasy of self-sufficiency and mastery that much of our current turmoil begins, from environmental ruin to political division. This fantasy leads us to believe we can act without attending to the interdependencies that sustain us, and that we can make a clean break from the world in which we are enmeshed. Haraway offers a sharp rebuke – 'we cannot denounce the world in the name of an ideal world'[10] – and calls for a tricky but necessary alternative, of 'staying with the trouble', where we remain alive to the fact that our actions inescapably depend on others, and remain accountable to them – where 'decisions must take place somehow in the presence of those who will bear their consequences'.[11]

When we recognise the joint commitments that sustain us – staying with the trouble of our current world – and seek to forge new ones, our political stances begin to look different. Taking account of joint commitments does not eliminate difference, but brings differences down to earth. This can be seen, for instance, among anti-abortion activists. Abortion is a topic that can attract supercharged emotions. While most democratic nations have a solid share of people who are uncertain, or who see abortion as acceptable in some circumstances but not others, there are a great many people who take a stark view. In America, in 2020, nearly half the population fell into one of these camps, with 20 per cent of people believing abortion should be 'illegal in all circumstances', and 29 per cent saying that it should be 'legal in all circumstances'.[12]

If the issue can elicit such radically conflicting views, then we might expect pro- or anti-abortion activists to have the most stringent views of all. In the UK, for instance, the unequivocally anti-abortion camp is much smaller. Over the past several decades, when the question has been asked, typically less than 10 per cent – and by some measures only 3 per cent – have opposed abortion outright.[13] Despite their smaller numbers, however, some anti-abortion activists are clearly very vehement – for instance prompting local councils to ban protests outside of clinics, given the levels of 'intimidation, harassment and distress' protests were causing.[14]

For decades, this was the line taken by social scientists – that pro- or anti-abortion activists were motivated by strongly held beliefs. But at the turn of the millennium, the American sociologist Ziad Munson made a striking discovery. He spent time getting to know both anti-abortion activists and those who had strong anti-abortion views, but were not activists themselves. Not unlike Shoshan's far-right extremists in Berlin, who didn't know who Germany's chancellor was, Munson found that most non-activists claimed to have strong opinions, but lacked the capacity to back these up. He writes: 'Nonactivists express incoherent and vague beliefs about the issue. They can seldom articulate even basic pro-life ideas, such as why abortion is wrong or whether abortion should be illegal.'[15] Meanwhile, those who became activists did not necessarily start out holding strong opinions at all. Some were 'at best ambivalent' about abortion, 'and in many cases decidedly pro-choice'.[16] Why, then, did they become activists?

Munson found that, for activists, participation in anti-abortion communities and organisations typically came before the development of strong anti-abortion views, not the other way around. Participation in such groups was often motivated by unrelated reasons. As an illuminating example, Munson shares the story of Ruth, a former paediatric nurse living in Minneapolis–Saint Paul, who left her job to become a full-time parent. As her children grew up, Ruth began to look for opportunities to volunteer, and settled on becoming a volunteer probation officer where she worked with young offenders facing complex issues. Despite her Catholic upbringing, over the course of this work she regularly referred young people to abortion services without qualm. One of the services they could refer people to was named 'Birthright', but it was listed with a note: 'Only refer if they're carrying to term.'[17] Ruth ended up getting in touch with them to learn more about their work, motivated by the desire to maintain good links with partner organisations and to build up her own understanding for the sake of the young people she worked with. She attended a Birthright training session on how to counsel women with crisis pregnancies, and stayed in touch with them. This led to a gradual process of absorbing Birthright's belief that abortion represented not only a loss of life, but a loss of human potential. As she put it, 'When I got with Birthright I found out what they did, that they weren't in the political arena, and they didn't show pictures of aborted fetuses; they didn't get into the destruction, they got into the positive points.'[18] Ultimately, she left her position as a probation officer to become a counsellor, and then later a local leader with Birthright – coming to spend more than thirty hours a week on pro-life activities.

It's when people like Ruth become involved in organisations associated with pro-life causes that they come to develop stronger and more clearly informed beliefs. These commitments, however, are of a different sort than those who adopt pro-life views in the abstract, without direct involvement. A frequent charge against anti-abortion politicians is that they adopt the term pro-life, while remaining happy for children to be born into immensely difficult – even life-threatening – circumstances, without support. As in Ruth's case, however, by coming to pro-life beliefs through participation, activists are often more likely to recognise the different personal stakes and difficult dilemmas that surround abortion. This can lead to its own distinct pattern of views, as Munson notes: 'On the one hand, activists' beliefs seldom line up consistently as either conservative or liberal as defined by current American political divisions. On the other hand, activism itself changes the way activists look at other issues. For example, many in the pro-life movement have come to oppose the death penalty as part of their efforts to be "consistently pro-life."[19] Likewise, in contrast to non-activists with strong anti-abortion beliefs, activists were more opposed to cutting social welfare. For activists, then, the idea of being anti-abortion was not simply an abstract principle, but a more worldly commitment, shaped in relation to others. To engage in the work of activism – to face up to young offenders grappling with teenage pregnancy, or to witness the difficulties of raising a child with few resources – required recognition of the way abortion was entangled with other issues. Claims that abortion was wrong could not be made in the abstract. They had to be made – at least to some degree – in relation to the needs, perspectives and understandings of others, who might not agree. What Munson describes is a situation where activists were compelled to stay with the trouble. They had to make their case in a way that opened up possibilities for others, rather than closing them down.

Public resources are often seen as substitutes for private ones. Trains and buses are alternatives to private car ownership, for instance. For champions of public resources, typically on the left, these alternatives involve forms of economic rebalancing, reducing the risks and expenses faced by disadvantaged citizens, while attempting to minimise the public costs of private actions – such as the pollution from cars. For opponents of public resources, typically on the right, public resources standardise life, constraining personal choice at the taxpayer's expense. Both these perspectives value public resources in relation to freedom – either in terms of freedom from economic and social constraints, or in terms of a freedom to choose. Thinking of public resources as commons – as products of joint commitments – subtly shifts this perspective. The cultivation of joint commitments does not so much open up or close down freedom – it reshapes it in relation to others. Joint commitments allow for new possibilities to emerge, opening a space of freedom. These possibilities, however, inescapably depend on others. Freedom becomes a collective capacity.

Not long after our walk, where the group drinking on the benches ceded the space to us, Len emailed me, forwarding a grateful letter from the woman whose wheelchair I had helped push. It began: 'A sense of community is a wonderful thing and I felt it in spades on Wednesday.' She remarked that although she didn't know anyone in the group, save for the friend who had invited her, she was 'chatting easily' with everyone by the end of the outing. It wasn't only the new connections she valued, however – her letter detailed the various discoveries she made along the way, including listing off a range of local projects and services at community centres dotted around the neighbourhood. Explaining that she had been housebound for some time, and that these projects showed her the types of things she could be getting out for, she concluded: 'See what I mean about a sense of community? These people get it. You are happy to know your neighbours. You are not isolated. And as you get older this gathers importance.'

※

Megan-Phelps Roper left the Westboro Baptist Church at the age of twenty-eight. Two things made this possible. The first was the influence of a few strangers on Twitter. Among her usual combative encounters online, she had begun to encounter others who showed genuine interest in her beliefs. Although they seemed sceptical or disapproving, Megan could tell that these acquaintances were holding back on expressing their own perspective in order to learn more about hers, drawing her out with general, searching questions in lieu of confrontational challenges. She credits the Jewish blogger David Abitbol, who blogged under the handle 'Jewlicious', for one of the first moments when she came to question her church's doctrine.

When Megan was attempting to defend Westboro's call for homosexuality to be made a capital offence, Abitbol surprised her by quoting the words of Jesus: 'He that is without sin among you, let him first cast a stone at her.' Though Megan was familiar with the passage, she remarks that, 'I had seen this as a general call to humility, and I couldn't believe I had never connected that Jesus was specifically arguing against the death penalty.' From these experiences, she was able to identify four important things that got her to engage and listen. She notes first of all that those she was receptive to didn't assume bad intent on her part – they disagreed with her views, but also recognised that, 'I sincerely believed I was doing the right thing.' Secondly, they asked questions rather than directly criticising her, or asserting their own values. Third, they stayed calm and patient, de-escalating conversations when they hit on irreconcilable differences. Finally, she stresses, they didn't treat their own positions as self-evident but, like David, took the trouble to make the argument.

Twitter exchanges, however, weren't enough. Although online conversations opened Megan up to other perspectives, she would almost reflexively shrug these off. What fully ignited her scepticism was the way her close family was treated. First, her mother, long at the heart of the church, was nearly ostracised in a bid by a group of male 'elders' to seize control as her grandfather aged. Megan witnessed how being castigated by a church they had loved their whole lives almost broke her parents. Next, the elders targeted Megan's younger sister Grace, framing her bubbly, friendly mannerisms as deliberate sexual provocation. These admonishments, and the threat to expel both her mother and Grace if they didn't show greater obedience, were, as always, justified through scripture and the rock-solid certainty Westboro was known for. Yet for Megan, these justifications began to ring hollow. For the first time she truly began to question things, drawing on her online exchanges with outsiders as a critical resource. The accusations against Grace surfaced in the summer, and after a difficult period of soul-searching, by November she and Grace were gone.

The places Ostrom studied rarely had just one use. A forest could be a source of lumber and firewood and a place to forage and to hunt. A fishery may be balanced between commercial fishing and scientific research. In drawing on and stewarding these resources, the communities attached to them became attuned to their possibilities. They often learnt to manage these according to more general notions of sustainability that kept a range of different possibilities open. In other words, successful stewards often recognised natural commons as versatile, and tended to them as such.

When it comes to the diversity commons, versatility remains important, but its scope widens. Diversity commons are composed not only of physical resources, but also of symbolic and practical ones. All three can be flexible, capable of accommodating or generating a range of different possibilities, and this is often a product of how these resources play off one another. Creating versatility involves layering different sorts of understandings and relationships, and the different possibilities that flow from them.

In Chapter Two we visited a scrappy community café set on the Caldwell estate. The café was well known as one of the most diverse spaces in the area, attracting parents – mainly mothers – whose families hailed from all over the world. The café was set up in the hall of a church, which offered a range of other services and activities – from debt advice to fitness classes. But for Emma and Jacob – the husband-and-wife team who ran the church – the café sat at the heart of their work. In fact, Emma once told me, it was the café that made much of their other work possible.

If you visited on a typical Friday afternoon, you might be forgiven for not immediately understanding why Emma thought the café was so important. Held in a sunny, but ageing, multipurpose church hall, the café was at once modest and chaotic. Half the room was filled with folding tables and sturdy church chairs, tightly arranged to maximise space, where parents sat, chatted and ate. The other half was given over to their children, who raced around this designated play space. Not unlike The Door – which we visited in Chapter Seven – the café was a decidedly versatile space. It was where mothers met their closest friends – sometimes people they had grown up with – but it was also somewhere to encounter strangers. It was a place for swapping parenting tips or griping about husbands, but somewhere, too, to step away from being a parent for a while. It was also a space that was without purpose. In turn, all these different possibilities inflected one another. It was a space of both familiarity and encounter, belonging and uncertainty, directed support and general openness.

It was this blending of possibility at the café, Emma once explained, that made her and Jacob able to do more difficult forms of work. She illustrated this in relation to the debt advice they offered – where debt could often be a stressful issue, surrounded by stigma and, often, a sense of futility. Debt was hard to discuss, and even harder to be fully honest about. This meant that most debt-advice services struggled to attract clients and tended to dispense more generic advice that could often feel ill-fitting. In contrast, Emma once told me that 'you find once you have a connection and trust with people, they became more open to you helping with the critical problems in their life'. The café was such an important space, because it allowed for the patient, uncertain work of building trust.

There was a catch, however. Typical support services required people to self-refer, to have a clear understanding of their situation for themselves and to immediately feel comfortable sharing the messy details. This screened many people out. Emma and Jacob faced the opposite challenge: they couldn't present what they were offering as a service at all. Instead, they committed to an open-ended and uncertain process, where perhaps some café visitors would eventually come forward with concerns around debt, while others realised they needed support with education, parenting or dealing with abusive or criminal partners – while others still simply came for the friendly atmosphere. Many of these were issues Emma and Jacob could and did help with, but following this approach there was no way of knowing what would arise – no way of setting targets, or making promises to funders or partner organisations. In fact, even treating the café as a space for coaxing out issues was self-defeating. Emma emphasised that to focus on people's problems, whether by over-advertising their services, or by asking probing questions before people had become comfortable, tended to close things down. What worked, she stressed, was treating the café first and foremost as a place of gathering, and then committing to the open-ended possibilities that came out of this.

Emma explained this to me by recalling a conversation she had with the director of another social support charity, who had been impressed by their success rate, but grew increasingly frustrated as Emma explained their approach, until finally she snapped: '"We can't possibly compete with you! ... The problem is it's not a job to you lot, is it?"' Emma continued reflectively, 'I think that's huge because that's really true. I don't get paid. I get a living stipend that allows me to be here and do what I do, but that's very different, isn't it?' Paradoxically, by taking an open-ended approach and not focusing on chasing specific goals, she and Jacob were better able to produce the sorts of outcomes that were desirable to more narrowly focused, tight-fisted organisations.

When Megan and Grace fled the Westboro Baptist Church, they left feeling utterly shattered. If it was the abject treatment of those they cared about that drove them out, then it was the care shown by others that allowed them to rebuild a life. After they left, the sisters soon ended up in a bed and breakfast in

Deadwood, South Dakota. Megan and Grace's time in Deadwood was marked by the care and understanding shown to them by relative strangers – from Cora, a bartender at a local casino who escaped a similarly controlling, highly spiritual mother, to Laura and Dustin, who owned the bed and breakfast, and who not only took Megan and Grace in for an extended period, but who would sit with them, talk through their questions and doubts. Unusually, Megan's online interactions were marked by a similar sort of care and commitment – something reflected in the lessons she outlines. David not only brushed over her past – the wielding of 'God hates Jews' signs – and talked through Megan's doubts, but invited her to Los Angeles, where an Orthodox Jewish rabbi and his wife took them in, receiving them with kindness and warmth. In New York, Megan met up with two gay men she had sparred with online, who helped her talk through the pain of breaking from your family. The gentlest, perhaps most effective support, however, came from a tall, quiet man hailing from Norway, who Megan initially knew only as C.G. Through his sincerely curious questioning, his firmly humane but demurring disagreement, and his persistent recognition of everything that made her human, C.G., or Chad, eventually became her husband.

Care has tremendous power to transform lives. The Dutch sociologist and philosopher Annemarie Mol defines it as 'persistent tinkering in a world full of complex ambivalence and shifting tensions'. For Mol, care is a form of understanding and acting that commits to meeting people where they are – resisting pregiven solutions in favour of close, sensitive attention to changeable personal circumstances. Care cuts through abstract categories to try to address us in terms of our own sense of self and belonging. With Megan, it was others taking her as she was that allowed her to find a different sense of self. Today, Megan works as an activist and educator, campaigning to fight divisiveness. Her capacity to do so relies on her ability to stay with the trouble of her past. Megan writes: 'I couldn't allow bitterness to steal the beauty in my family, or love to conceal the destructiveness in it. I wouldn't rewrite history. I would hold the whole messy truth of it to myself all at once.' Yet for Megan, the forms of care that made this possible were incidental – made possible by the bravery and kindness of others. Versatility represents a way for institutions, rather than individuals, to cultivate relations of care. When institutions, such as the Caldwell community café, allow people to use them on their own terms, they create a space where people feel capable of being open. In turn, by holding together different possibilities – debt advice and parenting classes, friendship and support – they allow people to explore these possibilities in relation to their sense of who they are.

Just as those who reached out to Megan when she was still in the Church displayed courage, there is courage in building versatile institutions. In fact, there is something radical about it. Versatility requires holding open plural possibilities without knowing in advance which of these will be useful. Versatile institutions therefore resist straightforward valuation. It can be hard to see what their point is; they can look chaotic. It is no surprise, then, that the institutions that best embodied this in Kilburn often struggled to attract enough funding or revenue to remain in operation. Versatility offers a challenge to the logic of state and market, where value is most often determined in relation to clear-cut categories. Typically, when purchasing goods, we are told in advance what we are getting, and how much it will cost. The value of versatility cannot be established in advance – it emerges over time. Yet it's an error to overlook this value or categorise it as wasteful. As Emma and Jacob show, it's a commitment to openness that allows organisations to enact change. In fact, by folding recognition and belonging with practical support, versatile organisations enact *deeper* forms of change.

The possibilities for community, care and connection are rarely apparent in advance. Committing to them requires courage and entails risk. In Chicago, the psychologists Nicholas Epley and Juliana Schroeder conducted an experiment with the help of commuters. They asked some of their volunteers to strike up a conversation with strangers on public transport, others to avoid interaction and a third group to 'commute as normal' (which tended towards avoiding interaction). People predicted they would have a more positive experience when left to themselves, but, in fact, those who were forced to connect reported more positive experiences.[20] In the still-emerging aftermath of the Covid-19 pandemic, while some are anxious to return to offices and public streets, others are relishing the prospect of greater solitude. In the UK and US, the pandemic saw an exodus from cities to the suburbs and countryside, and an increase in remote working that is unlikely to be wholly reversed.[21] These shifts are taking place in a context where public space and opportunities for connection are rapidly vanishing. In the UK, for instance, over the past decade, over a quarter of all libraries have either been closed or are run by volunteers. Spaces such as youth centres are increasingly outsourced to private management, leading to restricted opening hours and services that prioritise profitability. Church halls are turned into nightclubs, community centres into flats. Internationally, other countries face similar challenges. In the US, where cars have long dominated city planning, the vast majority of Americans live in neighbourhoods where it is not possible to access most amenities or public spaces by walking.[22] In China's fast-growing megacities, many 'public' spaces are designed within the courtyards of building complexes or atop high buildings, open only to those with the right keys. These transformations are often seen as desirable – championed by city planners and citizens alike. Yet being cut off from others does not seem to make city dwellers happy.[23] Like the participants in Epley and Schroeder's Chicago study, it seems as if we mistake familiarity for preference when it comes to our private lives. In turn, when faced with challenges in living with others, our growing tendency is to retreat into private space, rather than trying to cultivate new ways of inter-acting in public.

❋

The commons Ostrom studied were collectively stewarded, but they were not open to just anyone. Communities sustained these resources through carefully established, collectively nego-tiated rules and conventions. Sustainable, inclusive commons, Ostrom stressed, were those with clear boundaries governing access and management.

An insistence on boundaries may seem counterintuitive. Yet the importance of boundaries emerges in relation to how the potential of commons unfolds over time. As we have seen, joint commitments emerge gradually. The same is true of the value drawn from commons, where the 'persistent tinkering' of everyday care enables people to figure out what they need and how to support one another. But if commitment and value only emerge slowly, what gets people to engage in the first place?

Boundaries play their first crucial role here. In dividing up the world, in specifying who belongs where, and on what terms, boundaries make things legible. Back at the Caldwell's community café, despite the general diversity of its patrons, it was dominated almost exclusively by women. A few weeks into volunteering at the café, Jenny – part of the tight-knit squad of British, European and Caribbean women, who always managed to grab the corner table – invited me to join her and her friends for lunch. When talk turned to parenting, and I admitted to not having children myself, a game quickly developed. Trading bemused glances, or fixing me with mock-serious looks, Jenny and her friends bounced between topics – the trauma of child-birth, nappy mishaps, sex, attractive men and 'useless' husbands – to see if they could make me squirm. In the following weeks,

I witnessed other male visitors encounter similar teasing. It was clear that regulars treated the café as a mothers' space. Yet this bounding also made the café a space where mothers could presume shared understanding – whether in venting about family quarrels, parental exhaustion or troubles with in-laws. In doing so, it not only closed things down, but opened them up.

Among Jenny's circle of friends was Klara. Klara was German and her husband Congolese. They had been raised with traditional views of marriage and gender roles. When their son was born, Klara decided to stay at home to take care of him. Now that he had started school, Klara was feeling restless and unfulfilled. She was anxious, however – unsure how to approach getting a job. Nor was she sure how to broach the topic with her husband, who she worried might be resistant. At the heart of Klara's anxieties was a lingering feeling that going back to work – even just *wanting* to go back to work – made her a bad mother, and perhaps a bad wife as well. She worried that working would contravene her own understanding of motherhood, and the tacit agreements around family roles on which her marriage had been built. When Klara would raise these anxieties, others responded with fragments of their own experience: Jenny would crack exasperated jokes about the absurdity of navigating mixed cultural traditions. Others would talk about overbearing relatives, struggles to find a job, or about the nervousness they felt sending their children off to school. These different contributions evoked different visions of family life, grounded in different cultural traditions. Some were happy as staunch traditionalists, others voiced different forms of restlessness. Yet the shared assumption that everyone was, in the end, talking about the same thing, enabled Klara to reassemble her understanding of motherhood over time, by borrowing bits and pieces from friends and acquaintances. Within a few months, Klara had found a way to discuss her ambitions and anxieties with her husband, and had begun to apply for jobs.

Boundaries played an important role in orienting the mothers towards each other. If, to some extent, the sorts of understandings that emerge in close, face-to-face encounters are always caught up in the flow of life, continually emerging, continually being rewritten, boundaries stand in for the possibility of resolution. Many of the places and people we've visited in this book managed to hold together different understandings of a common project – different relationships to Islam, different visions of the public realm, different understandings of the environment – by relying on some form of boundary-marking. When the world's plurality pulls in different directions, boundaries provide a framework for drawing differences together. It's this drawing together that underwrites more substantive transformations – the slow reworking of values and identities demonstrated by Klara, visitors to the Caldwell's creative hub or the young Muslims who frequent The Door. Boundaries weave forms of difference and fluidity together into ethical and political projects across time.

Boundaries are important, but they need not be fixed. Rather, boundaries themselves can be subject to processes of collective exploration and reworking. When Emma and Jacob first started running the church centre where the Caldwell's community café was based, they were focused on creating a primarily Christian space. The couple, however, struggled to engage the local community until their children were born. This prompted them to approach the centre less as a strictly religious space, and more as a resource for building the sort of community they wanted their children to grow up in. Offering everything from debt advice to elderly fitness classes enabled Emma and Jacob to revitalise the centre. It also transformed their sense of faith. They came to see connecting to and supporting those around them as crucial expressions of faith, above and beyond the work of proselytising or serving a community of believers. For them, it became important to create and sustain community in its own right.

Boundaries, suggests the anthropologist Vered Amit, are 'good to think with'.[24] They need not be taken as permanent, but are useful for getting people to think they're playing the same game. Any one form of closure, though, will inevitably include some over others. This tension means that there is no universal template for community, no one way to be together. Perhaps, also, there is a fundamental limit on the scope of difference any one community can accommodate within a given moment. The need for boundaries, then, points to the need to foster a wide range of community resources – to not content ourselves with singular visions of togetherness, but to let a thousand flowers bloom.

※

For critics alive to its historical failings and struggles, liberal universalism is sometimes imagined as an unfinished project.[25] Past political orders were marked by their limits and exclusions but it's still possible to learn from them. We can develop a more inclusive vision of humanity upon which new political orders might be founded. In some cases, the quest to overcome these limits has led to some especially creative propositions. The influential British philosopher Paul Gilroy, for instance, has called for a 'planetary humanism' that breaks with the idea of a world divided into races, cultures or nations, by simply taking humanity to encompass the whole of the globe, lacking any essential form.[26] Yet, even if it were one day possible to reach these utopian horizons, dilemmas of difference remain. Without a fixed definition of humanity, it becomes difficult, if not impossible, to publicly adjudicate injustices. If humanity is *not* defined by some core equivalence – if, for instance, we dispense with standards of human rationality, or dignity – then how are we to say what qualifies as unreasonable or unjust? How are we supposed to balance rights and duties, punishment and redress, state intervention and forms of autonomy, without a common set of weights and measures?[27] If we *do* define humanity according to certain standards, then the anthropological challenge remains: these standards are culturally specific. They will always have an outside.

This dilemma has created a constant stumbling block for those fighting for a fairer society. One result is that an increasingly deeper wedge has been driven between politics and everyday life, and between liberal and republican traditions. The quest for truly universal justice, truly universal inclusion, has led social movements and politicians towards an abstract, top-down vision of humanity. Today, however, these universal horizons have come to be embraced not only by projects vying for equality, but by political actors of all stripes – making politics an imposing, oppositional affair, marked by clashes between different universal visions.

Meanwhile, as the formal institutions of republican politics have crumbled, we have seen the proliferation of a sort of fragmented, private republicanism. Here, citizens insist on the primacy of personal, negotiated understandings of truth and justice, grounded in everyday worlds and relations, but closed off to those beyond them. These private convictions are often asserted as truths that others cannot legitimately challenge, no matter what they say. They are used to make public claims, without accepting public terms of adjudication.

This growing gulf can be seen as a process of radicalisation of both the liberal and civic republican traditions, as each redefines itself in increasingly stark opposition to the other. Opposed to one another, both traditions provide ways of seeing difference as tied to conflict, as something that depletes us. The world is full of different cosmos: we can think of the Inuit understanding that all things have spirits and moral standing; Orthodox Jewish laws governing when men and women ought not to mix; New Age conspiracy theories; or Yoruba notions of predetermined fate. For a liberalism that insists on having the final word on the nature of humanity, such claims to inhabiting a different world are suspect. They threaten the singular order of the universe that underpins public politics. Ultimately, liberalism has an impulse to eliminate such differences. Insofar as diverse cultures and ways of knowing have something to say about the nature of humankind or our common world, they remain a public threat and – at best – need to be cut down to size, reduced from truth or knowledge to private 'belief', 'opinion' or 'preference'.

Meanwhile, for a republicanism that exclusively looks inwards for the source of political and ethical truth, the only world it becomes possible to inhabit is one marked by near-constant conflict. The truth is under threat from countless alternatives. Historically, civic republicanism has struggled to define the scope of the political community, when its vision of politics relies on face-to-face connection and negotiation. Today, this has led to a deep fragmentation where we have come to occupy different social, cultural and political worlds, each of which considers itself a self-contained source of moral authority.

Even within Western democratic states, and within the confines and challenges of our present moment, this state of tension is not the only way. As we have seen, the liberal and civic republican traditions do not exhaust our capacities to connect – although they may draw on and channel them in distinct ways. More importantly, it's clear that these traditions have never been singular, and that they can be built on in different ways. Across the democratic world, in places such as Kilburn, people have been engaged in experiments in living. This everyday inventiveness allows us to stay with the potential and the trouble of our democratic societies, to rework them from within.

In attempting to hold the liberal and republican traditions in tension, then, there is one final principle from Elinor Ostrom that can set us on our way. Ostrom recognised the importance of bounded, committed communities but also acknowledged that not all issues can be addressed at a local scale. She proposed a system of 'nested' commons, blending face-to-face and representation-based politics. Ostrom's proposal would marry a high level of local autonomy with layered structures for oversight, negotiation and coordination. Local communities would send delegates to wider assemblies. These wider assemblies would also operate according to the principles of the commons – treating resource management as a collective, negotiated affair. Yet delegates within these gatherings must also work to *represent* their original communities, distilling their messy concerns and complex practices into clearer positions that can be easily communicated. Ostrom's proposal is effectively one for *much more* democracy – democracy wherever common interests are at stake.

This principle of nesting serves as a bottom-up counterpart to the principle of translation explored in the previous chapter. If translation enables collective stories to be filtered across different communities, and rewritten in the language of their everyday affairs and concerns, nesting makes the everyday negotiation of personal relationships and commitments dependent, in part, on how these join up with wider political concerns. In practice, applied to the diversity commons, this would mean creating bodies that work to mediate disputes, negotiate differences and allocate resources, composed of locally accountable community representatives. It would involve approaching community not as a mosaic of independent groups, but as an interwoven tapestry.

❊

Only a few months after I had arrived in Kilburn, when I still felt out of my depth – spending my days running between community groups, dizzy from the evident diversity of the neighbourhood, and unsure of how to fit it all together – I noticed something odd. Prior to moving to Kilburn, a friend had taught me an old anthropological research trick: at the end of every conversation, try to ask for an introduction to someone else. Although it sometimes felt uncomfortable, I tried to make a habit of doing so. It wasn't long, however, before others started doing this back – responding by asking me for suggestions of my own. Environmental activists wanted to see if they were overlooking potential allies, parent groups wanted tips on who to invite to their next event and residents' associations wanted support in confronting the council over the neglected public realm.

I think back to the first time I visited Kilburn, to attend the 'pop-up university' where architects and academics spoke about all neighbourhoods being defined by distinctive patterns and a particular character. As I got to know the area better, my sense that this statement didn't quite fit this super-diverse corner of London never quite left me. I don't think there ever was a singular pattern. Yet seeing the local community in action, learning from those who sought to make the neighbourhood their own and to open it up to others, I'm not convinced there needs to be one. Kilburn took shape, not through a single story, nor as an uncontainable jumble of difference, but through strands of connection, which wove diverse lives together – and allowed them to be rewoven, anew.

NOTES

Chapter One: Journeys

1   This challenge comes from Stuart Hall, 'Culture, Community, Nation', 1993, p. 361 – 'The capacity to live with difference is, in my view, the coming question of the 21st century' – who seems to be riffing off W. E. B. Du Bois's own era-defining statement that 'the problem of the twentieth century is the problem of the colour line'. (First voiced at a speech to the First Pan-African Conference in London in July 1900, and then reiterated in his 1903 book *The Souls of Black Folk*.) The historical transformations that inform the differences between these two statements – marked by both continuity and change – provide the basic frame for this book.

2   Foa et al., 'The Global Satisfaction with Democracy Report 2020', 2020.

3   See Pildes, 'Romanticizing Democracy', 2015; Rooduijn et al., 'Expressing or Fuelling Discontent?', 2016; Pellikaan et al., 'The Centre Does Not Hold', 2016; Elchardus and Spruyt, 'Populism, Persistent Republicanism and Declinism', 2014.

4   For a useful framing of this issue, see Harsin, 'Regimes of Posttruth', 2015. To be clear, evidence suggests that the majority of news consumers (online as well as off) tend to rely on an overlapping set of mainstream sources (Fletcher and Nielsen, 'Are News Audiences Increasingly Fragmented?', 2017; Mukerjee et al., 'Networks of Audience Overlap', 2018) and that fragmentation is likely to characterise only a small fringe, who may be disproportionately vocal or politically active (Nelson and Taneja, 'The Small, Disloyal Fake News Audience', 2018; Tewksbury and Riles, 'Polarization as a Function of Citizen Predispositions', 2015). Gaps in *trust* (as opposed to consumption), however, may

be more significant, with the greatest trust associated with the most frequently consumed media, particularly for committed partisans (Kantar Media, 'Brand and Trust in a Fragmented News Environment', 2017; Suiter and Fletcher, 'Polarization and Partisanship', 2020), while there is evidence of an overall erosion of trust in mainstream media, independent of polarisation – i.e. people are simply becoming more uncertain overall (Guess et al., 'The Consequences of Online Partisan Media', 2021) – and an increasingly polarised or sensationalised tone to both mainstream and non-mainstream reporting (Van Aelst et al., 'Political Communication in a High-Choice Media Environment', 2017).

5   In the UK, for instance, a recently released report on racial inequality, commissioned by the government following the 2020 Black Lives Matter protests, claimed there was 'no evidence of systemic or institutional racism' in the UK (Sewell, 'Commission on Race and Ethnic Disparities', 2021, p. 77). The report was widely criticised for coming to this conclusion by arguing that other factors, such as geography, poverty and familial structure were better predictors of disadvantage – when in fact all of these factors have been shown to be strongly influenced by ethnic background. In effect, it shifted the terms of reference to define away racism.

6   Smith, *NW*, 2012, pp. 40–1.

7   Hickman et al., *Migration and Social Cohesion in the UK*, 2012.

8   Vertovec, 'Super-Diversity and its Implications', 2007.

9   In the 2011 Census, 31 per cent of the Kilburn population was recorded as 'White British'. The next largest group, at 18 per cent, are the European migrants of various nationalities who get lumped together as 'Other White'. In third place are black Africans, at 11 per cent, while the rest of Kilburn is made up of a mix of fifteen other groups. London is already one of the world's most diverse cities and Kilburn is even more diverse than London both in terms of ethnic and language groups. (Here diversity is understood in terms of the number of different groups present alongside their relative share of the population.)

10 Fryer, *Staying Power*, 1984, p. 372.

11 Specifically, the British Nationality Act 1981 permits this power insofar as there is a reasonable expectation that the deprivation of

British citizenship would not then render the person stateless. In its actual application and in case law, this has been established not to require the person in question to actually hold another passport, but simply to be considered potentially eligible for citizenship elsewhere. Thus, while the law does not explicitly single out those of migrant backgrounds, its provisions only hold for such people.

12 Massey, *A Global Sense of Place*, 1991, p. 28.

13 Willcox, *International Migrations*, 1929.

14 Colonial authorities did not always keep records of migration between colonial territories, making non-European mobility in this era harder to assess.

15 Meredith, *The Fortunes of Africa*, 2014.

16 Czaika and de Haas, 'The Globalization of Migration', 2014.

17 Ibid.; Castles et al., *The Age of Migration*, 2014; Flahaux and de Haas, 'African migration', 2016.

18 Frey, *Diversity Explosion*, 2014.

19 Lomax et al., 'What the UK Population Will Look Like', 2019.

20 See various examples from: Meissner and Vertovec, 'Comparing Superdiversity', 2015; Scholten et al., *Coming to Terms with Superdiversity*, 2018; Acosta-García and Martínez-Ortiz, 'Mexico Through a Superdiversity Lens', 2015. The data and visualisations at superdiv.mmg.mpg.de allow for an in-depth exploration of this trend across data from Canada, Australia and New Zealand.

21 Wallman, *Eight London Households*, 1984; Dürrschmidt, *Everyday Lives in the Global City*, 2013.

22 Li et al., 'Does Ethnic Diversity Affect Well-Being?', 2021; Jonsson and Demireva, 'Does the Ethno-Religious Diversity of a Neighbourhood Affect the Perceived Health of its Residents?', 2018.

23 See reviews in Portes and Vickstrom, 'Diversity, Social Capital, and Cohesion', 2011; and Dinesen et al., 'Ethnic Diversity and Social Trust', 2020 – both of which survey a range of studies, noting that a minority of studies seem to find the opposite effect but that there is a general overall tendency towards negative relationships between diversity and trust/participation.

24 See Habyarimana et al., *Coethnicity*, 2009; Koopmans and Veit, 'Cooperation in Ethnically Diverse Neighborhoods', 2013; Gereke

et al., 'Ethnic Diversity, Poverty and Social Trust in Germany', 2018; Koning, *Immigration and the Politics of Welfare Exclusion*, 2019.

25 Pickett and Wilkinson, 'Income Inequality and Health', 2015. See also note 4, esp. Peter Van Aelst et al.

26 Wilkes and Wu, 'Ethnicity, Democracy, Trust', 2018.

27 Norris et al., 'The Paranoid Style of American Elections', 2019; Myers and Levy, 'Racial Population Projections', 2018.

28 Blinder and Richards, 'UK Public Opinion Toward Immigration', 2020.

29 Clarke et al., *Brexit*, 2017; Arnorsson and Zoega, 'On the Causes of Brexit', 2018.

30 E.g. Hatton, 'Public Opinion on Immigration in Europe', 2017; Ruedin, 'Attitudes to Immigrants in South Africa', 2019.

31 See note 23, especially Dinesen et al.

32 Main, 'We Knew Platypuses were Incredible', 2020; Buehler, 'Flying Squirrels Secretly Glow Pink', 2019; Cronin and Bok, 'Photoreception and Vision in the Ultraviolet', 2016.

33 Bateson, *Steps to an Ecology of Mind*, 1972.

34 See Regier and Kay, 'Language, Thought, and Color', 2009; Davidoff et al., 'Colour Categories in a Stone-Age Tribe', 1999; Roberson et al., 'Color categories', 2005.

35 Shore, *Culture in Mind*, 1998 p. 3.

36 Ibid.; Keane, *Ethical Life*, 2015.

37 Carsten, 'The Substance of Kinship', 1995. Carsten describes Malay notions of kinship as a matter of degree rather than kind. Birth creates the strongest relation, followed by breastfeeding, then by the feeding of rice from a family hearth. At the same time, the strength of birth-based kinship can diminish if children are not breastfed or fed at the family hearth.

38 Blackless et al., 'How Sexually Dimorphic Are We?', 2000.

39 Pison and D'Addato, 'Frequency of Twin Births', 2012. Note, the data for this and Blackless et al., 2000 cover similar time periods, allowing for comparison.

40 Davies, *Gender Diversity in Indonesia*, 2010; Peletz, 'Transgenderism and Gender Pluralism in Southeast Asia', 2006.

41 Vowel, *Indigenous Writes*, 2016.

42 Renne and Bastian, 'Reviewing Twinship in Africa', 2001.

43 Smith et al., 'A Time of Revolution?', 2016.
44 Williamson, *Sprawl, Justice, and Citizenship*, 2010.
45 Allen, 'A Decade of Immigration in the British Press', 2016.
46 See Chapter Eight, note 17.

Chapter Two: Near and Far
1   Carrey, *William Golding*, 2012, p. 82.
2   Ibid., p. 127.
3   Golding and Baker, 'An Interview with William Golding', 1982.
4   Weidman, 'Do Humans Really Have a Killer Instinct?', 2020.
5   Powell, *Freedom and Reality*, 1969. Powell estimated that by the millennium, there would be 5–7 million people in Britain from immigrant backgrounds. In the 2001 census, 4.9 million people were recorded as foreign born. The children of immigrants were not counted as such, meaning that Powell's estimate was likely correct, or perhaps even low.
6   Deveney, *Callaghan's Journey*, 2010, p. 32.
7   I borrow this name from Zadie Smith. My research in Kilburn involved an agreement to anonymise all names, as well as, in some instances, to disguise other potentially identifying details. As such, identifying locations have also been changed in important cases, including this one. In Smith's novel *NW*, she likewise writes of the 'Caldwell' estate, inserting the fictional estate into the otherwise true-to-life geography of Kilburn in her novel.
8   Dinesen et al., 2020; Kaufmann and Harris, 'White Flight', 2015.
9   Dunbar, 'Neocortex Size as a Constraint on Group Size in Primates', 1992; Dunbar, 'Coevolution of Neocortical Size', 1993; Dunbar, 'The Social Brain Hypothesis', 1998.
10 Lamm and Majdandžić, 'The role of Shared Neural Activations', 2015; Firth and Firth, 'Mechanisms of Social Cognition', 2012; Decety and Jackson, 'The Functional Architecture of Human Empathy', 2004.
11 Meltzof, '"Like me"', 2007; Reddy, 'On Being the Object of Attention', 2003; Zeedyk, 'From Intersubjectivity to Subjectivity', 2006.
12 Csibra and Gergely, 'Social Learning and Social Cognition', 2006;

Flom and Johnson, 'The Effects of Adults' Affective Expression', 2011.

13 Soussignan et al., 'Mimicking Emotions', 2018.

14 Broesch et al. 'Cultural Variations in Children's Mirror Self-Recognition', 2011; Keller et al., 'Parenting Styles and the Development of the Categorical Self', 2005; Ross et al., 'Cultural Differences in Self-Recognition', 2017.

15 Bayliss and Tipper, 'Predictive Gaze Cues and Personality Judgments', 2006; Bayliss et al., 'Gaze Cuing and Affective Judgments', 2006.

16 Lyons et al., 'The Scope and Limits of Overimitation', 2011; Nicola McGuigan et al., 'From Over-Imitation to Super-Copying', 2011; Horner and Whiten, 'Causal Knowledge and Imitation/Emulation Switching', 2005.

17 Keupp et al., 'Why Do Children Overimitate?', 2013; Hoehl et al., 'Over-imitation', 2019.

18 Firth and Firth, 2012.

19 Willerslev, *Soul Hunters*, 2007; Willerslev, 'Not Animal, Not Not Animal', 2004.

20 There's a certain resonance with what psychologists have termed 'contact theory' here – the well-evidenced finding that contact with those marked as different can improve attitudes and trust towards the groups they are seen as representing (see Hewstone and Swart, 'Fifty-odd Years Of Inter-Group Contact', 2011, and Pettigrew and Tropp, 'A Meta-Analytic Test of Intergroup Contact Theory', 2006, for overviews). However, an understanding of the effects of contact on everyday behaviour beyond reported attitudes is still lacking. As Gill Valentine ('Living with Difference', 2008) notes, what matters more are not simply generic attitudes, but the actual patterns of everyday relations that take hold – which are likely to reflect significantly more complexity than reported attitudes. The forms of friendship built at the café, for instance, were not without their tensions or moments of misunderstanding or friction created by different cultural backgrounds, and did not necessarily reflect a sense that differences simply did not matter, but friendship often entailed a willingness to work through or bracket forms of tension.

21 Mitchell, *The Kaleka Dance*, 1956.

22 Behrends et al., 'Moving In and Out of Synchrony', 2012; McGarry, 'Mirroring in Dance/Movement Therapy', 2011.

23 Perry, 'The View from the Boys', 2014; Perry, *The Lost Boys*, 2018. In other work (*Behind the Shock Machine*, 2013) Perry reaches similar conclusions regarding Stanley Milgram's famous experiments where he asked volunteers to administer electric shocks to a stranger. Milgram's experiment was reportedly a response to witnessing the trial of Adolf Eichmann, the chief architect of the Holocaust, where Eichmann claimed to be merely following orders. Milgram framed his study as an investigation into the human tendency to obey authority. Comparing different versions of Milgram's experiment, Perry found a relationship between how sincerely volunteers believed themselves to be administering shocks to a real person, and their tendency to disobey instructions. She also documented volunteers talking about how aggressively they were pushed to obey – challenging Milgram's claim that what was being measured was obedience (as opposed to coercion).

24 Weathers et al., 'Differences in the Communication of Affect', 2002; Soto and Levenson, 'Emotion Recognition Across Cultures', 2009; Beaupré and Hess, 'Cross-Cultural Emotion Recognition', 2005; Elfenbein and Ambady, 'On the Universality and Cultural Specificity of Emotion Recognition', 2002.

25 Thibault et al., 'The Effect Of Group-Identification on Emotion Recognition', 2006; see also Friesen et al., 'Perceiving Happiness in an Intergroup Context', 2019.

26 Avenanti et al., 'Racial Bias Reduces Empathic Sensorimotor Resonance with Other-Race Pain', 2010; see Chiao and Mathur, 'Intergroup Empathy', 2010, for an overview of similar studies.

27 Mazzarella, 'The Anthropology of Populism', 2019, p. 53.

28 Bloom, *Against Empathy*, 2017.

29 Tomasello et al., 'Two Key Steps in the Evolution of Human Cooperation', 2012.

30 Chiao and Mathur, 2010; Richeson et al., 'African Americans' Implicit Racial Attitudes', 2005; Richeson and Trawalter, 'Why Do Interracial Interactions Impair Executive Function?', 2005.

31 Schläpfer et al., 'The Scaling of Human Interactions', 2014. The population figures I use are from the time of the study.

32 A strand of recent work within social science has argued for a
    view of cognition where culture in general, and representations
    in particular, play a lesser role (i.e. non-representational theory).
    Psychologically informed anthropology has consistently resisted
    this conclusion. Recent work, for instance, reveals the ways in
    which different theories of mind – of how humans understand
    themselves and one another – channel experience, emotion and
    understanding in widely varied ways (see Luhrmann, 'Mind and
    Spirit', 2020). Partly, as Webb Keane ('Signs Are Not the Garb of
    Meaning', 2005) suggests, this emphasis on non-representational
    thinking comes from a narrow understanding of representation,
    confined to the symbolic dimension of language, and excluding the
    material world. Here, I am trying to walk a fine line. I do not aim
    to present symbolic and empathic reasoning as ways of thinking
    that can be wholly separated from one another, but I do suggest
    that particular thought processes may be *more* empathic or *more*
    symbolic than others. The quality of symbolic reasoning becoming
    more symbolic, I understand as abstraction – which can be taken as
    my key axis of comparison.

33 Rappaport, *Ritual and Religion in the Making of Humanity*, 1999, p. 8.

34 Oatley, 'Worlds of the possible', 2013.

35 Dunbar, 'The Social Brain', 2003; Dunbar, *The Human Story*, 2004.

36 Especially when it comes to media such as oral epics, visual art and
    so on, but in general for communication, symbolic representation
    is rarely the only thing going on. In linguistic terms, forms of
    communication also frequently involve iconic qualities and
    indexical gestures. Yet what I am pointing to here is the capacity
    of media, of any form, to prompt reflection on the nature of
    referential meaning – which necessarily operates in a symbolic
    register. (Or, put differently, the *ideas* of iconicity and indexicality
    themselves operate symbolically.)

37 Mithen, *The Prehistory of the Mind*, 1996; Olson, 'Literacy and the
    Languages of Rationality', 2013. Olson focuses on literacy but
    emphasises that this does not mean that non-literate people do
    not understand that words have (variable) meanings, but rather
    that 'reading and literacy involve a metalinguistic knowledge of
    phonemes, words and sentences, that is, knowledge about the

words as countable objects with definitions extracted over contexts of use with relations of synonymy, antonymy and hyponymy among them.' (p. 434) These forms of knowledge can be cultivated and transmitted by other means, beyond writing.

38 Hockett, *The Origin of Speech*, 1982, p. 6.

39 Bateson, 1972.

40 Laugrand and Oosten, *Hunters, Predators and Prey*, 2014.

41 Ravin and Leacock, 'Polysemy: An Overview', 2000.

42 Krupnik and Müller-Wille, 'Franz Boas and Inuktitut Terminology for Ice and Snow', 2010. One issue in determining the truth of this claim has been that many Inuit dialects are polysynthetic, allowing words to be extensively modified by appending other words as suffixes – to the point where single words can communicate the same meaning as a whole English sentence. Krupnik and Müller-Wille make a point of only looking at base words, and conclude Boas likely did the same in making his initial claim.

43 Not in unqualified ways – see Keen, *Empathy and the Novel*, 2007; Bal and Veltkamp, 'How Does Fiction Reading Influence Empathy?', 2013; Panero et al., 'Does Reading a Single Passage of Literary Fiction Really Improve Theory of Mind?', 2016.

44 Västfjäll et al., 'Compassion Fade', 2014; Galesic and Garcia-Retamero, 'The Risks We Dread', 2012. Galesic and Garcia-Retamero argue explicitly that when it comes to one's own community, perception of risk or loss does increase in line with the number of people affected, up to a level of around the 'average' community, but then do not increase proportionally or at all at larger scales.

Chapter Three: Us and Them

1 The term 'double bind' is from anthropologist Gregory Bateson's 1973 book *Steps to an Ecology of Mind*, where he uses the term to describe contradictory pressures generated by the same process. John Nagle (*Multiculturalism's Double Bind*, 2008) has used this term to demonstrate the pressure faced by Western minorities who are included within multicultural states only on the basis of their difference, and are thus, on the one hand, expected to integrate and build cross-cultural connections, and on the other hand

are only included by others on the basis of ascribed difference. Other scholars describe similar tensions, often emphasising how understandings of enduring or innate difference are more often imposed from outside groups, alongside demands to integrate (Hage, *White Nation*, 1999; Nayak, 'Race, Religion and British Multiculturalism', 2012).

2   Griffiths, 'Fragmentation and Consolidation', 2000; Griffiths, *Somali and Kurdish Refugees in London*, 2002; Hopkins, 'Somali Community Organizations in London and Toronto', 2006.

3   Sharp, 'Tribe', 2003. Janet Carsten's *After Kinship* (2004) likewise characterises this as the preoccupying concern of mid-century British social anthropology. The key work which generalised the descent-based seminary lineage system as a model for all non-state societies was Meyer Fortes's and Edward Evan Evans-Pritchard's *African Political Systems* (2006 [originally 1940]). This approach gave way to a debate between 'descent'-based approaches to kinship – characterised by authors such as Evans-Pritchard, Radcliffe-Brown and Fortes, focused on African case studies, and 'alliance'-based approaches, characterised by the work of Claude Levi-Strauss, which focused on the exchange of women in marriage, and the symbolic and social alliances forged by such exchange. The Somali case held interest within this debate into the 1990s, partly due to the prominent role given both to the reckoning of ancestral descent and to the forging of new alliances through marriage – though prominent accounts, until recently, tended to subordinate the latter to the former (see Lewis, *Blood and Bone*, 1994; and Lewis, *Understanding Somalia and Somaliland*, 2008, where he draws on this conception of clan in accounting for the Somali civil war).

4   These latter two groups are sometimes counted together.

5   Mukhtar, 'Islam in Somali History', 1995; Cassanelli, 'Speculations on the Historical Origins of the 'Total Somali Genealogy', 2010.

6   Lewis, *Blood and Bone*, 1998, p. 233.

7   Barth, *Ethnic Groups and Boundaries*, 1969.

8   Horowitz, *Ethnic Identity*, 1975.

9   Ibid.

10 Powell, 1969, p. 237.

11 Many years later, Lila Abu-Lughod (*Writing Against Culture*, 1991,

p. 137) would highlight the same persistent tendency, remarking that '"culture" operates in anthropological discourse to enforce separations that inevitably carry a sense of hierarchy'.

12 Quoted in Krieger, *The Kosovo Conflict*, 2001, p. 10.

13 Tone, *Being Muslim the Bosnian Way*, 1995; Gellner, *Nations and Nationalism*, 2008; Denich, 'Dismembering Yugoslavia', 1994; Halpern and Kideckel, *Neighbors at War*, 2000.

14 Greenberg, *Language and Identity in the Balkans*, 2004. As Greenberg notes, whether Serbian, Bosnian and Croatian can 'originally' be thought of as one language or three is a matter of ongoing debate, which turns in part on different understandings of what defines a common language. Taking a more nuanced approach, Greenberg highlights active attempts to create and support language unification or mutual intelligibility in the 1800s and the Communist era, as well as the tensions within such efforts and the resistance to them, and likewise traces active attempts to create distinctiveness in the 1990s.

15 Bailyn, 'To What Degree Are Croatian and Serbian the Same Language?', 2010.

16 Mukhtar, 1994, p. 14.

17 Mohamed, 'Kinship and Contract in Somali Politics', 2007; Cassanelli, 2010; Kusow, 'The Somali Origin: Myth or Reality?', 1995.

18 This is especially the case in disciplines and approaches influenced by postmodern and deconstructionist approaches (see, Cahoone, *Introduction*, 2003). In some cases, this notion that an opposition to otherness is fundamentally constitutive of the self is even presented as disciplinary common sense. For instance, in the *International Encyclopedia of Human Geography*, Jean-François Staszak (2008, p. 44) writes: 'The ethnocentric bias that creates otherness is doubtlessly an anthropological constant. All groups tend to value themselves and distinguish themselves from Others whom they devalue.' However, there is also plenty of subtle and overt variation in how scholars have conceived otherness and its relation to the self (as more or less absolute, more or less constitutive, more or less opposed and so on). My intention here is

not to paint a homogenous picture, but to highlight one prominent strand of thinking.

19 Bird-David, *Us, Relatives*, 2017, p. 201.

20 Berger, *And Our Faces, My Heart, Brief as Photos*, 1984.

21 In defining belonging in this way (including, later, attending to its exclusions and the capacity to evoke a sense of wholeness), I most closely follow Floya Anthias ('Thinking Through the Lens of Translocational Positionality', 2008; 'Belongings in a Globalising and Unequal World', 2006).

22 Coleman, *The Art of Work*, 1988.

23 Ibid., p. 37.

24 Over, 'The Origins of Belonging', 2016.

25 Here I intend a gentle challenge to the social-psychological model of belonging (e.g. in Over, 2016), to incorporate an understanding of positive connections not just to people but instead to recognise that culture, language and materiality are inextricably intertwined in the forming of social bonds, security and self-identity, and can thus become grounds for belonging themselves.

26 Hutchins, *Cognition in the Wild*, 1995; Ingold, *The Perception of the Environment*, 2000.

27 Anthias, 2006, p. 21.

28 Here she draws prominently on Peter Burke, who gives an account focused on Europe (*Languages and Communities in Early Modern Europe*, 2004).

29 Mitchell, *Language, Emotion, and Politics in South India*, 2009.

30 Anthias, 2008, p. 8. This may seem like the whole story. If belonging is such a deep-seated and compelling need, if breakdowns or challenges to belonging can be a powerful motivator, and if encounters with other ways of being in the world can work to trigger such feelings of breakdown, then this may seem like a strong explanation for why our collective identities can be so compelling. That is to say, we might be tempted to conclude that people primarily become motivated to act to defend or assert their identities when their sense of belonging is felt or imagined to be under threat from the outside. Yet, on the one hand, the lives of those living in diverse places such as Kilburn show that feelings of threat need not follow from witnessing different claims

on the world. On the other hand, the account in this chapter is partly one of identity as a coordinating frame for social life – which would suggest a certain intrinsic value for identity, regardless of opposition or threat.

31 Anthias, 2006, p. 21. Preceding the quote from Berger above (note 20), he likewise first attempts to reject any idea of untroubled belonging, declaring: 'All origins are unattainable – just as, on a personal scale, it is impossible to imagine a self before conception.'

32 Abu-Lughod, *Veiled Sentiments*, 2016; Abu-Lughod, 'The Romance of Resistance', 1990.

33 Cohen, *The Symbolic Construction of Community*, 1985; see also Cohen, 'Of symbols and boundaries', 1986.

34 Cohen, 1985, pp. 14–15.

35 Early work reflecting this approach comes prominently from the Manchester School, including Mitchell (1956) and Epstein (*Politics in an Urban African Community*, 1958).

36 Southall, quoted in Astuti et al., 'Constraints on Conceptual Development', 2004, p. 19.

37 Astuti, 'Food for Pregnancy', 1993; Astuti, 'It's a Boy, It's a Girl!', 1998.

38 Astuti et al., 2004, p. 22, and see Astuti, 'The Vezo Are Not a Kind of People', 1995.

39 Wimmer, *Ethnic Boundary Making*, 2013. Here I take a pared-down reading of Wimmer's more systematic framework, focusing on his overarching argument about the shaping of groups internally through hegemonic consensus, and then his focus on institutions and power (leaving out 'networks' but recognising this as an element that mostly mediates access to power, in his original formulation). Wimmer's work builds on a relatively rationalist understanding of ethnic interest as comparative gain in political power and wealth – though dignity is also sometimes acknowledged as part of this picture. I would argue that this approach fails to account for the many ways in which people act in the names of their identities that do not produce a direct overall benefit. This approach struggles to account for many of the cases of collective ritual, socialisation and other actions to promote belonging that take place within groups, as well as certain cases

of inter-group conflict where groups act against their overall interest in the name of identity. Nonetheless his focus on power and institutions is useful, and can be situated within a discussion of belonging-driven action.

40 Baumann, *Contesting Culture*, 1996.

41 Stasch, *Society of Others*, 2009.

Chapter Four: We the People

1 Calculations are my own, with numbers of churches and mosques obtained from Full Fact ('Don't Trust Claims', 2019) and numbers of Christians/Muslims from the London Data Store ('Population by Religion', 2018), with population figures taken for the same year as the church/mosque data.

2 Arendt, *Eichmann in Jerusalem*, 2006.

3 A good summary of the debate around Arendt's depiction of Eichmann, and of her concept of the banality of evil, is provided by Berkowitz ('Misreading "Eichmann in Jerusalem"', 2013).

4 Stonebridge, *Placeless People*, 2018.

5 Arendt, *The Origins of Totalitarianism*, p. 381.

6 Stonebridge, 2018.

7 Whitehead, *Process and Reality*, 1978, p. 39.

8 Plato, *Plato in Twelve Volumes*, Vols. 5 & 6, 1969, via Perseus Digital Library, Plat. Rep. 6.500e. I have swapped 'outline' for 'lineaments' here to avoid the archaic term, and since 'outline' has been used in other translations.

9 This dramatic dimension has been emphasised by a number of classics scholars (see Finley, 'Athenian Demagogues', 1962; Hammer, 'Plebiscitary Politics in Archaic Greece', 2005).

10 Arendt, 'We Refugees', 2009.

11 Arendt, *The Human Condition*, 2013, p. 41.

12 Classical republicanism in the modern era has been refracted into a range of semi-distinct traditions, which get named in inconsistent ways. Sometimes civic republicanism is used as a term for both neo-Athenian and neo-Roman approaches, sometimes it is used only for the latter, with the former termed civic humanism. Communitarianism and 'virtue ethics' are sometimes each taken as identical to neo-Athenian/civic-humanism approaches, whereas

in other cases they are distinguished from these – respectively by emphasising ascribed or inherited community membership as a prerequisite for political participation, and by putting a heavier emphasis on the shaping of ethical subjects, within given cosmological traditions. These distinctions become especially salient in relation to questions of political process, inclusion and justice. Here, because I focus on how these traditions imagine human difference and offer ways of relating to it, I use 'civic republicanism' as a loose umbrella term – although my explanation focuses especially (if not exclusively) on neo-Athenian / civic-humanist approaches. More broadly, I follow Habermas ('Three Normative Models of Democracy', 1994) both in broadly recognising liberalism and republicanism as the two prevailing democratic traditions and in dialoguing with these to try to formulate an alternative.

13 The term 'recognition' itself is fraught, and contested. The dominant academic usage (especially in discussing 'the politics of recognition') tends to focus on recognition on the basis of categorical identities, i.e. recognition *as* something – *as* Muslim, gay, black, etc. This is often critiqued for allocating rights and responsibilities on the basis of putting people into narrow and fixed boxes. This is not my intended use here. Instead, I work with a more everyday usage, of recognition as acknowledgement (which can take different forms). Patchen Markell (*Bound by Recognition*, 2003) champions precisely such a 'politics of acknowledgment' (which he contrasts to a politics of (categorial) recognition), likewise building on Arendt. He elaborates the dynamics of acknowledgement in two ways, firstly insisting that, 'In this picture, democratic justice does not require that all people be known and respected as who they really are. It requires, instead, that no one be reduced to any characterization of his or her identity for the sake of someone else's achievement of a sense of sovereignty or invulnerability, regardless of whether that characterization is negative or positive … It demands that each of us bear our share of the burden and risk involved in the uncertain, open-ended, sometimes maddeningly and sometimes joyously surprising activity of living and interacting with other people.'

(p. 7). Secondly, he emphasises how both justice and personal identity emerge from the process of continually figuring others out, continually working to attune to them: 'Rather than treating identities as antecedent facts about people that govern their action, Arendt conceives of identities as the results of action and speech in public, through which people appear to others and thereby disclose who they are ... Arendt makes it clear that identity itself comes into being through the public words and deeds through which actors "make their appearance" in the world.' (p. 13). I nonetheless insist on the term 'recognition' here for its clearer connotations of ongoing alertness towards others, and simply in order to centre everyday language over specialised academic usage.

14 Overing, 'In Praise of the Everyday', 2003, p. 293.

15 Overing and Passes, *The Anthropology of Love and Anger*, 2000.

16 Overing, 2003, p. 300. Linking the Piaroa with civic republicanism is not an arbitrary choice. To analyse the Piaroa practices she describes, Overing finds her guide in the philosopher Annette Baier, who takes a decidedly feminist reading of the virtue ethics offshoot of modern republican philosophy. Baier's approach cuts against the importance placed on tradition and replaces this with a dynamic model of trust – as something continually built and rebuilt – which sits much closer to the *civic* republican approach I try to sketch here.

17 Marcelo González Gálvez, 'The Truth of Experience and its Communication', 2015, p. 145.

18 Ibid., p. 147.

19 Ibid., p. 151.

20 Calhoun, 'Civil Society and the Public Sphere', 2015.

21 This need to maintain habituated consensus was expressed by the famous conservative commentator Roger Scruton: 'Our most necessary beliefs may be both unjustified and unjustifiable from our own perspective, and the attempt to justify them will lead merely to their loss.' ('Why I Became a Conservative', 2003) Scruton, however, expresses a much greater tolerance of critical reasoning in elites (see, e.g. 'In Defense of Elitism', 2014), providing a sense of the aristocratic bent of the republican tradition as well, where critical reasoning was considered both essential to

democracy and corrosive of consensus, and thus often imaged as best wielded by a cultural elite who were invested in the preservation of a cultural status quo.

22 Catlos, *Kingdoms of Faith*, 2018.

23 Tronto, *Moral Boundaries*, 1993.

24 Ibid., p. 33.

25 Ibid., p. 31.

26 Smith, *An Inquiry into the Nature and Causes of the Wealth of Nations*, 2008.

27 Although consistent with Tronto's account, I borrow the exposition of 'recognition' as central to Smith from Kalyvas and Katznelson (*Liberal Beginnings*, 2008). My interpretation of Smith is additionally guided by Montes ('Adam Smith's Foundational Idea of Sympathetic Persuasion', 2019).

28 Tronto, 1993.

29 Srividhya Swaminathan ('Adam Smith's Moral Economy', 2007, p. 483) notes: '*The Theory of Moral Sentiments* and *The Wealth of Nations* put forth ideas that abolitionists appropriated, and this appropriation forced slavery apologists to question and re-appropriate or counter Smith to serve their own ends.'

30 Brett, *Changes of State*, 2011.

31 Tronto notes that the feminisation of sympathy and sentiment only followed after sentiment had been demoted as an important foundation of political life, in favour of calculative rationality: 'Prior to the eighteenth century, there was little discussion of women's capacities to reason, nor a sustained discussion of their capacity to feel. Feeling has not always been the preserve of women; during the eighteenth century in English-speaking countries, the capacity for sentiment was initially conceived as an important quality of the virtuous man.' (1993, p. 52). The broader point is that what may appear to be the progressive (i.e. increasingly inclusive or fair) reworking of liberalism may in fact involve the entrenchment of vested interests, and that such entrenchment may not only be opposed to forms of liberal 'progress' but may develop symbiotically with it. Possible liberal horizons are always multiple, and the choice between them always political.

32 Povinelli, *The Cunning of Recognition*, 2002; Povinelli, 'Beyond Good and Evil', 2009; Povinelli, *Economies of Abandonment*, 2011.

33 These possibilities and limits are often two sides of the same coin. For instance, the take-up of Adam Smith's vision of human flourishing grounded in the pursuit of rational self-interest (primarily within capitalist markets) offered a forceful argument against certain forms of bondage – whether slavery in the nineteenth century, or extreme poverty in the twentieth. Simultaneously, it suggested that once free from the direst constraints, all humans ought to be able to thrive independently. This double-edged perspective was a major guide for twentieth-century humanitarian efforts, which simultaneously sought to alleviate the most extreme factors presumed to impede independence – such as disease or a lack of sanitation – but then has also insisted, often coercively, on market-based reforms as the basis for any further improvements in well-being.

34 Arendt, 2006, p. 252.

Chapter Five: Waiting

1 Quoted in translation in Martinez-Alier, *Marriage, Class, and Colour in Nineteenth-century Cuba*, 1989, p. 72.

2 Hickman, 'The Devil and the One Drop Rule', 1997.

3 Stoler, *Carnal Knowledge*, 2020, p. 86.

4 Ibid., p. 81.

5 Hanchard, *The Spectre of Race*, 2018; Hall et al., *Policing the Crisis*, 1978.

6 Back ('VIEWPOINT: There Ain't No Black', 2019), who reminds us 'The title is taken from a football chant sung during the 1970s and 1980s by England fans: "There ain't no black in the Union Jack, send the bastards back."'

7 Alexander, 'Beyond Black', 2002; Alexander, 'Breaking Black', 2018.

8 Ungar, 'Campus Speech Protests Don't only Target Conservatives', 2018.

9 Haider, *Mistaken Identity*, 2018, p. 31.

10 Press and Ehrenreich, 'On the Origins of the Professional-Managerial Class', 2019.

11 Pardy, 'The Shame of Waiting', 2009, p. 198.

12 Lorde, *Sister Outsider*, pp. 147–8.

13 Ahmed, *Cultural Politics of Emotion*, 2014.

14 Most of this research has been done on American students. See Tenenbaum and Ruck ('Are Teachers' Expectations Different?', 2007) for an analysis of overall trends.

15 Strand, 'The White British–Black Caribbean achievement gap', 2012.

16 Rubie-Davies et al., 'Expecting the Best for Students', 2010.

17 Gershenson and Papageorge, 'The Power of Teacher Expectations', 2018; Papageorge et al., 'Teacher Expectations Matter', 2020; Sorhagen, 'Early Teacher Expectations Disproportionately Affect Poor Children's High School Performance', 2013; Howe and Abedin, 'Classroom dialogue', 2013.

18 Ouazad, 'Assessed by a Teacher Like Me', 2014.

19 Zschirnt and Ruedin, 'Ethnic Discrimination in Hiring Decisions', 2016; Quillian et al., 'Meta-Analysis of Field Experiments', 2017; Ndobo, 'The Ethno-Racial Segmentation Jobs', 2018.

20 Profit et al., 'Racial/Ethnic Disparity in NICU Quality of Care Delivery', 2017.

21 Zebrowitz and Montepare, 'Social Psychological Face Perception', 2008.

22 Frumkin and Stone, 'Not All Eyewitnesses Are Equal', 2020

23 Werker and Tees, 'Cross-Language Speech Perception', 1984; Njoroge et al. ('What Are Infants Learning About Race?', 2009) note that this is likely to be the earliest way in which infants notice difference. More broadly, they also note the abundance of psychological work focusing on the development of racial identities in minority (especially African American) children, and the general lack of similar research on white children. There is even less cross-cultural research. The picture presented here is thus necessarily suggestive.

24 Kelly et al., 'Three-Month-Olds, but Not Newborns', 2005; Dunham et al., 'The Development of Implicit Intergroup Cognition', 2008.

25 Meltzoff, 2007.

26 Katz and Kofkin, 'Race, Gender, and Young Children', 1997.

27 Kendi, *Stamped from the Beginning*, 2016.

28 Jhally and Hall, 'Race, the Floating Signifier', 1997.
29 Kendi, 2016.
30 Amin-Smith, 'Grunwick Changed Me', 2016.
31 Ibid.; Anitha and Pearson, *Striking Women*, 2018. The Labour government of the time also played a role in the division between unionists. Worried about the unpopularity of the strike, they pressured national union leaders not to participate, insinuating that doing so would damage their own standing and power with the government. See Travis ('Callaghan had Scargill watched', 2007).
32 Anitha and Pearson, 2018, p. 7.
33 Hall, 'The Long Civil Rights Movement', 2005.
34 Korstad and Lichtenstein, 'Opportunities Found and Lost', 1988.
35 Ibid., p. 791.
36 Ibid.
37 On Fortune, I rely on Susan Carle ('Debunking the Myth', 2008), who shares the concerns I trace here.
38 The *Age* started off under Fortune's editorship as the *Rumor*, and went through several name changes before persisting as the *New York Age* from 1887 to 1960.
39 Carle, 2009, p. 1511.
40 Freeman, 'Delivering the goods', 1978.
41 Bernstein, 'Racism, Railroad Unions, and Labor Regulations', 2000.
42 Hill, 'The Problem of Race in American Labor History', 1996.
43 Ibid.
44 Du Bois, *Black Reconstruction in America*, 1998, p. 357.
45 Fryer, 1984.
46 Waters, '"Dark Strangers" in Our Midst', 1997.
47 Paul, *Whitewashing Britain*, 1997; Fryer, 1984.
48 Hall et al., 1978.
49 Bain, *Industrial Relations in Britain*, 1983.
50 Amin-Smith, 2016.
51 Evans, '"The Aboriginal People of England"', 2012, p. 62.
52 Korstad and Lichtenstein, 1988.
53 Carle, 2009; Brown-Nagin, 'Race as Identity Caricature', 2003. But see Kenneth W. Mack ('Rethinking Civil Rights Lawyering', 2005), who challenges the claim that civil rights lawyers focused on high-level policy change, particularly around ending segregation,

arguing that many lawyers were more focused on combating inequality and improving everyday circumstances. Although complicating the narrative, Mack nonetheless reinforces the centrality of litigation, legal change and ultimate equality imposed from above, to the civil rights movement.

54 Dobbin, *Inventing Equal Opportunity*, 2009.
55 Hall, 2005; Dickens, 'Gender, Race and Employment Equality in Britain', 1997; Orleck, *Common Sense and a Little Fire*, 2000.
56 Skocpol, *Diminished Democracy*, 2013.
57 See, e.g. Hill, 'Fosterites and Feminists', 1998; Hancock, *Solidarity Politics for Millennials*, 2011.
58 Brown-Nagin, 2003.
59 Morrison, 'Portland State, Black Studies Center public dialogue', 1975.
60 King, 'I Have a Dream', 1963.
61 Markell, 2003, p. 11.
62 hooks, 'Homeplace', 1990.

Chapter Six: Love and the Limits of Equality
1 Baldwin, *The Price of the Ticket*, 1985, p. 690.
2 Gates, 'The Fire Last Time', 1992.
3 Baldwin, *The Fire Next Time*, 1990, pp. 81–82.
4 This is not to suggest all black leaders held onto this vision of independent sovereignty – even at the time many debated the limits of this vision and advocated for radically different notions of freedom and nationhood. See Adom Getachew (*Worldmaking after Empire*, 2019).
5 Rose et al., 'Consolidated Brief of Amici Curiae', 2014.
6 Rudder, 'Race and Attraction', 2014.
7 See Bedi, *Private Racism*, 2019.
8 Bonilla-Silva, *Racism without Racists*, 2006. See also: Brewster and Rusche, 'Quantitative Evidence of the Continuing Significance of Race', 2012; Coates, 'Covert Racism in the USA and Globally', 2008.
9 Díaz-Morales, 'Gender-Based Perspectives about Women's and Men's Health', 2017.
10 Patnaik, 'Revisiting the "Drain"', 2017.
11 Davis, *Late Victorian Holocausts*, 2001.

12 Jordan, 'Little Public Support for Slave Trade Reparations', 2014;
    Williams and Nasir, 'AP-NORC Poll', 2019.
13 Jefferson, *Notes on the State of Virginia*, 1787, p. 234 (original text
    accessible via Google Books).
14 Honig and designboom, '25 Countries Photoshop Esther Honig to
    Make Her Beautiful', 2014.
15 Aristotle, *Aristotle in 23 Volumes*, Volume 19, 1934, via Perseus Digital
    Library, Aristot. Nic. Eth.
16 Honneth has played a major role in exploring the understanding
    of recognition within Hegel and Mead, across a range of their
    respective works, particularly his *The Struggle for Recognition* (1996)
    and in Fraser and Honneth, *Redistribution or Recognition?* (2003).
    Taylor's 1992 essay on 'Multiculturalism and "The Politics of
    Recognition"' (*Multiculturalism*, 1994) is widely seen as sparking the
    scholarly interest in recognition.
17 Nancy, *The Inoperative Community*, 1991, p. 12.
18 Nancy, *Being Singular Plural*, 2000, p. 3.
19 Here I am thinking especially of the work of Joan Tronto (1994),
    Selma Sevenhuijsen (*Citizenship and the Ethics of Care*, 1998) and
    Annemarie Mol (*The Logic of Care*, 2008; Mol et al., 'Care', 2010).
20 I use the term 'gang' in scare quotes here to emphasise firstly that
    this was not how many young people involved in forms of street
    sociality and criminality saw their involvement (although some
    did), and secondly that this was typically a label imposed by the
    police and media. For many young people, there was no clear-cut
    line between street and 'straight' life. The 'street' (or, more often,
    'the road') could simply refer to hanging out with friends, or a
    particular style, as much as it could refer to taking part in criminal
    activity. Some of those who did engage in crime did so only on
    occasion. Although the Caldwell estate was considered to be
    involved in a violent rivalry with at least two nearby estates, even
    young people involved with the street community varied as to how
    committed they felt to their rivalry – or, alternatively, as to how
    much they were seen as viable targets by rival groups hoping to
    avenge past acts or enhance their reputation. All of this is to stress
    that commitment, participation and organisation in the Caldwell's
    street community were much more ambiguous and fluid than the

label 'gang' would indicate – even as this label continued to be imposed, and used as a basis for policing, commentary and policy.
21 Baldwin, *Nothing Personal*, 2021, pp. 49–50.

Chapter Seven: Enchantments

1   Here, I primarily follow John Law and Vicky Singleton, 'ANT, multiplicity and policy', 2014.
2   See also Kao, 'The Role of Mathematical Modelling', 2002.
3   Ibid., p. 286.
4   Taylor, 'Review of the Use of Models', 2003.
5   Ipsos Mori, 'Perils of Perception 2015', 2015; Ipsos Mori, 'The Perils of Perception 2017', 2017; Ipsos Mori, 'The Perils of Perception 2020', 2020.
6   Cook et al., 'Consensus on Consensus', 2016.
7   Ipsos Mori, 'Have We Had Enough of Climate Experts?', 2017.
8   Ipsos Mori, 'Britons Hugely Underestimate How Hot Planet has Become', 2019; Ipsos Mori, 'Ipsos Perils of Perception: climate change', 2021.
9   Cohen, 'Covid-19 Vaccine Hesitancy is Worse In E.U. Than U.S.', 2021.
10 Woolford, *This Benevolent Experiment*, 2015; Parry, 'Identifying the Process', 1995.
11 I am taking some poetic licence here to navigate a tricky set of concerns. 'The Door', is a pseudonym for this organisation, meant to ensure anonymity, and the organisation's real name did not derive from this poem at all. In addition, despite Al-Khayr being the most likely author, this poem is more commonly attributed to Jalāl ad-Dīn Rūmī, with different English translations involving fairly significant variations – especially in terms of the central metaphor, where the 'door' has also been taken as a caravan or (royal) court. In one conversation, this poem (attributed to Rumi) was pointed out to me by staff and volunteers at 'The Door' as something which exemplified their ethos (much like their actual name did), and so, when searching for pseudonyms, I thought this poem would be a good source. My choice of English translation from Nevit Ergan (Rumi, *Crazy As We Are*, 2017) differs from the one brought up in conversation, as it allows for a pseudonym that

resonates both within Islamic tradition and which would seem intriguing or inviting to a secular audience – again rather like the original name.

12 Estimate based on Camden half only, based on BBC ward-level calculations. Data downloaded from Rosenbaum ('Local Voting Figures Shed New Light on EU Referendum', 2017).

13 Jefferson, A Bill for the More General Diffusion of Knowledge, 1950 [1779], p. 526.

14 Quoted in Schall, *Schall on Chesterton*, 2010.

15 Adorno, *Minima Moralia*, 2005.

16 Mill, *On Liberty*, 1859, p. 189.

17 de Tocqueville, *Democracy in America*, 1889, pp. 126–7.

18 Reflecting this, the last figures seen as fitting the Renaissance-era ideal of the polymath were active around the late 1700s and early 1800s, including Thomas Young and Hermann von Helmholtz (see Schmidgen, *The Last Polymath*, 2018; Robinson, *The Last Man Who Knew Everything*, 2007).

19 Jasanoff, 'Science and Democracy', 2017.

20 Arendt, 2013, p. 3.

21 Kahan et al., 'Motivated Numeracy', 2013; see also Kahan, 'Ideology, Motivated Reasoning', 2012.

22 Kahan et al., 'The Polarizing Impact of Science Literacy', 2012.

23 Kahan et al., '"They Saw a Protest"', 2012.

24 Barber and Pope, 'Does Party Trump Ideology?', 2018. Barber and Pope found this effect held for several groups: low-knowledge respondents, strong Republicans, Trump-approving respondents and self-described conservatives. While this result suggests a stronger tendency to favour party over policy for conservatives, it is somewhat limited by the focus only on policies from Trump. Other studies (see notes 25–6 below) contain mixed findings – with some finding this effect more evenly across the political spectrum, and others finding a similar tendency for conservatives to judge or select information more heavily based on political labelling.

25 Cohen, 'Party over Policy', 2003; Slothuus and de Vreese, 'Political Parties, Motivated Reasoning, and Issue Framing Effects', 2010; Lenz, *Follow the Leader?*, 2013.

26 Firmer et al., 'Liberals and Conservatives are Similarly Motivated', 2017.

27 Here and below, I follow Maureen O'Malley ('Microbiology, Philosophy and Education', 2016; Hooks and O'Malley, 'Dysbiosis and Its Discontents', 2017; O'Malley and Soyer, 'The Roles of Integration in Molecular Systems Biology', 2012.

28 Donna Haraway (*Staying with the Trouble*, 2016) points to some of the work being done in this regard.

29 O'Malley, 2016.

30 Latour, *Down to Earth*, 2018, p. 23.

31 Someone once even explicitly invoked the post-colonial theorist Homi Bhabha's notion of Third Space (*The Location of Culture*, 1994), using it to emphasise a sense of in-betweenness.

32 Evans-Pritchard, *Witchcraft, Oracles and Magic*, 1976. In discussing Evans-Pritchard, I take a cue from the ethics-focused reading offered by Keane as well as Laidlaw (*The Subject of Virtue*, 2013, p. 198) where he quotes Evans-Pritchard to stress that 'witchcraft was not "a necessary link in a sequence of events but something external to them that participates in them and gives them a peculiar value"'. Instead of offering a form of investigation into the *primary* cause of events, Laidlaw stresses how speculation on witchcraft adds an additional ethical dimension.

33 Keane, 2015, p. 173.

34 Arendt, 2013, p. 77.

35 Mattingly, *Moral Laboratories*, 2014, p. 15.

36 Asad, *Formations of the Secular*, p. 27.

37 Here, it's helpful to read Asad in relation to Latour (*We Have Never Been Modern*, 2003).

Chapter Eight: Rewriting History

1 Hickman et al., 2012.

2 Anderson, *A Life Beyond Boundaries*, 2016.

3 Anderson, *Imagined Communities*, 1991, p. 7.

4 See Chapter One, notes 22–3.

5 Williams, 'The French Origins', 2017. A key text for this movement is Alain de Benoist and Charles Champetier's *Manifesto for a European Renaissance* (2012).

6   Hancock, 2011; Alexander, 2002, 2018; Spencer and Patterson, 'Abridging the acronym', 2017; Winant, *The World is a Ghetto*, 2001.

7   Lilla, *The Once and Future Liberal*, 2018; Haidt and Lukianoff, *The Coddling of the American Mind*, 2018.

8   Hoewer, *Crossing Boundaries During Peace and Conflict*, 2014, pp. 77–8.

9   Ibid., p. 78.

10   Ibid., pp. 80–1.

11   Both Les Back (*New Ethnicities and Urban Culture*, 1996) and Gillian Evans (*Educational Failure*, 2006), who have produced important ethnographic studies of London neighbourhoods, point to local identities as a particularly important frame for holding together or shifting focus away from other differences, although Evans puts greater stress on how localism may be imagined in race-tinted terms. In Kilburn, I found more often that the frames for bringing people together varied across spaces, experiences, needs and opportunities – and that while local identities were often evoked and sometimes celebrated, they were also often treated as too limited to contain the whole of people's lives, or all of what might bring them together. As I stress in what follows, what mattered most were narrative affordances.

12   Nic Craith, 'Living Heritage and Religious Traditions', 2013.

13   Kearney, 'Frank Cottrell-Boyce on The Return of Colmcille', 2013.

14   Gordon-Nesbitt, 'Analysing UK City of Culture', 2013; Doak, 'Beyond Derry or Londonderry', 2014; Doak, 'Cultural Policy as Conflict Transformation?', 2020; Boland et al., 'Neoliberal Place Competition and Culturephilia', 2020.

15   Campbell, *Setting the Truth Free*, 2014, which points to many of the key primary documents but also the historical work done to uncover these.

16   EUROM, 'John Kelly', 2015; Alfaro, 'The Rhythms of Temporal Displacement', 2018.

17   On benefits, see O'Grady ('How Politicians Created', 2017). On the overall tone of newspaper coverage see Blinder and Allen ('Constructing Immigrants', 2018) and Baker et al. ('A Useful Methodological Synergy?', 2008). On assessing how this tone impacts public opinion see Blinder and Jeannet ('The "Illegal" and the Skilled', 2018).

18 Shoshan, *The Management of Hate*, 2016, p. 25.

19 Damon is a little off on the specific conditions, but not wrong
    about the basic fact that citizenship can and has been revoked from
    citizens with migrant backgrounds. The 1981 British Nationality
    Act made it possible to revoke British citizenship in cases where
    doing so would not result in statelessness, and where the secretary
    of state deemed that doing so was 'conducive to the public good'.
    The 2014 Immigration Act extended these powers to make it
    possible to rescind citizenship even when doing so would leave
    people stateless, as long as those in question had been deemed to
    act in a manner 'seriously prejudicial to the vital interests of the
    United Kingdom'. In practice the UK government has frequently
    applied the 1981 act in cases where UK citizens have a migrant
    background, and a *possible* entitlement to citizenship on paper in
    the country of their birth or that of their parents – even if such
    citizenship has never been sought, and may later be denied for
    political or procedural reasons.

20 Knuth, 'Extinction Rebellion', 2019; DeChristopher, 'It's Not as
    Simple as Rebellion', 2020.

Chapter Nine: New Republics

1 Here, and for other details regarding Megan Phelps-Roper, I rely
   on Phelps-Roper, *Unfollow*, 2019; *I Grew Up in the Westboro Baptist
   Church*, 2017.

2 Phelps-Roper, 2019, p. 11. Emphasis in original.

3 Gidley, 'Landscapes of Belonging', 2013.

4 Hardin, 'The Tragedy of the Commons', 1968.

5 Hardin, 'Lifeboat Ethics', 1974.

6 Powell, 1969, p. 237.

7 In this case backed up by the US supreme court.

8 Here, I draw on the 'design principles' Ostrom sets out in *Governing
   the Commons* (1990), but take some liberty in translating these to
   apply not only to natural-resource commons, but more broadly
   to the diversity commons. 'Joint commitments' is my reworking
   of Ostrom's rule three, that 'most individuals affected by the
   operational rules can participate in modifying the operational
   rules' (p. 90). 'Versatility' is likewise a reworking of her rule

two, that there must be 'congruence between appropriation and provision rules and local sanctions' (p. 90). Both these principles, as I approach them here, incorporate further insights from Ostrom's other rules as well as from other thinkers. 'Boundedness' and 'nesting', meanwhile, are more direct restatements of Ostrom's rules one and eight respectively, although again my thinking on these is influenced by others beyond Ostrom.

9   Gilbert, *Remarks on Collective Belief*, 1994; Gilbert, *Joint Commitment*, 2013.

10   Haraway, 2016, p. 12.

11   Ibid.

12   Gallup, 'Abortion', 2007.

13   This is my very rough gloss on a range of different data sets, reviewed by Clements and Field ('Abortion and Public Opinion in Great Britain', 2018), some of which do record forms of relatively stark disapproval slightly (but not dramatically or consistently) above 10 per cent. However, somewhat strangely, a larger proportion of people (e.g. 31 per cent in 1981, 23 per cent in 2008) agree that abortion can never be *justified* – which differs from supporting its availability or restriction.

14   Perraudin, 'Council Ban on Protests Outside Abortion Clinic', 2019.

15   Munson, *The Making of Pro-life Activists*, 2010, p. 20.

16   Ibid., p. 5.

17   Ibid., p. 28.

18   Ibid., p. 29.

19   Ibid., p. 25.

20   Epley and Schroeder, 'Mistakenly Seeking Solitude', 2014.

21   Gallagher, 'Escape to the Country', 2020; Patino et al., 'Where Americans Are Moving', 2021; Farhat, 'London's Suburbs Draw Young People Looking for Space in Pandemic', 2021; Sidders, 'London Home Buyers Are Heading for the Suburbs in Record Numbers', 2021.

22   Schmitt, 'Public Health Experts Give America an "F" on Walkability', 2017.

23   Steuteville, 'Preference for Walkable Communities Strong', 2021.

24   Amit, 'Part I: An Anthropology Without Community?', 2002.

25   One of the best-developed (and pointedly critical) articulations of

this approach comes from Charles W. Mills (see especially *Black Rights/White Wrongs*, 2017).

26 Tellingly, he refers to this as 'postanthropological' – i.e. beyond a specific vision of humanity (*Against Race*, 2002, p. 271). It's also worth noting that, not unlike Mills, although Gilroy is a fierce critic of current forms of liberalism, he nonetheless (in the same work) locates his project firmly in the tradition of the Enlightenment. His, too, is a project of attempting to purify and refine this tradition.

27 Robotham, 'Cosmopolitanism and Planetary Humanism', 2005.

REFERENCES

Abu-Lughod, Lila, 'The Romance of Resistance: Tracing Transformations of Power Through Bedouin Women', *American Ethnologist* 17 (1), (1990), pp. 41–55.
────── 'Writing Against Culture', in *Recapturing Anthropology: Working in the Present*, edited by Richard G. Fox (Santa Fe, School of American Research Press, 1991), pp. 137–62.
────── Veiled Sentiments: *Honor and Poetry in a Bedouin Society* (Oakland, University of California Press, 2016).
Acosta-García, Raúl, and Esperanza Martínez-Ortiz, 'Mexico through a Superdiversity Lens: Already-Existing Diversity Meets New Immigration', *Ethnic and Racial Studies* 38 (4), (2015), pp. 636–49 DOI: 10.1080/01419870.2015.980289.
Adorno, Theodor W., *Minima Moralia: Reflections on a Damaged Life* (London & New York, Verso, 2005).
Aelst, Peter Van, Jesper Strömbäck, Toril Aalberg, Frank Esser, Claes de Vreese, Jörg Matthes, David Hopmann et al., 'Political Communication in a High-Choice Media Environment: A Challenge for Democracy?', *Annals of the International Communication Association* 41 (1) (2017), pp. 3–27 DOI: 10.1080/23808985.2017.1288551.
Ahmed, Sara, *The Cultural Politics of Emotion*, Second Edition (Edinburgh, Edinburgh University Press, 2004).
Alan, Travis, 'Callaghan Had Scargill Watched as Grunwick Dispute Escalated', *Guardian*, 28 December 2007, sec. UK news. theguardian.com/uk/2007/dec/28/past.politics4.
Alexander, Claire, 'Beyond Black: Re-Thinking the Colour/Culture Divide', *Ethnic and Racial Studies* 25 (4), (2002), pp. 552–71 DOI: 10.1080/01419870220136637.

References

————— 'Breaking Black: The Death of Ethnic and Racial Studies in Britain', *Ethnic and Racial Studies* 41 (6), (2018), pp. 1034–54 DOI: 10.1080/01419870.2018.1409902.

Alfaro, Garikoitz Gomez, 'The Rhythms of Temporal Displacement. On Space and Memory in Post-Conflict Derry'. Paper given at 'The social life of time: power, discrimination and transformation' (2018), University of Edinburgh.

Allen, William, 'A Decade of Immigration in the British Press', Migration Observatory (2016), University of Oxford migrationobservatory.ox.ac.uk/resources/briefings/uk-public-opinion-toward-immigration-overall-attitudes-and-level-of-concern/.

Amin-Smith, Maya, 'Grunwick Changed Me', BBC Radio 4 (2016) bbc.co.uk/programmes/b07npvfh.

Amit, Vered, 'Part I: An Anthropology without Community?' in *The Trouble with Community: Anthropological Reflections on Movement, Identity and Collectivity*, edited by Vered Amit and Nigel Rapport (London, Pluto Press, 2002).

Anderson, Benedict, *Imagined Communities: Reflections on the Origin and Spread of Nationalism* (London & New York, Verso, 1991).

————— *A Life Beyond Boundaries: A Memoir* (London & New York, Verso, 2016).

Anitha, Sundari, and Ruth Pearson, *Striking Women: Struggles & Strategies of South Asian Women Workers from Grunwick to Gate Gourmet* (London, Lawrence & Wishart, 2018).

Anthias, Floya, 'Belongings in a Globalising and Unequal World: Rethinking Translocations' in *The Situated Politics of Belonging*, edited by Nira Yuval-Davis, Kalpana Kannabiran and Ulrike Vieten. (London, Thousand Oaks & New Delhi, SAGE, 2006).

————— 'Thinking through the Lens of Translocational Positionality: An Intersectionality Frame for Understanding Identity and Belonging', *Translocations: Migration and Social Change* 4 (January 2008), pp. 5–20.

Arendt, Hannah, *Eichmann in Jerusalem: A Report on the Banality of Evil* (New York, Penguin, 2006).

————— 'We Refugees' in *The Jewish Writings*, edited by Jerome Kohn and Ron H. Feldman (New York, Knopf Doubleday Publishing Group, 2009).

────── *The Human Condition* (Chicago, University of Chicago Press, 2013).

────── *The Origins of Totalitarianism* (London, Penguin, 2017).

Aristotle, *Aristotle in 23 Volumes*, Volume 19, translated by H. Rackham (Cambridge, MA, Harvard University Press, 1975).

Arnorsson, Agust, and Gylfi Zoega, 'On the Causes of Brexit', *European Journal of Political Economy* 55 (December 2018), pp. 301–23 DOI: 10.1016/j.ejpoleco.2018.02.001.

Asad, Talal, *Formations of the Secular: Christianity, Islam, Modernity* (Stanford, Stanford University Press, 2003).

Astuti, Rita, 'Food for Pregnancy: Procreation, Marriage and Images of Gender among the Vezo of Western Madagascar', *Social Anthropology* 1 (3), (1993), pp. 277–90 DOI: 10.1111/j.1469–8676.1993. tb00257.x.

────── '"The Vezo Are Not a Kind of People": Identity, Difference, and "Ethnicity" among a Fishing People of Western Madagascar', *American Ethnologist* 22 (3), (1995), pp. 464–82.

────── '"It's a Boy, It's a Girl!": Reflections on Sex and Gender in Madagascar and Beyond', in *Bodies and Persons: Comparative Perspectives from Africa and Melanesia*, edited by Michael Lambek and Andrew Strathern (Cambridge, Cambridge University Press, 1998).

Astuti, Rita, Gregg E. A. Solomon and Susan Carey, 'Constraints on Conceptual Development: A Case Study of the Acquisition of Folkbiological and Folksociological Knowledge in Madagascar', *Monographs of the Society for Research in Child Development* 69 (3), (2004), pp. i–161.

Avenanti, Alessio, Angela Sirigu and Salvatore M. Aglioti, 'Racial Bias Reduces Empathic Sensorimotor Resonance with Other-Race Pain', *Current Biology* 20 (11), (2010), pp. 1018–22 DOI: 10.1016/j. cub.2010.03.071.

Back, Les, *New Ethnicities and Urban Culture: Racisms and Multiculture in Young Lives* (London, UCL Press, 1996).

────── 'VIEWPOINT: There Ain't No Black in the Union Jack @ Thirty', Discover Society (blog), 2 January 2019 archive.

References

discoversociety.org/2019/01/02/viewpoint-there-aint-no-black-in-the-union-jack-thirty/.

Bailyn, John Frederick, 'To What Degree Are Croatian and Serbian the Same Language? Evidence from a Translation Study', *Journal of Slavic Linguistics* 18 (2), (2010), pp. 181–219.

Bain, George Sayers (ed.), *Industrial Relations in Britain*, First Edition (Oxford, Blackwell Publishers, 1983).

Baker, Paul, Costas Gabrielatos, Majid KhosraviNik, Michał Krzyżanowski, Tony McEnery and Ruth Wodak, 'A Useful Methodological Synergy? Combining Critical Discourse Analysis and Corpus Linguistics to Examine Discourses of Refugees and Asylum Seekers in the UK Press', *Discourse & Society* 19 (3), (2008), pp. 273–306 DOI: 10.1177/0957926508088962.

Bal, P. Matthijs, and Martijn Veltkamp, 'How Does Fiction Reading Influence Empathy? An Experimental Investigation on the Role of Emotional Transportation', *PLOS ONE* 8 (1), (2013), e55341 DOI: 10.1371/journal.pone.0055341.

Baldwin, James, *The Price of the Ticket: Collected Nonfiction, 1948–1985* (London & New York, St Martin's Press, 1985).

——— *The Fire Next Time* (London, Penguin, 1990).

——— *Nothing Personal* (Boston, Beacon Press, 2021).

Baquiran, Chin Lorelei C., and Elena Nicoladis, 'A Doctor's Foreign Accent Affects Perceptions of Competence', *Health Communication* 35 (6), (2020), pp. 726–30 DOI: 10.1080/10410236.2019.1584779.

Barber, Michael, and Jeremy C. Pope, 'Does Party Trump Ideology? Disentangling Party and Ideology in America', *American Political Science Review* 113 (1), (2019), pp. 38–54 DOI: 10.1017/S0003055418000795.

Barth, Fredrik, *Ethnic Groups and Boundaries: The Social Organization of Culture Difference* (Boston, Little Brown and Company, 1969).

Bateson, Gregory, *Steps to an Ecology of Mind: Collected Essays in Anthropology, Psychiatry, Evolution, and Epistemology* (Chicago, University of Chicago Press, 1972).

Baumann, Gerd, *Contesting Culture: Discourses of Identity in Multi-Ethnic London* (Cambridge, Cambridge University Press, 1996).

Bayliss, Andrew P., Matthew A. Paul, Peter R. Cannon and Steven P. Tipper, 'Gaze Cuing and Affective Judgments of Objects: I Like

What You Look At', *Psychonomic Bulletin & Review* 13 (6), (2006), pp. 1061–6 DOI: 10.3758/BF03213926.

Bayliss, Andrew P., and Steven P. Tipper, 'Predictive Gaze Cues and Personality Judgments: Should Eye Trust You?' *Psychological Science* 17 (6), (2006) pp. 514–20 DOI: 10.1111/j.1467–9280.2006.01737.x.

Beaupré, Martin G., and Ursula Hess, 'Cross-Cultural Emotion Recognition among Canadian Ethnic Groups', *Journal of Cross-Cultural Psychology* 36 (3), (2005), pp. 355–70 DOI: 10.1177/0022022104273656.

Bedi, Sonu, *Private Racism* (Cambridge, Cambridge University Press, 2019).

Behrends, Andrea, Sybille Müller and Isabel Dziobek, 'Moving in and out of Synchrony: A Concept for a New Intervention Fostering Empathy through Interactional Movement and Dance', *The Arts in Psychotherapy* 39 (2), (2012), pp. 107–16 DOI: 10.1016/j.aip.2012.02.003.

Benoist, Alain de, and Charles Champetier, *Manifesto for a European Renaissance* (London, Arktos, 2012).

Berger, John, *And Our Faces, My Heart, Brief as Photos* (London, Writers and Readers, 1984).

Berkowitz, Roger, 'Misreading "Eichmann in Jerusalem"', *The New York Times*, 7 July 2013 opinionator.blogs.nytimes.com/2013/07/07/misreading-hannah-arendts-eichmann-in-jerusalem/.

Bernstein, David E., 'Racism, Railroad Unions, and Labor Regulations', ID 249309, Law and Economics Working Papers Series. Rochester, NY, George Mason University School of Law (2000) DOI: 10.2139/ssrn.249309.

Bhabha, Homi K., *The Location of Culture* (London & New York, Routledge, 1994).

Bird-David, Nurit, *Us, Relatives: Scaling and Plural Life in a Forager World* (Oakland, University of California Press, 2017).

Blackless, Melanie, Anthony Charuvastra, Amanda Derryck, Anne Fausto-Sterling, Karl Lauzanne and Ellen Lee, 'How Sexually Dimorphic Are We? Review and Synthesis', *American Journal of Human Biology* 12 (2), (2000), pp. 151–66 DOI: 10.1002/(SICI)1520–6300(200003/04)12:2<151::AID-AJHB1>3.0.CO;2-F.

Blinder, Scott, and William L. Allen, 'Constructing Immigrants: Portrayals of Migrant Groups in British National Newspapers,

References

2010–2012', *International Migration Review* 50 (1), (2016), pp. 3–40 DOI: 10.1111/imre.12206.

Blinder, Scott, and Anne-Marie Jeannet, 'The "Illegal" and the Skilled: Effects of Media Portrayals on Perceptions of Immigrants in Britain', *Journal of Ethnic and Migration Studies* 44 (9), (2018), pp. 1444–62 DOI: 10.1080/1369183X.2017.1412253.

Blinder, Scott, and Lindsay Richards, 'UK Public Opinion toward Immigration: Overall Attitudes and Level of Concern', Migration Observatory (2018), University of Oxford migrationobservatory.ox.ac.uk/resources/briefings/uk-public-opinion-toward-immigration-overall-attitudes-and-level-of-concern/.

——— 'UK Public Opinion toward Immigration: Overall Attitudes and Level of Concern – 7th Revision', Migration Observatory (2020), University of Oxford migrationobservatory.ox.ac.uk/resources/briefings/uk-public-opinion-toward-immigration-overall-attitudes-and-level-of-concern/.

Bloom, Paul, *Against Empathy: The Case for Rational Compassion* (London, Bodley Head, 2017).

Boland, Philip, Brendan Murtagh and Peter Shirlow, 'Neoliberal Place Competition and Culturephilia: Explored through the Lens of Derry~Londonderry', *Social & Cultural Geography* 21 (6), (2020), pp. 788–809 DOI: 10.1080/14649365.2018.1514649.

Bonilla-Silva, Eduardo, *Racism without Racists: Color-Blind Racism and the Persistence of Racial Inequality in the United States* (Oxford, Rowman & Littlefield Publishers, 2006).

Brett, Annabel S., *Changes of State: Nature and the Limits of the City in Early Modern Natural Law* (Princeton, Princeton University Press, 2011).

Brewster, Zachary W., and Sarah Nell Rusche, 'Quantitative Evidence of the Continuing Significance of Race: Tableside Racism in Full-Service Restaurants', *Journal of Black Studies* 43 (4), (2012), pp. 359–84 DOI: 10.1177/0021934711433310.

Bringa, Tone, *Being Muslim the Bosnian Way: Identity and Community in a Central Bosnian Village* (Princeton, Princeton University Press, 1995).

Broesch, Tanya, Tara Callaghan, Joseph Henrich, Christine Murphy and Philippe Rochat, 'Cultural Variations in Children's Mirror

Self-Recognition', *Journal of Cross-Cultural Psychology* 42 (6), (2011), pp. 1018–29 DOI: 10.1177/0022022110381114.

Brown-Nagin, Tomiko, 'Race as Identity Caricature: A Local Legal History Lesson in the Salience of Intraracial Conflict', *University of Pennsylvania Law Review* 151 (6), (2003), p. 1913.

Buehler, Jake, 'Flying Squirrels Secretly Glow Pink, Thanks to Fluorescence', *National Geographic*, 31 January 2019 nationalgeographic.com/animals/article/flying-squirrels-fluorescent-secretly-glow-pink.

Burke, Peter, *Languages and Communities in Early Modern Europe* (Cambridge, Cambridge University Press, 2004).

Cahoone, Lawrence E., 'Introduction' in *From Modernism to Postmodernism: An Anthology Expanded*, edited by Lawrence E. Cahoone (London, Wiley, 2003).

Calhoun, Craig, 'Civil Society and the Public Sphere: History of the Concept', in *International Encyclopedia of the Social & Behavioral Sciences*, Second Edition, edited by James D. Wright (London, Elsevier, 2015), pp. 701–6 DOI: 10.1016/B978-0-08-097086-8.03070-1.

Campbell, Julieann, *Setting the Truth Free: The Inside Story of the Bloody Sunday Justice Campaign* (Dublin, Liberties Press, 2014).

Carey, John, *William Golding: The Man Who Wrote Lord of the Flies* (London, Faber & Faber, 2012).

Carle, Susan, 'Debunking the Myth of Civil Rights Liberalism: Visions of Racial Justice in the Thought of T. Thomas Fortune, 1880–1890', *Fordham Law Review* 77 (4), (September 2008), pp. 1479–1533.

Carsten, Janet, 'The Substance of Kinship and the Heat of the Hearth: Feeding, Personhood, and Relatedness among Malays in Pulau Langkawi', *American Ethnologist* 22 (2), (1995), pp. 223–41.

—— *After Kinship* (Cambridge, Cambridge University Press, 2004).

Cassanelli, Lee, 'Speculations on the Historical Origins of the 'Total Somali Genealogy' in *Peace and Milk, Drought and War: Somali Culture, Society and Politics: Essays in Honour of I. M. Lewis*, edited by Markus V. Hoehne and Virginia Luling (London, Hurst, 2010).

Castles, Stephen, Hein de Haas and Mark J. Miller, *The Age of Migration: International Population Movements in the Modern World*, fifth edition (Basingstoke, Palgrave Macmillan, 2014).

References

Catlos, Brian A., *Kingdoms of Faith: A New History of Islamic Spain* (Oxford, Oxford University Press, 2018).

Chiao, Joan Y., and Vani A. Mathur, 'Intergroup Empathy: How Does Race Affect Empathic Neural Responses?' *Current Biology* 20 (11), (2010), R478–80 DOI: 10.1016/j.cub.2010.04.001.

Clarke, Harold D., Matthew Goodwin, and Paul Whiteley, *Brexit: Why Britain Voted to Leave the European Union* (Cambridge, Cambridge University Press, 2017).

Clements, Ben, and Clive D. Field, 'Abortion and Public Opinion in Great Britain: A 50-Year Retrospective', *Journal of Beliefs & Values*, (March 2018) tandfonline.com/doi/full/10.1080/13617672.2018.1441 351.

Coates, Rodney D., 'Covert Racism in the USA and Globally', *Sociology Compass* 2 (1), (2008), pp. 208–31 DOI: 10.1111/j.1751–9020.2007.00057.x.

Cohen, Anthony, 'Of Symbols and Boundaries, or, Does Ertie's Greatcoat Hold the Key?' in *Symbolising Boundaries: Identity and Diversity in British Cultures*, edited by Anthony Cohen (Manchester, Manchester University Press, 1986).

Cohen, Anthony Paul, *The Symbolic Construction of Community* (Chichester, Ellis Horwood Limited, 1985).

Cohen, Geoffrey L., 'Party over Policy: The Dominating Impact of Group Influence on Political Beliefs', *Journal of Personality and Social Psychology* 85 (5), (2003), pp. 808–22 DOI: 10.1037/0022–3514.85.5.808.

Cohen, Joshua, 'Covid-19 Vaccine Hesitancy Is Worse In E.U. Than U.S.', *Forbes*, 8 March 2021 forbes.com/sites/joshuacohen/2021/03/08/covid-19-vaccine-hesitancy-is-worse-in-eu-than-us/.

Coleman, Roger, *The Art of Work: An Epitaph to Skill* (London, Pluto Press, 1988).

Cook, John, Naomi Oreskes, Peter T. Doran, William R. L. Anderegg, Bart Verheggen, Ed W. Maibach, J. Stuart Carlton et al., 'Consensus on Consensus: A Synthesis of Consensus Estimates on Human-Caused Global Warming', *Environmental Research Letters* 11 (4), (2016), 048002 DOI: 10.1088/1748–9326/11/4/048002.

Cronin, Thomas W., and Michael J. Bok, 'Photoreception and Vision in the Ultraviolet', *Journal of Experimental Biology* 219 (18), (2016), pp. 2790–2801 DOI: 10.1242/jeb.128769.

Csibra, Gergely, and György Gergely, 'Social Learning and Social Cognition: The Case for Pedagogy', in *Processes of Change in Brain and Cognitive Development: Attention and Performance XXI*, edited by Yuko Munakata and Mark Johnson (Oxford, Oxford University Press, 2006).

Czaika, Mathias, and Hein de Haas, 'The Globalization of Migration: Has the World Become More Migratory?' *International Migration Review* 48 (2), (2014), pp. 283–323 DOI: 10.1111/imre.12095.

Davidoff, Jules, Ian Davies and Debi Roberson, 'Colour Categories in a Stone-Age Tribe', *Nature* 398 (6724), (1999), pp. 203–4 DOI: 10.1038/18335.

Davies, Sharyn Graham, *Gender Diversity in Indonesia: Sexuality, Islam and Queer Selves* (Abingdon, Routledge, 2010).

Davis, Mike, *Late Victorian Holocausts: El Niño Famines and the Making of the Third World* (London & New York, Verso, 2001).

Decety, Jean, and Philip L. Jackson, 'The Functional Architecture of Human Empathy', *Behavioral and Cognitive Neuroscience Reviews* 3 (2), (2004), pp. 71–100 DOI: 10.1177/1534582304267187.

DeChristopher, Tim, 'It's Not as Simple as Rebellion', *YES! Magazine*, 11 May 2020 yesmagazine.org/issue/coronavirus-community-power/2020/05/11/its-not-as-simple-as-rebellion.

Denich, Bette, 'Dismembering Yugoslavia: Nationalist Ideologies and the Symbolic Revival of Genocide', *American Ethnologist* 21 (2), (1994), pp. 367–90 DOI: 10.1525/ae.1994.21.2.02a00080.

Deveney, Paul J., *Callaghan's Journey to Downing Street* (Basingstoke, Springer, 2010).

Díaz-Morales, Juan F., 'Gender-Based Perspectives About Women's and Men's Health', in *The Psychology of Gender and Health*, edited by M. Pilar Sánchez-López and Rosa M. Limiñana-Gras, pp. 55–83 (San Diego, Academic Press, 2017) DOI: 10.1016/B978-0-12-803864-2.00002-X.

Dickens, Linda, 'Gender, Race and Employment Equality in Britain: Inadequate Strategies and the Role of Industrial Relations Actors', *Industrial Relations Journal* 28 (4), (1997), pp. 282–91 DOI: 10.1111/1468-2338.00064.

Dinesen, Peter Thisted, Merlin Schaeffer and Kim Mannemar

References

Sønderskov, 'Ethnic Diversity and Social Trust: A Narrative and Meta-Analytical Review', *Annual Review of Political Science* 23 (1), (2020), pp. 441–65 DOI: 10.1146/annurev-polisci-052918–020708.

Doak, Peter, 'Beyond Derry or Londonderry: Towards a Framework for Understanding the Emerging Spatial Contradictions of Derry~Londonderry – UK City of Culture 2013', *City* 18 (4–5), (2014), pp. 488–96 DOI: 10.1080/13604813.2014.939469.

———— 'Cultural Policy as Conflict Transformation? Problematising the Peacebuilding Potential of Cultural Policy in Derry~Londonderry – UK City of Culture 2013', *International Journal of Cultural Policy* 26 (1), (2020), pp. 46–60 DOI: 10.1080/10286632.2018.1445727.

Dobbin, Frank, *Inventing Equal Opportunity* (Princeton, Princeton University Press, 2009).

Du Bois, W. E. B., *Black Reconstruction in America 1860–1880* (New York, Free Press, 1998).

Dunbar, R. I. M., 'Neocortex Size as a Constraint on Group Size in Primates', *Journal of Human Evolution* 22 (6), (1992), pp. 469–93 DOI: 10.1016/0047–2484(92)90081-J.

———— 'Coevolution of Neocortical Size, Group Size and Language in Humans', *Behavioral and Brain Sciences* 16 (4), (1993), pp. 681–94 DOI: 10.1017/S0140525X00032325.

Dunbar, R. I. M., 'The Social Brain: Mind, Language, and Society in Evolutionary Perspective', *Annual Review of Anthropology* 32 (1), (2003), pp. 163–81 DOI: 10.1146/annurev.anthro.32.061002.093158.

Dunbar, Robin, *The Human Story* (London, Faber & Faber, 2011).

Dunbar, Robin I. M., 'The Social Brain Hypothesis', *Evolutionary Anthropology: Issues, News, and Reviews* 6 (5), (1998), pp. 178–90 DOI: 10.1002/(SICI)1520–6505(1998)6:5<178::AID-EVAN5>3.0.CO;2–8.

Dunham, Yarrow, Andrew S. Baron and Mahzarin R. Banaji, 'The Development of Implicit Intergroup Cognition', *Trends in Cognitive Sciences* 12 (7), (2008), pp. 248–53 DOI: 10.1016/j.tics.2008.04.006.

Elchardus, Mark, and Bram Spruyt, 'Populism, Persistent Republicanism and Declinism: An Empirical Analysis of Populism as a Thin Ideology', *Government and Opposition* 51 (1), (2016), pp. 111–33 DOI: 10.1017/gov.2014.27.

Elfenbein, Hillary Anger, and Nalini Ambady, 'On the Universality and Cultural Specificity of Emotion Recognition: A Meta-Analysis',

Psychological Bulletin 128 (2), (2002), pp. 203–35
DOI: 10.1037/0033–2909.128.2.203.

Epley, Nicholas, and Juliana Schroeder, 'Mistakenly Seeking Solitude',
Journal of Experimental Psychology: General, 143 (5), (2014), pp. 1980–
99. DOI: 10.1037/a0037323.

Epstein, Arnold Leonard, *Politics in an Urban African Community*
(Manchester, Manchester University Press, 1958).

EUROM, 'John Kelly, Education and Outreach Officer at the Museum
of Free Derry, Ireland/UK', European Observatory on Memories
(2015) vimeo.com/134717451.

Evans, G., *Educational Failure and Working Class White Children in Britain*
(Basingstoke, Springer, 2006).

Evans, Gillian, '"The Aboriginal People of England": The Culture of
Class Politics in Contemporary Britain', *Focaal: Journal of Global
and Historical Anthropology* (62), (2012), pp. 17–29 DOI: 10.3167/
fcl.2012.620102.

Evans-Pritchard, E. E., *Witchcraft, Oracles and Magic among the Azande*,
abridged edition (Oxford: Oxford University Press, 1976).

Farhat, Eamon Akil, 'London's Suburbs Draw Young People
Looking for Space in Pandemic', BloombergQuint, 18 July 2021
bloombergquint.com/global-economics/london-s-suburbs-draw-
young-people-looking-for-space-in-pandemic.

Finley, M. I., 'Athenian Demagogues', *Past & Present* no. 21, (1962),
pp. 3–24.

Flahaux, Marie-Laurence, and Hein de Haas, 'African Migration:
Trends, Patterns, Drivers', *Comparative Migration Studies* 4 (1),
(2016), p. 1 DOI: 10.1186/s40878–015–0015–6.

Fletcher, Richard, and Rasmus Kleis Nielsen, 'Are News Audiences
Increasingly Fragmented? A Cross-National Comparative
Analysis of Cross-Platform News Audience Fragmentation and
Duplication', *Journal of Communication* 67 (4), (2017), pp. 476–98
DOI: 10.1111/jcom.12315.

Flom, Ross, and Sarah Johnson, 'The Effects of Adults' Affective
Expression and Direction of Visual Gaze on 12-Month-Olds' Visual
Preferences for an Object Following a 5-Minute, 1-Day, or 1-Month
Delay', *British Journal of Developmental Psychology* 29 (Pt 1), (2011),
pp. 64–85 DOI: 10.1348/026151010X512088.

References

Foa, Roberto Stefan, Andrew Klassen, Micheal Slade, Alex Rand and Rosie Collins, 'The Global Satisfaction with Democracy Report 2020', Cambridge, Centre for the Future of Democracy (2020).

Fortes, Meyer, and Edward Evan Evans-Pritchard, *African Political Systems* (Redditch, Read Books, 2006).

Fraser, Nancy, and Axel Honneth, *Redistribution or Recognition?: A Political-Philosophical Exchange* (London & New York, Verso, 2003).

Freeman, Joshua, 'Delivering the Goods: Industrial Unionism during World War II', *Labor History* 19 (4), (1978), pp. 570–93 DOI: 10.1080/00236567808584513.

Frey, William H., *Diversity Explosion: How New Racial Demographics Are Remaking America* (Washington DC, Brookings Institution Press, 2014).

Friesen, Justin P., Kerry Kawakami, Larissa Vingilis-Jaremko, Regis Caprara, David M. Sidhu, Amanda Williams, Kurt Hugenberg, Rosa Rodríguez-Bailón, Elena Cañadas and Paula Niedenthal, 'Perceiving Happiness in an Intergroup Context: The Role of Race and Attention to the Eyes in Differentiating between True and False Smiles', *Journal of Personality and Social Psychology* 116 (3), (2019), p. 375–95 DOI: 10.1037/pspa0000139.

Frimer, Jeremy A., Linda J. Skitka and Matt Motyl, 'Liberals and Conservatives Are Similarly Motivated to Avoid Exposure to One Another's Opinions', *Journal of Experimental Social Psychology* 72 (September 2017), pp. 1–12. DOI: 10.1016/j.jesp.2017.04.003.

Frith, Chris D., and Uta Frith, 'Mechanisms of Social Cognition', *Annual Review of Psychology* 63 (1), (2012), pp. 287–313 DOI: 10.1146/annurev-psych-120710-100449.

Frumkin, Lara A., and Anna Stone, 'Not All Eyewitnesses Are Equal: Accent Status, Race and Age Interact to Influence Evaluations of Testimony', *Journal of Ethnicity in Criminal Justice* 18 (2), (2020), pp. 123–45 DOI: 10.1080/15377938.2020.1727806.

Fryer, Peter, *Staying Power: The History of Black People in Britain* (Edmonton, University of Alberta, 1984).

Full Fact, 'Don't Trust Claims about the Change in the Number of Churches and Mosques in London', Full Fact, 3 October 2019 fullfact.org/online/churches-and-mosques-london/.

Galesic, Mirta, and Rocio Garcia-Retamero, 'The Risks We Dread: A

Social Circle Account', *PLOS ONE* 7 (4), (2012), e32837 DOI: 10.1371/journal.pone.0032837.

Gallagher, Sophie, 'Escape to the Country: Will People Leave Cities behind Post-Pandemic?' *Independent*, 13 August 2020, sec. Lifestyle independent.co.uk/life-style/people-leaving-cities-london-manchester-coronavirus-pandemic-lockdown-a9612116.html.

Gallup, 'Abortion: Gallup Historical Trends', Gallup.com, 22 June 2007 news.gallup.com/poll/1576/Abortion.aspx.

Gates, Henry Louis, 'The Fire Last Time', *New Republic*, 1 June 1992 newrepublic.com/article/114134/fire-last-time.

Gellner, Ernest, *Nations and Nationalism* (Ithaca, Cornell University Press, 2008).

Gereke, Johanna, Max Schaub and Delia Baldassarri, 'Ethnic Diversity, Poverty and Social Trust in Germany: Evidence from a Behavioral Measure of Trust.' PLOS ONE 13 (7), (2018), e0199834 DOI: 10.1371/journal.pone.0199834.

Gershenson, Seth, and Nicholas Papageorge, 'The Power of Teacher Expectations: How Racial Bias Hinders Student Attainment,' *Education Next* 18 (1), (2018), pp. 65–70.

Getachew, Adom, *Worldmaking after Empire: The Rise and Fall of Self-Determination* (Princeton, Princeton University Press, 2019).

Gidley, Ben, 'Landscapes of Belonging, Portraits of Life: Researching Everyday Multiculture in an Inner City Estate', *Identities* 20 (4), (2013), pp. 361–76 DOI: 10.1080/1070289X.2013.822381.

Gilbert, Margaret, 'Remarks on Collective Belief', in *Socializing Epistemology: The Social Dimensions of Knowledge*, edited by Frederick F. Schmitt (London & New York, Rowman & Littlefield, 1994).

Gilroy, Paul, *Against Race: Imagining Political Culture Beyond the Color Line* (Cambridge, MA, Harvard University Press, 2000).

Golding, William, and James R. Baker, 'An Interview with William Golding', *Twentieth Century Literature* 28 (2), (1982), pp. 130–70 DOI: 10.2307/441151.

González Gálvez, Marcelo, 'The Truth of Experience and Its Communication: Reflections on Mapuche Epistemology', *Anthropological Theory* 15 (2), (2015), pp. 141–57 DOI: 10.1177/1463499614560947.

References

Gordon-Nesbitt, Rebecca, 'Analysing UK City of Culture: The Implications of Culture-Led Regeneration', *Fugitive Papers* (2013).

Greenberg, Robert D., *Language and Identity in the Balkans: Serbo-Croatian and Its Disintegration* (Oxford, Oxford University Press, 2004).

Griffiths, David J., 'Fragmentation and Consolidation: The Contrasting Cases of Somali and Kurdish Refugees in London', *Journal of Refugee Studies* 13 (3), (2000), pp. 281–302 DOI: 10.1093/jrs/13.3.281.

——— *Somali and Kurdish Refugees in London: New Identities in the Diaspora* (Aldershot, Ashgate Publishing, Ltd., 2002).

Guess, Andrew M., Pablo Barberá, Simon Munzert and JungHwan Yang, 'The Consequences of Online Partisan Media', Proceedings of the National Academy of Sciences 118 (14), (2021), e2013464118 DOI: 10.1073/pnas.2013464118.

Habermas, Jürgen, 'Three Normative Models of Democracy', *Constellations* 1 (1), (1994) pp. 1–10 DOI: 10.1111/j.1467-8675.1994.tb00001.x.

Habyarimana, James, Macartan Humphreys, Daniel N. Posner and Jeremy M. Weinstein, *Coethnicity: Diversity and the Dilemmas of Collective Action* (New York, Russell Sage Foundation, 2009) jstor.org/stable/10.7758/9781610446389.

Hage, Ghassan, *White Nation: Fantasies of White Supremacy in a Multicultural Society* (Sydney, Pluto Press, 1999).

Haider, Asad, *Mistaken Identity: Race and Class in the Age of Trump* (London & New York, Verso Books, 2018).

Haidt, Jonathan, and Greg Lukianoff, *The Coddling of the American Mind: How Good Intentions and Bad Ideas Are Setting Up a Generation for Failure* (New York, Penguin, 2018).

Hall, Jacquelyn Dowd, 'The Long Civil Rights Movement and the Political Uses of the Past', *Journal of American History* 91 (4), (2005), pp. 1233–63 DOI: 10.2307/3660172.

Hall, Stuart, 'Culture, Community, Nation', *Cultural Studies* 7 (3), (1993), pp. 349–63 DOI: 10.1080/09502389300490251.

Hall, Stuart, Chas Critcher, Tony Jefferson, John Clarke and Brian Roberts, *Policing the Crisis: Mugging, the State and Law and Order* (New York, Holmes & Meier, 1978).

Halpern, Joel Martin and David A. Kideckel, *Neighbors at War:*

Anthropological Perspectives on Yugoslav Ethnicity, Culture, and History (University Park, Pennsylvania State University Press, 2000).

Hammer, Dean, 'Plebiscitary Politics in Archaic Greece', *Historia: Zeitschrift Für Alte Geschichte* 54 (2), (2005), pp. 107–31.

Hanchard, Michael G., *The Spectre of Race* (Princeton, Princeton University Press, 2018).

Hancock, A., *Solidarity Politics for Millennials: A Guide to Ending the Oppression Olympics* (New York, Palgrave Macmillan, 2011).

Hardin, Garrett, 'The Tragedy of the Commons', *Science* 162 (3859), (1968), pp. 1243–48 DOI: 10.1126/science.162.3859.1243.

Hardin, Garrett, 'Lifeboat ethics: the case against helping the poor', *Psychology Today*, 8, (1974), pp. 38–43.

Haraway, Donna J., *Staying with the Trouble: Making Kin in the Chthulucene* (Durham, Duke University Press, 2016).

Harsin, Jayson, 'Regimes of Posttruth, Postpolitics, and Attention Economies', *Communication, Culture and Critique* 8 (2), (2015), pp. 327–33 DOI: 10.1111/cccr.12097.

Hatton, Timothy J., 'Public Opinion on Immigration in Europe: Preference versus Salience', IZA DP No. 10838, Bonn, IZA Institute of Labour Economics (2017).

Hewstone, Miles, and Hermann Swart, 'Fifty-Odd Years of Inter-Group Contact: From Hypothesis to Integrated Theory', *British Journal of Social Psychology* 50 (3), (2011), pp. 374–86 DOI: 10.1111/j.2044–8309.2011.02047.x.

Hickman, Christine B., 'The Devil and the One Drop Rule: Racial Categories, African Americans, and the U.S. Census', *Michigan Law Review* 95 (5), (1997), pp. 1161–1265 DOI: 10.2307/1290008.

Hickman, M., N. Mai and H. Crowley, *Migration and Social Cohesion in the UK* (Basingstoke, Palgrave Macmillan, 2012).

Hill, Herbert, 'The Problem of Race in American Labor History', *Reviews in American History* 24 (2), (1996), pp. 189–208.

Hill, Rebecca, 'Fosterites and Feminists, or 1950s Ultra-Leftists and the Invention of AmeriKKKa', *New Left Review* no. I/228 (April 1998), pp. 67–90.

Hockett, Charles F., 'The Origin of Speech' in *Human Communication: Language and Its Psychobiological Bases: Readings from Scientific*

American, edited by William S.-Y. Wang (San Francisco, W. H. Freeman, 1982).

Hoewer, M., *Crossing Boundaries during Peace and Conflict: Transforming Identity in Chiapas and in Northern Ireland* (Basingstoke, Palgrave Macmillan, 2014).

Honig, Esther and designboom, '25 Countries Photoshop Esther Honig to Make Her Beautiful', Designboom, 26 June 2014 designboom. com/art/25-countries-photoshop-esther-honig-make-her-beautiful-06-26-2014/.

Honneth, Axel, *The Struggle for Recognition: The Moral Grammar of Social Conflicts* (Cambridge, MA, MIT Press, 1996).

hooks, bell, 'Homeplace (A Site of Resistance)', in *Yearning: Race, Gender, and Cultural Politics* (Boston, South End Press, 1990).

Hooks, Katarzyna B., and Maureen A. O'Malley, 'Dysbiosis and Its Discontents', *MBio* 8 (5), (2017) DOI: 10.1128/mBio.01492-17.

Hopkins, Gail, 'Somali Community Organizations in London and Toronto: Collaboration and Effectiveness', *Journal of Refugee Studies* 19 (3), (2006), pp. 361–80 DOI: 10.1093/jrs/fei013.

Horner, Victoria, and Andrew Whiten, 'Causal Knowledge and Imitation/Emulation Switching in Chimpanzees (Pan Troglodytes) and Children (Homo Sapiens)', *Animal Cognition* 8 (3), (2005), pp. 164–81 DOI: 10.1007/s10071-004-0239-6.

Horowitz, Donald L., 'Ethnic Identity' in *Ethnicity: Theory and Experience*, edited by Nathan Glazer, Daniel Patrick Moynihan and Corinne Saposs Schelling (Cambridge, MA, Harvard University Press, 1975).

Howe, Christine, and Manzoorul Abedin, 'Classroom Dialogue: A Systematic Review across Four Decades of Research', *Cambridge Journal of Education* 43 (3), (2013), pp. 325–56 DOI: 10.1080/0305764X.2013.786024.

Hutchins, Edwin, *Cognition in the Wild* (Cambridge, MA, MIT Press, 1995).

Ingold, Tim, *The Perception of the Environment: Essays on Livelihood, Dwelling and Skill* London & New York, Routledge, 2000).

Ipsos Mori, 'Perils of Perception 2015', London, Ipsos Mori (2015).

——— 'Have We Had Enough of Climate Experts?', London, Ipsos Mori (2017).

———— 'The Perils of Perception 2017', London, Ipsos Mori (2017).

———— 'Britons Hugely Underestimate How Hot Planet Has Become', London, Ipsos Mori (2019).

———— 'The Perils of Perception 2020: Causes of Death', London, Ipsos Mori (2020).

———— 'Ipsos Perils of Perception: climate change', London, Ipsos Mori (2021)

Jasanoff, Sheila, 'Science and Democracy', in *The Handbook of Science and Technology Studies*, Fourth Edition, edited by Ulrike Felt, Rayvon Fouché, Clark Miller and Laurel Smith-Doerr (Cambridge, MA, MIT Press, 2017).

Jefferson, Thomas, 'A Bill for the More General Diffusion of Knowledge', in *The Papers of Thomas Jefferson, vol. 2, 1777–18 June 1779*, edited by Julian P. Boyd (Princeton, Princeton University Press, 1950)

———— *Notes on the State of Virginia* (London, J. Stockdale, 1787) books.google.pt/books?id=i3fSzN5RRyoC&.

Jhally, Sut, and Stuart Hall, 'Race, the Floating Signifier, Featuring Stuart Hall, Transcript', Northampton: Media Education Foundation (1997).

Jonsson, Kenisha Russell, and Neli Demireva, 'Does the Ethno-Religious Diversity of a Neighbourhood Affect the Perceived Health of Its Residents?', *Social Science & Medicine* 204 (May 2018), pp. 108–16 DOI: 10.1016/j.socscimed.2018.03.011.

Jordan, William, 'Little Public Support for Slave Trade Reparations', YouGov (blog), 15 March 2014 yougov.co.uk/topics/politics/articles-reports/2014/03/15/little-support-slave-trade-reparations.

Kahan, Dan M., 'Ideology, Motivated Reasoning, and Cognitive Reflection: An Experimental Study', SSRN Scholarly Paper ID 2182588, Rochester, NY, Social Science Research Network (2012) DOI: 10.2139/ssrn.2182588.

Kahan, Dan M., Ellen Peters, Erica Dawson and Paul Slovic, 'Motivated Numeracy and Enlightened Self-Government', SSRN Scholarly Paper ID 2319992. Rochester, NY, Social Science Research Network (2013) DOI: 10.2139/ssrn.2319992.

Kahan, Dan M., Ellen Peters, Maggie Wittlin, Paul Slovic, Lisa Larrimore Ouellette, Donald Braman and Gregory Mandel, 'The

Polarizing Impact of Science Literacy and Numeracy on Perceived Climate Change Risks', *Nature Climate Change* 2 (10), (2012), pp. 732–5 DOI: 10.1038/nclimate1547.

Kahan, Dan, David Hoffman, Donald Braman, Danieli Evans and Jeffrey Rachlinski,'"They Saw a Protest": Cognitive Illiberalism and the Speech-Conduct Distinction.' *Stanford Law Review* 64 (4), (2012), pp. 851–906.

Kalyvas, Andreas, and Ira Katznelson, *Liberal Beginnings: Making a Republic for the Moderns* (Cambridge, Cambridge University Press, 2008).

Kanovsky, Martin, 'Essentialism and Folksociology: Ethnicity Again', *Journal of Cognition and Culture* 7 (3–4), (2007), pp. 241–81 DOI: 10.1163/156853707X208503.

Kantar Media, 'Brand and Trust in a Fragmented News Environment', Reuters Institute for the Study of Journalism, University of Oxford (2017).

Kao, Rowland R., 'The Role of Mathematical Modelling in the Control of the 2001 FMD Epidemic in the UK', *Trends in Microbiology* 10 (6), (2002), pp. 279–86 DOI: 10.1016/S0966–842X(02)02371–5.

Katz, Phyllis A., and Jennifer A. Kofkin, 'Race, Gender, and Young Children' in *Developmental Psychopathology: Perspectives on Adjustment, Risk, and Disorder*, pp. 51–74 (New York, Cambridge University Press, 1997).

Kaufmann, Eric, and Gareth Harris, '"White Flight" or Positive Contact? Local Diversity and Attitudes to Immigration in Britain', *Comparative Political Studies* 48 (12), (2015), pp. 1563–90 DOI: 10.1177/0010414015581684.

Keane, Webb, 'Signs Are Not the Garb of Meaning: On the Social Analysis of Material Things', in *Materiality*, edited by Daniel Miller (Durham, Duke University Press, 2005).

——— *Ethical Life: Its Natural and Social Histories* (Princeton, Princeton University Press, 2015).

Kearney, Dominic, 'Frank Cottrell Boyce on The Return of Colmcille', Culture Northern Ireland, 7 February 2013 culturenorthernireland.org/features/performing-arts/frank-cottrell-boyce-return-colmcille.

Keen, Suzanne, *Empathy and the Novel* (Oxford, Oxford University Press, 2007).

Keller, Heidi, Joscha Kärtner, Joern Borke, Relindis Yovsi and Astrid Kleis, 'Parenting Styles and the Development of the Categorical Self: A Longitudinal Study on Mirror Self-Recognition in Cameroonian Nso and German Families', *International Journal of Behavioral Development* 29 (6), (2005), pp. 496–504 DOI: 10.1080/01650250500147485.

Kelly, David J., Paul C. Quinn, Alan M. Slater, Kang Lee, Alan Gibson, Michael Smith, Liezhong Ge and Olivier Pascalis, 'Three-Month-Olds, but Not Newborns, Prefer Own-Race Faces', *Developmental Science* 8 (6), (2005), pp. F31–F36 DOI: 10.1111/j.1467–7687.2005.0434a.x.

Kendi, Ibram X., *Stamped from the Beginning: The Definitive History of Racist Ideas in America* (New York, Bold Type Books, 2016).

Keupp, Stefanie, Tanya Behne and Hannes Rakoczy, 'Why Do Children Overimitate? Normativity Is Crucial', *Journal of Experimental Child Psychology* 116 (2), (2013), pp. 392–406 DOI: 10.1016/j.jecp.2013.07.002.

King, Martin Luther, 'I Have a Dream', National Public Radio (1963) npr.org/2010/01/18/122701268/i-have-a-dream-speech-in-its-entirety. soundcloud.com/portland-state-library/portland-state-black-studies-1?mc_cid=7a27cfd978&mc_eid=e2efbcffa9.

Knuth, Hannah, 'Extinction Rebellion: "Fast ein normales Ereignis"', *Die Zeit*, 20 November 2019, sec. Wirtschaft zeit.de/2019/48/extinction-rebellion-roger-hallam-klimaaktivist.

Koning, Edward A., *Immigration and the Politics of Welfare Exclusion: Selective Solidarity in Western Democracies* (Toronto, University of Toronto Press, 2019).

Koopmans, Ruud, and Susanne Veit, 'Cooperation in Ethnically Diverse Neighborhoods: A Lost-Letter Experiment', *Political Psychology* 35 (3), (2014), pp. 379–400 DOI: 10.1111/pops.12037.

Korstad, Robert, and Nelson Lichtenstein, 'Opportunities Found and Lost: Labor, Radicals, and the Early Civil Rights Movement', *Journal of American History* 75 (3), (1988), pp. 786–811 DOI: 10.2307/1901530.

Krieger, Heike, *The Kosovo Conflict and International Law: An Analytical*

Documentation 1974–1999 (Cambridge, Cambridge University Press, 2001).

Kusow, Abdi M., 'The Somali Origin: Myth or Reality?' in *The Invention of Somalia*, edited by Ali Jimale Ahmed (Lawrenceville, NJ, Red Sea Press, 1995).

Laidlaw, James, *The Subject of Virtue: An Anthropology of Ethics and Freedom* (Cambridge, Cambridge University Press, 2013).

Lamm, Claus, and Jasminka Majdandžić, 'The Role of Shared Neural Activations, Mirror Neurons, and Morality in Empathy – a Critical Comment', *Neuroscience Research* 90 (January 2015), pp. 15–24 DOI: 10.1016/j.neures.2014.10.008.

Latour, Bruno, *We Have Never Been Modern* (Cambridge, MA, Harvard University Press, 1993).

——— *Down to Earth: Politics in the New Climatic Regime* (Cambridge, Polity Press, 2018).

Laugrand, Frédéric, and Jarich Oosten, *Hunters, Predators and Prey: Inuit Perceptions of Animals* (New York, Berghahn Books, 2014).

Law, John, and Vicky Singleton, 'ANT, Multiplicity and Policy', *Critical Policy Studies* 8 (4), (2014), pp. 379–96 DOI: 10.1080/19460171.2014.957056.

Lenz, Gabriel S., *Follow the Leader?: How Voters Respond to Politicians' Policies and Performance.* (Chicago, University of Chicago Press, 2013).

Lewis, I. M., *Blood and Bone: The Call of Kinship in Somali Society* (Lawrenceville, NJ, Red Sea Press, 1994).

——— *Understanding Somalia and Somaliland: Culture, History, Society* (New York, Columbia University Press, 2008).

Li, Danying, Miguel R. Ramos, Matthew R. Bennett, Douglas S. Massey and Miles Hewstone, 'Does Ethnic Diversity Affect Well-Being and Allostatic Load among People across Neighbourhoods in England?', *Health & Place* 68 (March 2021) DOI: 10.1016/j.healthplace.2021.102518.

Lilla, Mark, *The Once and Future Liberal: After Identity Politics* (Oxford, Oxford University Press, 2018).

Lomax, Nik, Paul Norman, Philip Rees and Pia Wohland, 'What the UK Population Will Look like by 2061 under Hard, Soft or No Brexit Scenarios', *Conversation* (2019) http://theconversation.com/

what-the-uk-population-will-look-like-by-2061-under-hard-soft-or-no-brexit-scenarios-117475.

London Datastore and Office for National Statistics, 'Population by Religion, Borough', London Datastore (2018) data.london.gov.uk/dataset/percentage-population-religion-borough.

Lorde, Audre, *Sister Outsider: Essays and Speeches* (Berkeley, Ten Speed Press, 2012).

Luhrmann, T. M., 'Mind and Spirit: A Comparative Theory about Representation of Mind and the Experience of Spirit', *Journal of the Royal Anthropological Institute* 26 (S1), (2020), pp. 9–27 DOI: 10.1111/1467-9655.13238.

Lyons, Derek E., Diana H. Damrosch, Jennifer K. Lin, Deanna M. Macris and Frank C. Keil, 'The Scope and Limits of Overimitation in the Transmission of Artefact Culture', *Philosophical Transactions of the Royal Society B: Biological Sciences* 366 (1567), (2011), pp. 1158–67 DOI: 10.1098/rstb.2010.0335.

Mack, K. W., 'Rethinking Civil Rights Lawyering and Politics in the Era before Brown', *Yale Law Journal* 115 (November 2005), pp. 256–354.

Main, Douglas, 'We Knew Platypuses Were Incredible. Now We Know They Glow, Too', *National Geographic*, 11 November 2020 nationalgeographic.com/animals/article/glowing-platypus.

Markell, Patchen, *Bound by Recognition* (Princeton, Princeton University Press, 2009).

Martinez-Alier, Verena, *Marriage, Class, and Colour in Nineteenth-Century Cuba: A Study of Racial Attitudes and Sexual Values in a Slave Society* (Ann Arbor, University of Michigan Press, 1989).

Massey, Doreen, 'A Global Sense of Place', *Marxism Today*, June 1991.

Mattingly, Cheryl, *Moral Laboratories: Family Peril and the Struggle for a Good Life* (Oakland, University of California Press, 2014).

Mazzarella, William, 'The Anthropology of Populism: Beyond the Liberal Settlement', *Annual Review of Anthropology* 48 (1), (2019), pp. 45–60 DOI: 10.1146/annurev-anthro-102218-011412.

McGarry, Lucy M., and Frank A. Russo, 'Mirroring in Dance/Movement Therapy: Potential Mechanisms behind Empathy Enhancement', *The Arts in Psychotherapy* 38 (3), (2011), pp. 178–84 DOI: 10.1016/j.aip.2011.04.005.

McGuigan, Nicola, Jenny Makinson and Andrew Whiten, 'From

References

Over-Imitation to Super-Copying: Adults Imitate Causally Irrelevant Aspects of Tool Use with Higher Fidelity than Young Children', *British Journal of Psychology* 102 (1), (2011), pp 1–18 DOI: 10.1348/000712610X493115.

Meissner, Fran, and Steven Vertovec, 'Comparing Super-Diversity', *Ethnic and Racial Studies* 38 (4), (2015), pp. 541–55 DOI: 10.1080/01419870.2015.980295.

Meltzoff, Andrew N., '"Like Me": A Foundation for Social Cognition', *Developmental Science* 10 (1), (2007), pp. 126–34 DOI: 10.1111/j.1467-7687.2007.00574.x.

Meredith, Martin, *The Fortunes of Africa: A 5000-Year History of Wealth, Greed, and Endeavor* (London, Simon and Schuster, 2014).

Merry, Sally Engle, *Getting Justice and Getting Even: Legal Consciousness Among Working-Class Americans* (Chicago, University of Chicago Press, 1990).

Milam, Erika Lorraine, *Creatures of Cain* (Princeton, Princeton University Press, 2019) press.princeton.edu/books/hardcover/9780691181882/creatures-of-cain.

Milgram, Stanley, *Obedience to Authority: An Experimental View* (New York, Harper & Row, 1969).

Mill, John Stuart, *On Liberty* (London, Longmans, Green and Co., 1859). google.com/books/edition/On_Liberty/uWAJAAAAQAAJ

Mills, Charles Wade, *Black Rights/White Wrongs: The Critique of Racial Liberalism* (Oxford, Oxford University Press, 2017).

Mitchell, James Clyde, *The Kaleka Dance: Aspects of Social Relationships Among Urban Africans in Northern Rhodesia* (published on behalf of the Rhodes-Livingstone Institute by Manchester University Press, 1956).

Mitchell, Lisa, *Language, Emotion, and Politics in South India: The Making of a Mother Tongue* (Bloomington, Indiana University Press, 2009).

Mithen, Steven J., *The Prehistory of the Mind: The Cognitive Origins of Art, Religion and Science* (New York, Thames and Hudson, 1996).

Mohamed, Jama, 'Kinship and Contract in Somali Politics', *Africa: Journal of the International African Institute* 77 (2), (2007), pp. 226–49.

Mol, Annemarie, *The Logic of Care: Health and the Problem of Patient Choice* (Abingdon, Routledge, 2008).

Mol, Annemarie, Ingunn Moser and Jeannette Pols, 'Care: Putting

Practice into Theory', in *Care in Practice: On Tinkering in Clinics, Homes and Farms*, edited by Annemarie Mol, Ingunn Moser and Jeanne Pols (Bielefeld, transcript Verlag, 2010).

Montes, Leonidas, 'Adam Smith's Foundational Idea of Sympathetic Persuasion', *Cambridge Journal of Economics* 43 (1), (2019), pp. 1–15 DOI: 10.1093/cje/bex090.

Morrison, Toni, 'Portland State, Black Studies Center Public Dialogue. Pt. 2' (Portland State University, 1975). Available at: soundcloud. com/portland-state-library/portland-state-black-studies-1?mc_cid=7a27cfd978&mc_eid=e2efbcffa9.

Mukerjee, Subhayan, Sílvia Majó-Vázquez, and Sandra González-Bailón, 'Networks of Audience Overlap in the Consumption of Digital News', *Journal of Communication* 68 (1), (2018), pp. 26–50 DOI: 10.1093/joc/jqx007.

Mukhtar, Mohamed Haji, 'Islam in Somali History: Fact and Fiction' in *The Invention of Somalia*, edited by Ali Jimale Ahmed (Lawrenceville, NJ, Red Sea Press, 1995).

Müller-Wille, Ludger, and Igor Krupnik, 'Franz Boas and Inuktitut Terminology for Ice and Snow: From the Emergence of the Field to the "Great Eskimo Vocabulary Hoax"', in *SIKU: Knowing Our Ice: Documenting Inuit Sea Ice Knowledge and Use*, edited by Igor Krupnik, Claudio Aporta, Shari Gearheard, Gita J. Laidler and Lene Kielsen Holm (Dordrecht, Springer Science & Business Media, 2010).

Munson, Ziad W., *The Making of Pro-Life Activists: How Social Movement Mobilization Works* (Chicago, University of Chicago Press, 2010).

Nagle, John, *Multiculturalism's Double-Bind: Creating Inclusivity, Cosmopolitanism and Difference* (Farnham, Ashgate Publishing, Ltd., 2012).

Nancy, Jean-Luc, *The Inoperative Community* (Minneapolis & Oxford, University of Minnesota Press, 1991).

——— *Being Singular Plural* (Stanford, Stanford University Press, 2000).

Nayak, Anoop, 'Race, Religion and British Multiculturalism: The Political Responses of Black and Minority Ethnic Voluntary Organisations to Multicultural Cohesion', *Political Geography* 31 (7), (2012), pp. 454–63 DOI: 10.1016/j.polgeo.2012.08.005.

Ndobo, André, Alice Faure, Jeanne Boisselier and Stella Giannaki, 'The Ethno-Racial Segmentation Jobs: The Impacts of the Occupational

Stereotypes on Hiring Decisions', *Journal of Social Psychology* 158 (6), (2018), pp. 663–79. DOI: 10.1080/00224545.2017.1389685.

Nelson, Jacob L., and Harsh Taneja, 'The Small, Disloyal Fake News Audience: The Role of Audience Availability in Fake News Consumption', *New Media & Society* 20 (10), (2018), pp. 3720–37 DOI: 10.1177/1461444818758715.

Nic Craith, Máiréad, 'Living Heritage and Religious Traditions: Reinterpreting Columba/Colmcille in the UK City of Culture', *Anthropological Journal of European Cultures* 22 (1), (2013), p. 42–58 DOI: 10.3167/ajec.2013.220104.

Njoroge, Wanjiku, Tami Benton, Marva L. Lewis and Njoroge M. Njoroge, 'What Are Infants Learning about Race? A Look at a Sample of Infants from Multiple Racial Groups', *Infant Mental Health Journal* 30 (5), (2009), pp. 549–67 DOI: 10.1002/imhj.20228.

Oatley, Keith, 'Worlds of the Possible: Abstraction, Imagination, Consciousness', *Pragmatics & Cognition* 21 (3), (2013), pp. 448–68 DOI: 10.1075/pc.21.3.020at.

O'Grady, Tom, 'How Politicians Created, Rather than Reacted to, Negative Public Opinion on Benefits', British Politics and Policy at LSE (blog), 7 November 2017 http://blogs.lse.ac.uk/politicsandpolicy/public-opinion-towards-welfare/.

Olson, David R., 'Literacy and the Languages of Rationality', *Pragmatics & Cognition* 21 (3), (2013), pp. 431–47 DOI: 10.1075/pc.21.3.010ls.

O'Malley, Maureen A., 'Microbiology, Philosophy and Education', *FEMS Microbiology Letters* 363 (17), (2016) DOI: 10.1093/femsle/fnw182.

O'Malley, Maureen A., and Orkun S. Soyer, 'The Roles of Integration in Molecular Systems Biology', *Studies in History and Philosophy of Science Part C: Studies in History and Philosophy of Biological and Biomedical Sciences* 43 (1), (2012), pp. 58–68 DOI: 10.1016/j.shpsc.2011.10.006.

Orleck, Annelise, *Common Sense and a Little Fire: Women and Working-Class Politics in the United States, 1900–1965* (Chapel Hill & London, University of North Carolina Press, 2000).

Ostrom, Elinor, *Governing the Commons* (Cambridge: Cambridge University Press, 1990).

Ouazad, Amine, 'Assessed by a Teacher Like Me: Race and Teacher
Assessments', *Education Finance and Policy* 9 (3), (2014), pp. 334–72
DOI: 10.1162/EDFP_a_00136.

Over, Harriet, 'The Origins of Belonging: Social Motivation in Infants
and Young Children', *Philosophical Transactions of the Royal Society
B*, Biological Sciences 371 (1686), (2016), 20150072 DOI: 10.1098/
rstb.2015.0072.

Overing, Joanna, 'In Praise of the Everyday: Trust and the Art of
Social Living in an Amazonian Community', *Ethnos* 68 (3), (2003),
pp. 293–316 DOI: 10.1080/0014184032000134469.

Overing, Joanna, and Alan Passes, *The Anthropology of Love and
Anger: The Aesthetics of Conviviality in Native Amazonia* (London,
Routledge, 2002).

Panero, Maria Eugenia, Deena Skolnick Weisberg, Jessica Black,
Thalia R. Goldstein, Jennifer L. Barnes, Hiram Brownell and Ellen
Winner, 'Does Reading a Single Passage of Literary Fiction Really
Improve Theory of Mind? An Attempt at Replication', *Journal of
Personality and Social Psychology* 111 (5), (2016), pp. e46–e54
DOI: 10.1037/pspa0000064.

Papageorge, Nicholas W., Seth Gershenson and Kyung Min Kang,
'Teacher Expectations Matter', *Review of Economics and Statistics*
102 (2), (2020), pp. 234–51 DOI: 10.1162/rest_a_00838.

Pardy, Maree, 'The Shame of Waiting', in *Waiting*, edited by Ghassan
Hage (Carlton, Melbourne University Press, 2009).

Parry, Suzanne, 'Identifying the Process: The Removal of "Half-Caste"
Children from Aboriginal Mothers', *Aboriginal History* 19 (1/2),
(1995), pp. 141–53.

Patino, Marie, Aaron Kessler, Sarah Holder, Mira Rojanasakul
and Jackie Gu, 'Where Americans Are Moving', Bloomberg.
com. (n.d.), accessed 3 July 2021 bloomberg.com/
graphics/2021-citylab-how-americans-moved/.

Patnaik, Utsa, 'Revisiting the "Drain", or Transfers From India to
Britain in the Context of Global Diffusion of Capitalism' in
Agrarian and Other Histories: Essays for Binay Bhushan Chaudhuri,
edited by Shubhra Chakrabarti and Utsa Patnaik, pp. 277–318 (New
Delhi, Tulika Books, 2017).

Paul, Kathleen, *Whitewashing Britain: Race and Citizenship in the Postwar Era* (Ithaca, Cornell University Press, 1997).

Peletz, Michael G., 'Transgenderism and Gender Pluralism in Southeast Asia since Early Modern Times', *Current Anthropology* 47 (2), (2006), pp. 309–40 DOI: 10.1086/498947.

Pellikaan, Huib, Sarah L. de Lange and Tom W. G. van der Meer, 'The Centre Does Not Hold: Coalition Politics and Party System Change in the Netherlands, 2002–12', *Government and Opposition* 53 (2), (2018), pp. 231–55 DOI: 10.1017/gov.2016.20.

Perraudin, Frances, 'Council Ban on Protests Outside Abortion Clinic Upheld by Appeal Court', *Guardian*, 21 August 2019. theguardian. com/law/2019/aug/21/council-ban-on-protests-outside-abortion-clinic-upheld-by-court-of-appeal.

Perry, Gina, *Behind the Shock Machine: The Untold Story of the Notorious Milgram Psychology Experiments* (New York, New Press, 2013).

———— 'The View from the Boys', *Psychologist*, 2014.

———— *The Lost Boys: Inside Muzafer Sherif's Robbers Cave Experiment* (Brunswick, Scribe Publications, 2018).

Pettigrew, Thomas F., and Linda R. Tropp, 'A Meta-Analytic Test of Intergroup Contact Theory', *Journal of Personality and Social Psychology* 90 (5), (2006), pp. 751–83 DOI: 10.1037/0022-3514.90.5.751.

Phelps-Roper, Megan, 'I Grew Up in the Westboro Baptist Church. Here's Why I Left', *TEDNYC*, February 2017. ted.com/talks/ megan_phelps_roper_i_grew_up_in_the_westboro_baptist_ church_here_s_why_i_left

———— *Unfollow: a Memoir of Loving and Leaving the Westboro Baptist Church* (New York, Farrar, Strauss and Giroux, 2019).

Pickett, Kate E., and Richard G. Wilkinson, 'Income Inequality and Health: A Causal Review', *Social Science & Medicine* 128 (March 2015), pp. 316–26 DOI: 10.1016/j.socscimed.2014.12.031.

Pildes, Richard H., 'Romanticizing Democracy, Political Fragmentation, and the Decline of American Government', SSRN Scholarly Paper ID 2546042, Rochester, NY, Social Science Research Network (2015) papers.ssrn.com/abstract=2546042.

Pison, Gilles, and Agata V. D'Addato, 'Frequency of Twin Births in Developed Countries', *Twin Research and Human Genetics* 9 (2), (2006), pp. 250–9 DOI: 10.1375/twin.9.2.250.

Plato, *Plato in Twelve Volumes*, edited by Harold North Fowler, W. R. M. Lamb, Robert Gregg Bury and Paul Shorey (London & Cambridge, William Heinemann Ltd; Harvard University Press, 1969).

Portes, Alejandro, and Erik Vickstrom, 'Diversity, Social Capital, and Cohesion', *Annual Review of Sociology* 37 (1), (2011), pp. 461–79 DOI: 10.1146/annurev-soc-081309–150022.

Povinelli, Elizabeth A., *The Cunning of Recognition: Indigenous Alterities and the Making of Australian Multiculturalism* (Durham, Duke University Press, 2002).

———— 'Beyond Good and Evil, Whither Liberal Sacrificial Love?' *Public Culture* 21 (1), (2009), pp. 77–100 DOI: 10.1215/08992363–2008–022.

———— *Economies of Abandonment: Social Belonging and Endurance in Late Liberalism* (Durham, Duke University Press, 2011).

Powell, John Enoch, *Freedom and Reality* (Farnham, Elliot Right Way Books, 1969).

Press, Alex, and Barbara Ehrenreich, 'On the Origins of the Professional-Managerial Class: An Interview with Barbara Ehrenreich', *Dissent*, 22 October 2019 dissentmagazine.org/online_articles/on-the-origins-of-the-professional-managerial-class-an-interview-with-barbara-ehrenreich.

Profit, Jochen, Jeffrey B. Gould, Mihoko Bennett, Benjamin A. Goldstein, David Draper, Ciaran S. Phibbs and Henry C. Lee, 'Racial/Ethnic Disparity in NICU Quality of Care Delivery', *Pediatrics* 140 (3), (2017) DOI: 10.1542/peds.2017–0918.

Quillian, Lincoln, Devah Pager, Ole Hexel and Arnfinn H. Midtbøen, 'Meta-Analysis of Field Experiments Shows No Change in Racial Discrimination in Hiring over Time', *Proceedings of the National Academy of Sciences* 114 (41), (2017), pp. 10870–5.

Rappaport, Roy A., *Ritual and Religion in the Making of Humanity* (Cambridge, Cambridge University Press, 1999).

Ravin, Yael, and Claudia Leacock, 'Polysemy: An Overview' in *Polysemy: Theoretical and Computational Approaches*, edited by Yael Ravin and Claudia Leacock (Oxford, Oxford University Press, 2000).

Reddy, Vasudevi, 'On Being the Object of Attention: Implications for Self–Other Consciousness', *Trends in Cognitive Sciences* 7 (9), (2003), pp. 397–402 DOI: 10.1016/S1364–6613(03)00191–8.

References

Regier, Terry, and Paul Kay, 'Language, Thought, and Color: Whorf Was Half Right', *Trends in Cognitive Sciences* 13 (10), (2009), pp. 439–46 DOI: 10.1016/j.tics.2009.07.001.

Renne, Elisha P., and Misty L. Bastian, 'Reviewing Twinship in Africa', *Ethnology* 40 (1), (2001), pp. 1–11 DOI: 10.2307/3773885.

Richeson, Jennifer A., and Sophie Trawalter, 'Why Do Interracial Interactions Impair Executive Function? A Resource Depletion Account', *Journal of Personality and Social Psychology* 88 (6), (2005), pp. 934–47 DOI: 10.1037/0022-3514.88.6.934.

Richeson, Jennifer A., Sophie Trawalter and J. Nicole Shelton, 'African Americans' Implicit Racial Attitudes and the Depletion of Executive Function after Interracial Interactions', *Social Cognition* 23 (4), (2005), pp. 336–52 DOI: 10.1521/soco.2005.23.4.336.

Roberson, Debi, Jules Davidoff, Ian R. L. Davies and Laura R. Shapiro, 'Color Categories: Evidence for the Cultural Relativity Hypothesis', *Cognitive Psychology* 50 (4), (2005), pp. 378–411 DOI: 10.1016/j.cogpsych.2004.10.001.

Robinson, Andrew, *The Last Man Who Knew Everything* (London, Oneworld Publications, 2007).

Robotham, Don, 'Cosmopolitanism and Planetary Humanism: The Strategic Universalism of Paul Gilroy', *South Atlantic Quarterly* 104 (3), (2005), pp. 561–82 DOI: 10.1215/00382876-104-3-561.

Rooduijn, Matthijs, Wouter van der Brug and Sarah L. de Lange, 'Expressing or Fuelling Discontent? The Relationship between Populist Voting and Political Discontent', *Electoral Studies* 43 (September 2016), pp. 32–40 DOI: 10.1016/j.electstud.2016.04.006.

Rose, Sara, Brigitte Amiri and Jennifer Lee, 'Consolidated Brief of Amici Curiae Julian Bond, the American Civil Liberties Union and the American Civil Liberties Union of Pennsylvania in Support of Defendants-Appellants and Urging Reversal' (New York, American Civil Liberties Union Foundation, 2014) aclu.org/sites/default/files/field_document/06.17.14_aclu_amicus_brief.pdf

Rosenbaum, Martin, 'Local Voting Figures Shed New Light on EU Referendum', BBC News, 6 February 2017, sec. UK Politics bbc.com/news/uk-politics-38762034.

Ross, Josephine, Mandy Yilmaz, Rachel Dale, Rose Cassidy, Iraz Yildirim and M. Suzanne Zeedyk, 'Cultural Differences in

Self-Recognition: The Early Development of Autonomous and
Related Selves?', *Developmental Science* 20 (3), (2017) DOI: 10.1111/
desc.12387.

Rubie-Davies, Christine, John Hattie and Richard Hamilton, 'Expecting
the Best for Students: Teacher Expectations and Academic
Outcomes', *British Journal of Educational Psychology* 76 (3), (2006),
pp. 429–44 DOI: 10.1348/000709905X53589.

Rudder, Christian, 'Race and Attraction, 2009 – 2014', OkTrends (blog),
10 September 2014 web.archive.org/web/20150123110804/http://
blog.okcupid.com/index.php/race-attraction-2009–2014/.

Ruedin, Didier, 'Attitudes to Immigrants in South Africa: Personality
and Vulnerability', *Journal of Ethnic and Migration Studies* 45 (7),
(2019), pp. 1108–26 DOI: 10.1080/1369183X.2018.1428086.

Rumi, Mevlana Celaleddin, *Crazy As We Are*, translated by Nevit O.
Ergin (Chino Valley, Hohm Press, 2017).

Ryan, Louise, and Wendy Webster, *Gendering Migration: Masculinity,
Femininity and Ethnicity in Post-War Britain* (Aldershot, Ashgate
Publishing, Ltd., 2008).

Schall, James V., *Schall on Chesterton: Timely Essays on Timeless Paradoxes*
(Washington DC, Catholic University of America Press, 2010).

Schläpfer, Markus, Luís M. A. Bettencourt, Sébastian Grauwin, Mathias
Raschke, Rob Claxton, Zbigniew Smoreda, Geoffrey B. West and
Carlo Ratti, 'The Scaling of Human Interactions with City Size',
Journal of the Royal Society Interface 11 (98), (2014), pp. 20130789
DOI: 10.1098/rsif.2013.0789.

Schmidgen, Henning, 'The Last Polymath', *Nature* 561 (7722), (2018),
p. 175 DOI: 10.1038/d41586–018–06613–9.

Schmitt, Angie, 'Public Health Experts Give America an "F" on
Walkability', StreetsBlog USA (blog), 27 September 2017 usa.
streetsblog.org/2017/09/27/public-health-experts-give-america-
an-f-on-walkability/.

Scholten, Peter, Maurice Crul and Paul van de Laar, *Coming to Terms
with Superdiversity: The Case of Rotterdam* (Cham, Springer, 2018).

Scruton, Roger, 'Why I Became a Conservative', *New
Criterion*, February 2003 newcriterion.com/issues/2003/2/
why-i-became-a-conservative.

——— *In Defense of Elitism*, Hoffberger Center for Professional

Ethics, University of Baltimore, 2014 futuresymphony.org/in-defense-of-elitism/.

Sevenhuijsen, Selma, *Citizenship and the Ethics of Care: Feminist Considerations on Justice, Morality, and Politics* (London & New York, Routledge, 1998).

Sewell, Tony, 'Commission on Race and Ethnic Disparities: The Report', Commission on Race and Ethnic Disparities, London (2021).

Sharp, John, 'Tribe', in *The Social Science Encyclopaedia*, edited by Adam Kuper and Jessica Kuper (London, Routledge, 2003).

Shore, Bradd, *Culture in Mind: Cognition, Culture, and the Problem of Meaning* (Oxford, Oxford University Press, 1998).

Shoshan, Nitzan, *The Management of Hate: Nation, Affect, and the Governance of Right-Wing Extremism in Germany* (Princeton, Princeton University Press, 2016).

Sidders, Jack, 'London Home Buyers Are Heading for the Suburbs in Record Numbers', *Bloomberg*, 2 August 2021 bloomberg.com/news/articles/2021-08-01/london-home-buyers-are-heading-for-the-suburbs-in-record-numbers.

Skocpol, Theda, *Diminished Democracy: From Membership to Management in American Civic Life* (Norman, University of Oklahoma Press, 2013).

Slothuus, Rune, and Claes H. de Vreese, 'Political Parties, Motivated Reasoning, and Issue Framing Effects', *Journal of Politics* 72 (3), (2010), pp. 630–45 DOI: 10.1017/S002238161000006X.

Smith, Adam, *An Inquiry into the Nature and Causes of the Wealth of Nations: A Selected Edition* (Oxford & New York, Oxford University Press, 2008).

Smith, Neil Amin, David Phillips, Polly Simpson, David Eiser and Michael Trickey, 'A Time of Revolution? British Local Government Finance in the 2010s', Institute for Fiscal Studies, London (n.d.).

Smith, Zadie, *NW* (London, Penguin, 2012).

Sorhagen, Nicole S., 'Early Teacher Expectations Disproportionately Affect Poor Children's High School Performance', *Journal of Educational Psychology* 105 (2), (2013), pp. 465–77 DOI: 10.1037/a0031754.

Soto, José Angel, and Robert W. Levenson, 'Emotion Recognition across Cultures: The Influence of Ethnicity on Empathic Accuracy and Physiological Linkage', *Emotion* (Washington DC) 9 (6), (2009), pp. 874–84 DOI: 10.1037/a0017399.

Soussignan, Robert, Nicolas Dollion, Benoist Schaal, Karine Durand, Nadja Reissland and Jean-Yves Baudouin, 'Mimicking Emotions: How 3–12-Month-Old Infants Use the Facial Expressions and Eyes of a Model', *Cognition & Emotion* 32 (4), (2018), pp. 827–42 DOI: 10.1080/02699931.2017.1359015.

Spencer, Leland G., and G. Patterson, 'Abridging the Acronym: Neoliberalism and the Proliferation of Identitarian Politics', *Journal of LGBT Youth* 14 (3), (2017), pp. 296–316 DOI: 10.1080/19361653.2017.1324343.

Stasch, Rupert, *Society of Others: Kinship and Mourning in a West Papuan Place* (Berkeley, Los Angeles & London, University of California Press, 2009).

Staszak, Jean-François, 'Other/Otherness' in *International Encyclopedia of Human Geography*, edited by Rob Kitchin and Nigel Thrift (London, Elsevier, 2009).

Steuteville, Robert, 'Preference for Walkable Communities Strong, but Young Families Want a Bigger Home', *Public Square*, 28 January 2021 cnu.org/publicsquare/2021/01/28/walkable-community-stock-rises-young-families-want-bigger-home.

Stoler, Ann Laura, *Carnal Knowledge and Imperial Power: Race and the Intimate in Colonial Rule* (Berkeley and Los Angeles, University of California Press, 2010).

Stonebridge, Lyndsey, *Placeless People: Writings, Rights, and Refugees* (Oxford, Oxford University Press, 2018).

Strand, Steve, 'The White British–Black Caribbean Achievement Gap: Tests, Tiers and Teacher Expectations', *British Educational Research Journal* 38 (1), (2012), pp. 75–101 DOI: 10.1080/01411926.2010.526702.

Suiter, Jane, and Richard Fletcher, 'Polarization and Partisanship: Key Drivers of Distrust in Media Old and New?' *European Journal of Communication* 35 (5), (2020), pp. 484–501 DOI: 10.1177/0267323120903685.

Swaminathan, Srividhya, 'Adam Smith's Moral Economy and the Debate to Abolish the Slave Trade', *Rhetoric Society Quarterly* 37 (4), (2007), pp. 481–507.

References

Taylor, Charles, *Multiculturalism: Examining the Politics of Recognition* (Princeton, Princeton University Press, 1994).

Taylor, Nick, 'Review of the Use of Models in Informing Disease Control Policy Development and Adjustment', School of Agriculture, Policy and Development, University of Reading (2003) researchgate.net/publication/242463316_Review_of_the_use_of_ models_in_informing_disease_control_policy_development_and_ adjustment.

Tenenbaum, Harriet R., and Martin D. Ruck, 'Are Teachers' Expectations Different for Racial Minority than for European American Students? A Meta-Analysis', *Journal of Educational Psychology* 99 (2), (2007), pp. 253–73 DOI: 10.1037/0022-0663.99.2.253.

Tewksbury, David, and Julius Matthew Riles, 'Polarization as a Function of Citizen Predispositions and Exposure to News on the Internet', *Journal of Broadcasting & Electronic Media* 59 (3), (2015), pp. 381–98 DOI: 10.1080/08838151.2015.1054996.

Thibault, Pascal, Patrick Bourgeois and Ursula Hess, 'The Effect of Group-Identification on Emotion Recognition: The Case of Cats and Basketball Players', *Journal of Experimental Social Psychology* 42 (5), (2006), pp. 676–83 DOI: 10.1016/j.jesp.2005.10.006.

Tocqueville, Alexis de, *Democracy in America*, Volume 2 (London, Longman, Green, Longman, and Roberts, 1889).

Tomasello, Michael, Alicia P. Melis, Claudio Tennie, Emily Wyman and Esther Herrmann, 'Two Key Steps in the Evolution of Human Cooperation: The Interdependence Hypothesis', *Current Anthropology* 53 (6), (2012), pp. 673–92 DOI: 10.1086/668207.

Tronto, Joan C., *Moral Boundaries: A Political Argument for an Ethic of Care* (New York, Routledge, 1993).

Ungar, Sanford J., 'Campus Speech Protests Don't Only Target Conservatives, and When They Do, It's Often the Same Few Conservatives, Georgetown Free Speech Tracker Finds', Informed and Engaged (blog), 26 March 2018 medium.com/ informed-and-engaged/campus-speech-protests-dont-only-target-conservatives-though-they-frequently-target-the-same-few-bda3105ad347.

Valentine, Gill, 'Living with Difference: Reflections on Geographies of

Encounter', *Progress in Human Geography* 32 (3), (2008), pp. 323–37. DOI: 10.1177/0309133308089372.

Västfjäll, Daniel, Paul Slovic, Marcus Mayorga and Ellen Peters, 'Compassion Fade: Affect and Charity Are Greatest for a Single Child in Need', *PLOS ONE* 9 (6), (2014), e100115 DOI: 10.1371/journal.pone.0100115.

Vowel, Chelsea, *Indigenous Writes: A Guide to First Nations, Métis, and Inuit Issues in Canada* (Winnipeg, Portage & Main Press, 2016).

Wallman, Sandra, *Eight London Households* (London, Tavistock Publications, 1984).

Waters, Chris, '"Dark Strangers" in Our Midst: Discourses of Race and Nation in Britain, 1947–1963', *Journal of British Studies* 36 (2), (1997), pp. 207–38.

Weathers, Monica D., Elaine M. Frank and Leigh Ann Spell, 'Differences in the Communication of Affect: Members of the Same Race Versus Members of a Different Race', *Journal of Black Psychology* 28 (1), (2002), pp. 66–77 DOI: 10.1177/0095798402028001005.

Weidman, Nadine, 'Do Humans Really Have a Killer Instinct or Is That Just Manly Fancy?', August 2020 psyche.co/ideas/do-humans-really-have-a-killer-instinct-or-is-that-just-manly-fancy.

Werker, Janet F., and Richard C. Tees, 'Cross-Language Speech Perception: Evidence for Perceptual Reorganization during the First Year of Life', *Infant Behavior & Development* 7 (1), (1984), pp. 49–63 DOI: 10.1016/S0163–6383(84)80022–3.

Whitehead, Alfred North, *Process and Reality: An Essay in Cosmology* (London, Free Press, 1978).

Wilkes, Rima, and Cary Wu, 'Ethnicity, Democracy, Trust: A Majority-Minority Approach', *Social Forces* 97 (1), (2018), pp. 465–94 DOI: 10.1093/sf/soy027.

Willcox, Walter F., *International Migrations, Volume I: Statistics* (Cambridge, Massachusetts, NBER, 1929).

Willerslev, Rane, 'Not Animal, Not Not-Animal: Hunting, Imitation and Empathetic Knowledge Among the Siberian Yukaghirs', *Journal of the Royal Anthropological Institute* 10 (3), (2004), pp. 629–52 DOI: 10.1111/j.1467–9655.2004.00205.x.

———— *Soul Hunters: Hunting, Animism, and Personhood among the*

Siberian Yukaghirs (Berkeley, Los Angeles & London, University of California Press, 2007).

Williams, Corey, and Noreen Nasir, 'AP-NORC Poll: Most Americans Oppose Reparations for Slavery', AP News, 25 October 2019, sec. VA State Wire apnews.com/article/va-state-wire-us-news-ap-top-news-slavery-mi-state-wire-76de76e9870b45d38390cc40e25 e8f03.

Williams, Thomas Chatterton, 'The French Origins of "You Will Not Replace Us"', *New Yorker*, November 2017 newyorker.com/magazine/2017/12/04/the-french-origins-of-you-will-not-replace-us.

Williamson, Thad, *Sprawl, Justice, and Citizenship: The Civic Costs of the American Way of Life* (Oxford, Oxford University Press, 2010).

Wimmer, Andreas, *Ethnic Boundary Making: Institutions, Power, Networks* (Oxford, Oxford University Press, 2013).

Winant, Howard, *The World Is a Ghetto: Race and Democracy Since World War II* (New York, Basic Books, 2001).

Woolford, Andrew, *This Benevolent Experiment: Indigenous Boarding Schools, Genocide, and Redress in Canada and the United States* (Lincoln, University of Nebraska Press, 2015).

Zebrowitz, Leslie A., and Joann M. Montepare, 'Social Psychological Face Perception: Why Appearance Matters', *Social and Personality Psychology Compass* 2 (3), (2008), pp. 1497–1517 DOI: 10.1111/j.1751–9004.2008.00109.x.

Zschirnt, Eva, and Didier Ruedin, 'Ethnic Discrimination in Hiring Decisions: A Meta-Analysis of Correspondence Tests 1990–2015', *Journal of Ethnic and Migration Studies* 42 (7), (2016), pp. 1115–34 DOI: 10.1080/1369183X.2015.1133279.

ACKNOWLEDGEMENTS

It takes a village. Fittingly for a book where collective accomplishment is such a central theme, this book really is the product of countless conversations, inspirations and gifts given over many years.

I owe an immeasurable debt to all the people of Kilburn who opened their lives to me. A promise to disguise names may make for good research ethics, but it makes gratitude tricky. There are so many people I want to thank directly – not just for the stories recounted in this book, but for all the friendship, warmth and challenge they provided. My sixteen months in Kilburn were transformative in ways big and small. To those responsible for all this, I can only hope you know who you are and how grateful I am.

There are many, many stories from my time in Kilburn that did not make it into this book. Even for those who may not see themselves or their organisations in these pages, my gratitude remains the same. Everyone I met in Kilburn helped shape the story here.

I accumulated a second set of debts while writing. This book would be a shadow of itself were it not for the companionship, knowledge and insight of Hugh Williamson, Rosie Jones McVey and Taras Fedirko as well as Maha Atal, Pauline Kiesow and Katrina Harris. Anthropologists are fond of quoting Claude Lévi-Strauss and describing various things as 'good to think [with]'. I would put it more strongly: without such companions, I would have scarcely been able to think through this book at all. This is especially true of Hugh, Rosie and Taras – three of the sharpest anthropologists I know – who provided generous comments on a first draft.

Carrie Plitt at Felicity Bryant and Cecily Gayford at Profile believed in and championed *How To Live With Each Other* before I was even certain what it was about. This book would not exist without their immense effort and wisdom. Support from the Gates Cambridge Trust made the initial research for this book possible, and a fellowship at the Max Planck Institute for the Study of Religious and Ethnic Diversity allowed me to write it. Jack Ramm and Graeme Hall played crucial roles in editing.

Many scholars across the UK and Germany have provided threads of thought that helped weave this book together. At Cambridge I am indebted to my supervisor, Sian Lazar, as well as to Jonathan Woolley, Ed Pulford, Lily Tomson, Ethan Rubin, Johannes Lenhard and Marlen de la Chaux for a mosaic of wisdom and wit. I am deeply grateful to Jennie Middleton, not only for taking a chance on me and bringing me to the School of Geography and the Environment in Oxford as a non-geographer, but also for an intellectual collaboration that has played a vital role in shaping this book. At Oxford I also benefited from the reflections, support and suggestions of Bharath Ganesh, Ian Klinke, Ersilia Verlinghieri and Brendan Doody. I owe a similar debt to Steve Vertovec for bringing me to the Max Planck Institute for the Study of Religious and Ethnic Diversity, and for the insight and support he has offered. The Institute provided an intellectual community, especially over the strange years of the pandemic, and gave me an invaluable opportunity for focused, intense exchanges with Sabine Mohamed, Derek Denman, Lucas Drouhot, Michalis Moutselos, Tanita Engel and Elisa Lanari – who have left important marks on this book.

Finally, while completing this book, I was lucky enough to be working on a new project alongside organisers and leaders from the community-organising alliance Citizens UK, who provided new sources of insight and inspiration as I wrote. On top of the many local leaders who taught me vital lessons, I owe a particular debt of thanks to Alistair Rooms, Daniel Mackintosh, Charlotte Fischer, Claire Rodgerson, Jonathan Cox and Hannah Gretton, all of whom took interest in this project and provided crucial suggestions.

Again, fittingly for this sort of book, other debts are harder to pin down to time or place. Susannah Crockford has been invaluable as a roving American correspondent. Sophie Watson has a gift for putting things in perspective, and I have benefited from both her wisdom and friendship. Nikita Simpson provided generous feedback as a part of the LSE Covid and Care research team. Christina Woolner and Kenedid Hassan provided a valuable check on my account of Somali clan dynamics in Chapter Three, and Julia Steinhardt and Michelle Quay helped me understand the finer points of Persian poetry for Chapter Seven.

I have done my best to make this a worldly sort of book, full of life, stories and everyday wisdom that can be taken up and circulated. I have tried to trace ideas that stay with the trouble of our complicated world, and which might hold some potential to transform it from within. Hopefully, then, this book acts as an invitation for thinking and acting and living otherwise. May it lead you somewhere worthwhile.

INDEX